The Integrator

The Integrator
A Change Management Framework for Achieving Agile IT Project Success

Scott R. Coplan

Routledge
Taylor & Francis Group

A PRODUCTIVITY PRESS BOOK

First published 2022
by Routledge
605 Third Avenue, New York, NY 10158

and by Routledge
2 Park Square, Milton Park, Abingdon, Oxon, OX14 4RN

Routledge is an imprint of the Taylor & Francis Group, an informa business

ISBN: 978-1-032-22439-8 (hbk)
ISBN: 978-0-367-43165-5 (pbk)
ISBN: 978-1-003-00380-9 (ebk)

DOI: 10.4324/9781003003809

Typeset in Minion
by Apex CoVantage, LLC

I dedicate this book to the employees of Los Angeles County, California, who work tirelessly despite tremendous odds against them and yet successfully deliver help to communities in need.

Contents

Foreword

I carry around a piece of sub-optimized technology. It's my cell phone. It has far more functions than I can access, use, and integrate into my daily life. I spent $1,000 for the thing, while I use about $200 worth of email, text, and voice capability. Like everyone else, I'm enamored with all the latest features, but given my own personal challenges with technology, a 20% return on my investment is not impressive.

But let's say I spent $50 million on my new phone.

For over four decades, I've studied the integration of new technology into organizations. I would love to tell you that I planned all the work I did, but since over 70% of major systems projects did not achieve their benefits on time and on budget, much of my work was remedial. Organizations created their problems and resistance by the time I arrived.

There is one change management approach leaders consider an important contributor to technology project success. *Agile*: all leaders love that word, but Agile is not a training class or a technique. Agile is a change of mindset not solely for developers but for leaders and project sponsors as well. It requires leadership that embraces their role in Agile before their organization can transform and realize its benefits fully. You can't be Agile in development if you're not Agile in leadership decision making and sponsorship as well.

And once an organization adopts Agile, it must understand technology installation is not synonymous with implementation. Many technology teams believe they're done when they've achieved mission success at go-live. System lights go on, it hums, it runs, and users finish training. It's on to the next project. *Go-live* is mechanical. It has little to do with the human aspects of overcoming resistance and achieving readiness required for implementation success. Achieving such readiness is cheaper than the resistance that thwarts return on investment. Shortening the cycle time of adapting to new technology is key to maximizing true benefit achievement. The technology team finishes their job only when implementation results in ongoing realization of all benefits.

In this book, Scott R. Coplan brings a unique perspective, combining the frames of reference of organizational leadership, project sponsors, developers, and end users into a cohesive view of what successful integration of any new technology into an organization truly requires. I am proud to have contributed in some small way to Scott's thinking and this work.

Don Harrison
President, IMA, Inc

Preface

There are innumerable ways to tell a story. This book is a compilation of my experience, with artistic license used to explain key ideas and themes. The basis for this book is my 45+ years career in information technology (IT) project management, including nearly 30 years running my own company. As I tell my story, please note that any similarity to real people, living or dead, is entirely coincidental.

This story takes place in the health care industry but could occur in any industry. If you plan to work or have a career in IT project management, you can take advantage of what I share in this story in many other types of situations. I hope by sharing my past, I help the future of others.

Acknowledgments

While there is a lifetime of people who made this book possible, a select few exceptional individuals deserve additional praise. First, Don Harrison, the mastermind behind Accelerating Implementation Management (AIM) used throughout this book. I could not have completed client projects or this book without his brilliant contribution to organizational change management.

Second, Claire McCarthy, who introduced me to AIM, edited my manuscript, and supplied me with encouraging wisdom while I drafted this book. I am forever in her debt.

Third, Ashish Puri, a consummate information technology manager, who turned a floundering vendor solution into a customer success. His clear-sighted understanding of the client–vendor relationship during an Agile project helped me immeasurably.

Finally, and most importantly, my wife Elizabeth insisted I author a story instead of a textbook. As the best writer I know, her shrewd understanding and appreciation of dialogue introduced me to a whole new level of expression.

About the Author

Scott R. Coplan is a recognized change and project manager, educator, author, and speaker on industry proven practices. In 1991, he founded COPLAN AND COMPANY to focus on improving lives with IT project management.

His over 45 years of experience concentrates on successfully managing IT projects that transform or radically change the way clients deliver services to people in need. This includes changing organizations to achieve IT project management success involving planning, acquisition, transformation, implementation, quality assurance, and optimization. Examples include numerous Los Angeles County Department of Health Services inpatient and ambulatory systems, the Washington State Patrol Sexual Assault Kit Tracking system, and the Maricopa County Attorney's Office Victim Notification and Compensation system. Formerly with Deloitte and Booz Allen and Hamilton, Scott holds an MPA from the University of Washington and a BA from Beloit College. He is a Project Management Professional (PMP), Accredited Accelerating Implementation Methodology (AIM) practitioner, and Fellow member of the Healthcare Information Management Systems Society (HIMSS).

Scott co-authored the book *Project Management for Healthcare Information Technology* with David Masuda, M.D., McGraw-Hill, 2011, currently used as a higher education textbook on project management. He can be reached at scoplan@coplan.com.

Abbreviations and Acronyms

Abbreviations and Acronyms	Term
1115 Waiver	Medicaid waiver to change LA County health care delivery
ADT	Admission, Discharge, Transfer
AIM	Accelerating Implementation Management©
BOS	Board of Supervisors
CAP	Corrective Action Plan
CAST	Champion, Agent, Sponsor, Target
CDS	Clinical Decision Support
CEO	Chief Executive Officer
CFO	Chief Financial Officer
CIO	Chief Information Officer
CMO	Chief Medical Officer
CMT	Change Management Team
CNO	Chief Nursing Officer
COTS	Commercial-Off-the-Shelf
CPO	Chief Product Owner
DA	District Attorney
DHS	Department of Health Services
ED	Emergency Department
EHR	Electronic Health Record
EMPI	Enterprise Master Patient Index
FOR	Frame of Reference
GMIS	Global Management Information Systems
HDH	High Desert Hospital
HIM	Health Information Management
HIMSS	Health Information Systems Society
HR	Human Resources
HTAC	Health Technology Advisory Committee
IEEE	Institute of Electrical and Electronics Engineers

Abbreviations and Acronyms	Term
ISD	Information Services Department
IT	Information Technology
ITAS	IT Advisory Solutions
JIT	Just-in-Time
KDMC	King Drew Medical Center
LA	Los Angeles
LAC+USC	Los Angeles County at University of Southern California
LACnet	Los Angeles County Network
LAPD	Los Angeles Police Department
Medi-Cal	California Medicaid
NYHH	New York Health + Hospitals
PM	Project Manager
PMBOK Guide	Project Management Body of Knowledge Guide
PMO	Project Management Office
PMT	Project Management Team
PO	Product Owner
POC	Point of Care
QA	Quality Assurance
QM	Quality Management
RBM	Results-Based Management
RCM	Revenue Cycle Management
RLANRC	Rancho Los Amigos National Resource Center
SM	Scrum Master
SMART	Specific, Measurable, Realistic, Timebound
SME	Subject Matter Expert
SNOMED-CT or SNOMED	Systematic Nomenclature of Medicine Clinical Terms
SWEBOK Guide	Software Engineering Body of Knowledge Guide
UP	Upper Peninsula
WAM	Workflow Analysis Manager
WAT	Workflow Analysis Team
XP	Extreme Programming

Characters

Last Name	First Name	Title/Role	Organization/ Relationship
Adams	Steve	Owner	Island Hardware
Amato	Teri	Internal Auditor	Boeing
Avery	Tyler	Deputy CIO and Acting PM	KDMC
Bali	Sam	PM	GMIS
Berke	Oscar	Director	Recovery Project
Bernosky	Harry	Assistant CMO	LA County
Brewster	Dan	CMO	DHS
Campo	Renaldo	Acting CIO	LA County
Campo	Renaldo	CIO	LA County
Clemens	Miranda	Concierge	Downtown LA Omni Hotel
Cummings	Roger	CEO	Security Vendor
Davis	Billy	CPO	PO Team
Dice	Jack	Director	DHS
Graden	JoAnne	Deputy CIO	DHS
Green	Tina	CIO and PM	KDMC
Edwards	Samantha	Deputy CEO	LA County Executive Office
Ferguson	Joel	General Counsel	SampleDX
Fleming	George	PO	Product Owner Team
Holmes	Jane	CEO	LA County
Hursey	Nolan	SM	Scrum Team
Kumar	Zara	Tester	Scrum Team
Jen	Mike	Public Affairs Director	DHS
Jen	Mike	CEO	LA County
Jen	Mike	Senior Legislative Aide	LA County Board, 3rd District
Johnson	Alec	Friend	Max McLellan

Last Name	First Name	Title/Role	Organization/ Relationship
Jones	Cliff, *Jonesy*	Software Developer	Scrum Team
Jons	Homer	Deputy CIO	LA County
Jessup	Millie	Nurse	KDMC
Locke	Dave	Associate CEO	LA County Executive Office
Luis	Juan	CIO	DHS
Masis	Jorge	Door Attendant	Downtown LA Omni Hotel
Mayfield	Yolanda	Database Administrator	Scrum Team
McLellan	Eli	Youngest Son	Max and Jacqueline McLellan
McLellan	Jacqueline	Spouse	Max and Jacqueline McLellan
McLellan	Max	DELTA PM and QM	McLellan and Company
McLellan	Zach	Eldest Son	Max and Jacqueline McLellan
Ming	Walter	Chief Superuser	KDMC Project Superuser Team
Mongo	Gustavo	Consultant	McLellan and Company
Mulby	Marissa	Change Manager	CMT
Patel	Kabir	Senior Systems Engineer	PMT
Peabody	Loretta	Workflow Analyst	KDMC WAT
Powell	Jason	CEO	KDMC
Price	Keith	Doctor	Island Medical
Pullman	Georgia	Sister	Max McLellan's Sister-in-Law
Rossini	Jerry	Health Level Seven Specialist	McKesson

Last Name	First Name	Title/Role	Organization/ Relationship
Salvador	Paco	Programmer Analyst	GMIS LA Data Center
Smithers	Amanda	Assistant	Recovery Project
Sugarman	Rich	Private Attorney	Mitch Sugarman, LLC
Tarrel	Renee	Chief Technology Officer	McLellan and Company
Tuscan	Sylvia	Supervisor	LA County Board, 3rd District
Walker	Shirley	WAM	WAT
Washington	Layla	Change Agent and Chief Change Agent	Agent for KDMC's CEO and Chief of Change Agent Team
Wells	Cecilia	Secretary	Secretary for KDMC's CEO
Willoughby	Clarence	County CIO	LA County
Wolff	Sarah	Friend	Max McLellan
Worth	Grace	Senior Administrative Assistant	LA County Executive Office
Yasuda	Tomo	Superuser	Superuser Team
Yen	Catherine	Senior Associate CEO	LA County Executive Office
Zarifian	Eloisa	Director	LA County ISD

1

Failure

"Hello, Max. This is Jane Holmes, Los Angeles County. I need your help."

Wow! This is unprecedented. Jane personally calling me, not a member of her staff placing the call first. This meant something was seriously wrong. Incredulous, but without hesitation, I responded, "Good morning, Jane. What can I do for you?"

"The county is implementing fifteen new systems in all six of our hospitals, and something is out of control. Catherine and I do not know what it is, so we need your help."

Jane was the CEO of LA County. One of her associate CEOs, Catherine Yen, a brilliant and feisty fireball, controlled the county Department of Health Services' (DHS) $4 billion budget. Jane asked, "How fast can you come down here?"

With my office in Seattle and my home on a nearby island, I made travel arrangements to meet Jane. I did not wish to sound like I was anxiously awaiting client work. But I wanted Jane to know that I was ready to address her urgent situation as quickly as possible. I had a long history of working with LA County, and I knew the airline schedule without looking it up.

"I'll be at your office tomorrow at 1:00 p.m. What can I do to prepare for our meeting?"

"Catherine's senior associate, Dave Locke, will send you his research."

Adrenaline raced through my veins. I thanked Jane. I must admit I hoped the enormity of the challenge, the complexity of the work, and the resulting fees would allow us to finally open an LA office. We really needed a physical presence to better serve the county, our largest client, and a massive market.

When I arrived at Jane's office the following afternoon, Grace Worth, her senior administrative assistant, recognized me with a smile and politely

DOI: 10.4324/9781003003809-1

asked me to wait a moment. Grace checked with Jane and ushered me into the boardroom adjoining Jane's office.

Jane looked different. I hardly recognized her. She read my reaction and laughed in her usual infectious manner. She said, in her all-knowing tone, "I lost forty pounds!"

She reached forward, embracing me as a friend. I noticed no cigarette odor. She must have quit in addition to the weight loss. She honored me with her heartfelt greeting as we asked with genuine interest about our kids and spouses since seeing each other a year ago.

When we sat, Jane explained the county signed a contract with Global Management Information Systems (GMIS) to implement financial, administrative, and clinical applications. The county started implementing the financial software before continuing with the electronic health record (EHR) and administrative applications like scheduling, radiology management, patient tracking, and so on. The project included all county hospitals and outpatient clinics, the nation's second largest public health system.

Politics reign supreme in LA County, and this project was no exception. In fact, it sounded worse than I expected as Jane explained.

"The $145 million project financing is in municipal bonds. The county uses the funds from these bonds to issue payments to GMIS at project success milestones. Both the uninformed and malicious may assume the county will default on the municipal bonds if the project fails. While this is wrong, any ensuing public belief like this could affect the county's creditworthiness and lower its bond rating. The lower the bond rating, the higher the future borrowing cost to the county. This could cost the county millions of dollars."

My stomach twisted, and I feared Jane would read this internal reaction on my face. It was always hard to hide anything from Jane, given her decades of political experience and Ph.D.s in economics and psychology.

Then Jane delivered more unwelcome news. Did the county CIO, Clarence Willoughby, commit illegal acts accepting GMIS's box tickets to a Dodgers game during the procurement process? Are there other suspicious activities with the vendor? To me, Clarence was slippery. I never understood why Jane supported the board of supervisors (BOS) in hiring him. He was a bully at best and a crook at worst.

She ended her project description by saying I must tell her at once of any adverse issues involving Clarence so she could notify the district attorney (DA). These issues were the responsibility of DA investigators and not me.

I felt relieved. I am Max McLellan, an IT project manager (PM), not Sherlock Holmes, a detective. I gladly accepted referring any potential criminal activity to the DA.

Jane also noted I reported to her under county counsel attorney-privileged communication. Should a court case ensue due to this endeavor, I could claim everything I did was privileged. Jane explained this was a technicality. I would not report to county counsel under any circumstances. She suspected county counsel contributed to the current crisis. I reported to Jane only, at the board's direction.

I was always cautious on troubled projects. The findings in our work could end careers, or at least cause unwanted job changes. This was never something I relished. I made it clear our role was always to find the problem and deliver a solution while considering the impact on all of those involved. We were talking about people's lives and their income, families, and future. We never took this lightly. We confirmed our findings with at least two independent parties and documented our communication with the utmost care. We had a long history of client success on these kinds of projects. I certainly intended to keep it that way for this project, too.

INVESTIGATION

Jane sent me to meet with Catherine and Dave with an agreed-upon budget and an impossible 30-day schedule to conclude my investigation. I told Jane the schedule was not realistic. She acknowledged my response with, "We must live with this board directive, at least for now." That was hardly satisfactory, but I did not push it. She said *at least*, which gave me hope for future negotiations. However, the board was an intractable entity in most cases and always in a crisis. They wanted me to end this disaster so they could forget it as quickly as possible. BOS members used their current position as a stepping-stone to state and national offices. For example, Sylvia Tacsan, the current BOS member responsible for health care, had the highest-ranking elected position of any Latino female in the country. The outcome of this project could derail the political future of very influential people.

When I met Catherine, she smirked and said, "County Health was at it again. They could not do IT right. The only way DHS knew the scope, time, and cost of their projects was after they completed them. Most times DHS stopped just short of that with huge financial and time expenditures and not much else. So, in this situation, we're ahead of the game."

I laughed. Catherine was both tough and hilarious at the same time.

She introduced me to Dave, sending us to his office to follow up on the information he sent me for our meeting.

Dave was a gray-haired, no-nonsense senior advisor, who clearly knew how to minimize press involvement and the ensuing political nightmares that could occur at any moment. I embraced everything he offered, trusting his guidance implicitly.

He made it absolutely clear I must meet all players, including GMIS's PM and team members, DHS director, county counsel, hospital representatives, DHS and county CIOs, and others. He underscored they must honor my requests for an interview and for documentation, as I worked directly for Jane and the board.

Dave concluded our meeting, emphasizing I should start by assessing Oscar Berke. DHS recently designated Berke to direct this investigation, support my research, and execute my recommendations. Oscar was chief financial officer (CFO) of Rancho Los Amigos National Rehabilitation Center (RLANRC), one of the county's six hospitals already implementing the troubled GMIS system. Oscar expected to fill DHS's CFO position in the coming months. This was the pinnacle financial career position in DHS. The DHS CFO spent their time with the county CEO, BOS, governor, and Health and Human Services Cabinet secretary and president negotiating county health care funding. Oscar had a reputation as the person responsible for solving DHS's problems by getting things done with minimal political consequences, especially when there was a crisis.

It was warm, but the walk from Dave's office at the Hall of Administration to DHS was only short blocks downhill. While everyone drives a car in LA, I enjoyed staying at a hotel walking distance to the multiple block acreage of county offices.

DHS's headquarters was a nondescript dirty white office building longing for a change, like the organization within it. Despite the warm weather, twenty-somethings in hoodies clustered outside the front steps smoking cigarettes. I stayed clear, quickly skipping steps, as I climbed the stairs and entered the main lobby. There was a guard sitting behind a cheap metal desk, thrown in the middle of the elevator lobby to show a false security perimeter. The guard quickly stashed a porn magazine in the desk drawer and looked at me officiously. He gestured toward the clipboard, and I signed in while averting eye contact to avoid embarrassing him further.

DHS's elevators were in competition with all government buildings to see which were the slowest. Once an elevator arrived, dispirited employees slowly disembarked. It was a shabby world, apart from the bright sunny day outside. There was no reason to hurry as the elevator doors closed leisurely.

The smell of janitorial disinfectant greeted me as the elevator doors opened on the fifth floor. I stepped out into a narrow, bland hall with numbered office doors. I went sequentially to Oscar's office door. Should I knock or just enter? I decided to knock. Nothing happened. I waited a moment and then turned the knob and crossed the threshold.

Bright lights and a hum of activity enveloped me as I entered a crowded central room with multiple offices around its perimeter. It was like stepping into an alternate universe.

A short woman burst around a partition to greet me. She was fleshy and round, with a bowl haircut and a big smile. Amanda Smithers introduced herself as Oscar's assistant. She was expecting me and apologized for not answering the knock on the door. She explained she was just ending a call, which prevented her from greeting me properly.

Amanda showed me into Oscar's office. The first thing I noticed as I went in was his office door. Every conceivable inch included randomly posted layers of newspaper and magazine cartoons.

In contrast, Oscar was meticulous, with precisely organized papers on his desk and books on his metal shelf by a small window. He wore a perfectly pressed light purple shirt, matching tie, and dark purple suit and shoes. It was oddly subdued, and on him, it worked. This complemented his dark Mediterranean complexion. He had the tight and strong build of a long-distance runner. His most outstanding feature was his jet-black hair, swept back with a shock of silver on the right side of his forehead. He had a strong, warm, and confident presence.

Oscar shook my hand firmly, looking me straight on with a pleasant smile. He started at once, saying, "I know how to use IT, but not how to manage it." He then asked me how we should go ahead. I suggested he start telling me everything he knew to date about the project, including the organizations, names, roles, and responsibilities of the players.

Oscar was hard to read. He pleasantly reported facts, but with little verbal or nonverbal elaboration. He gave nothing away, clearly politically savvy. To great personal relief, I soon learned he used this political skill to advance the best interests of the public, not necessarily that of DHS or county government entities.

Oscar was intelligent and capable. Whether he was the right person for the project fix remained unknown. I needed to find the right person soon. I wanted success from someone in the department's ranks, like Oscar, not the result of an outsider. DHS would never recover fully unless it fixed this mess on its own.

Following Oscar's introduction, I read documentation he supplied and then started my interviews. During the following two weeks, I crammed in four to five two-hour group interviews each day. These were mostly in small teams responsible for key areas, requirements management, GMIS application analysis and development, project leadership, and so on. I also completed one-on-one interviews with the likes of the DHS director, hospital CEOs, hospital, department, and county CIOs, county counsel, and GMIS PM. Taking notes on my computer throughout each interview, I highlighted and summarized my findings before starting the next one. It was exhausting, but the BOS's 30-day schedule demanded it.

My DHS director interview was most telling. Jack Dice, Ph.D., was a distinguished, tall, muscular, and professorial man. He had a baritone voice and inquisitive blue eyes, focusing unwaveringly on whomever he met. I sat in his large office overlooking downtown LA. The Dorothy Chandler Pavilion, which had hosted the Academy Awards eight times over 13 years, was visible from his top-floor office windows. While Dr. Dice had an engaging manner, he received me peevishly. I was a nuisance.

Instead of providing substantive responses to my questions, Dr. Dice answered me with quick, single words like *yes* or *no*. He refused to elaborate, so I took a different tack. I said, "What will you tell the people of LA about the state of this current project?" He looked at me with his penetrating blue eyes, letting silence hang between us. Finally, he said, "There are a minimum of ten number-one priorities I am responsible for at any one time, and this one failed to meet expectations."

I had no idea how to respond. It was not possible to have more than one number-one priority. This was deliberate ambiguity meant for a press conference. It was not a genuine assessment of the current situation. There was no insightful information on how to recover from this crisis. In fact, it clarified, in large part, why there was a crisis.

I smiled, and he tried to smile back, but it did not take. I spoke again with, "How do you imagine doing this project if you get a chance to do it over?" This time, he looked out the window at the concrete reflecting pool in front of the Department of Water and Power. Finally, he turned his face directly toward me and said, "I'd start with a vendor I trusted, rely on their partnership with DHS, and deliver a successful solution."

All I could think of was that there is no such thing as "a customer and vendor partnership." It's far more complex than that. Vendors are sellers, and customers are buyers. This does not have to be an uneasy relationship, but it isn't a partnership, because it goes beyond just mutual interests. In part, it's a competitive relationship built on self-interest. Vendors need to make money from customers while minimizing costs. Customers must obtain the best product from their vendors at the lowest possible price. At the same time, it's a relationship with some mutual interests. Sustainable vendors must be profitable, and customers require product satisfaction. The customer and vendor relationship requires understanding and balancing both mutual and self-interests.

What Dr. Dice did not say was most revealing. The project and DHS lacked leadership. It was his responsibility. While I did not expect him to admit to his lack of leadership, I did hope for substance. No wonder DHS's reputation was about failure!

I was heading for a disaster. I learned a long time ago from a senior PM that if you did not know the outcome of your data gathering and analysis by the halfway mark in your schedule, you were in deep trouble. I was past that point here, and I didn't know the outcome.

I knew, like all project failures, it was rarely a technical issue, and all involved parties shared responsibility for the adverse outcome. There was insufficient clarity to define a meaningful corrective action plan (CAP) at this point. I could not just blame the project failure on the director's lack of leadership. There was more, but it escaped me so far. I was extremely uncomfortable.

I met with Dave, explaining my dilemma. Dave was not sympathetic. He impatiently said to go back and get more information. I acknowledged his directive by responding that this was a schedule issue. I could confirm a meaningful set of factors causing project failure and recommend county corrective action. But I could not complete this scope of work within the 30-day schedule with less than two weeks remaining. Using silence to my advantage, we sat quietly. Finally, Dave said he would speak with Jane. He asked, "How much more time do you need?"

I requested another 30 days. Dave frowned as if I was foolish asking for so much time. The telephone rang, and he picked up the receiver. Putting his hand over the microphone, he dismissed me, saying he would let me know about any schedule extension tomorrow after the board meeting.

I received only 15 more days. In the remaining time, I had to gather a whole lot more data, analyze and formulate it into meaningful findings, draw logical conclusions from these findings, and prepare recommendations. This had to include an achievable CAP, project schedule, and budget. I called Gustavo Mongo at our Seattle office. I told him to read everything I posted to Dropbox and start in Los Angeles by 1:00 tomorrow afternoon. In the meantime, I went to see Oscar.

By now Oscar and I had an amiable relationship where we spent time reviewing the facts collected to date. These meetings always started no earlier than 6:00 p.m., while they often lasted three to four hours. Oscar appeared to never eat or take a break for any reason.

Oscar had a wife, a young daughter, and a teenage son from an earlier marriage. He had breakfast with his wife and daughter every morning. He then took his daughter to before-school activities and arrived at work by 7:15.

He always had a new crisis assigned to him. I had no idea how he did it, but I had concerns about his workload and extended hours. This project, and all its tentacles, had to be his foremost responsibility if he was going to execute and successfully implement the CAP. Despite this, I was ready to tell Dave that Oscar was the right person for the job. However, I needed time to sort out whether this would prevent Oscar's future DHS CFO promotion.

Confirming DHS's choice of Oscar as the right person to manage the CAP disturbed me. I did not see myself as an arbiter of people's livelihood. There was a problem. There was a solution. My job was to bring them together, but I did not want to destroy Oscar's career future.

The DHS CFO spends their time in Sacramento and Washington, D.C., negotiating state and federal funding. The county supplied direct funds for only 15% of the department's budget, relying on direct and indirect state and federal funding for everything else. I had to talk this recommendation through with Oscar. I could not just drop it on him, even if he suspected I was going to recommend him for this assignment.

Oscar and I discussed the findings of facts known to us and agreed upon logical conclusions flowing from them. I told Oscar about my experience with Dr. Dice. In his usual manner, Oscar initially showed little expression other than to suggest he considered this project critical, and the director had his hands full. Oscar concurred the director's leadership was a requirement for project success without confirming it was absent and a significant contributing factor to the current crisis. He then just looked at me and said, "The BOS already identified the current director's replacement."

I was so surprised that I just continued our review on how the GMIS contract did not meet county needs. For example, there were no requirements referenced in the agreement, so there was no clear definition of the final solution or a measurable way to achieve acceptance. In fact, the DHS CIO, Juan Luis, independently added modules to the contract during negotiations, using referenced GMIS brochures to *clarify* what additions the county was acquiring. Oscar just nodded without any verbal response. Juan acted inappropriately. I previously shared this with Jane. I also confirmed her suspicion that county counsel did not negotiate a suitable IT contract.

I then explained to Oscar that Juan also authorized multiple GMIS payments for failed deliverables. Juan accepted deliverables that included impermissible defects, authorized GMIS payments, and later approved unwarranted payments for defect corrections while these deliverables continued to fail. It was not clear what was happening. Both the GMIS PM and DHS CIO denied any wrongdoing. Oscar stared at me. He finally broke the stare, saying Juan was already incurring dissent from DHS top leadership. Oscar did not elaborate. While to date, I had no reason to report any potential criminal activity about the county CIO to Jane, the GMIS PM and DHS CIO acted inappropriately.

To compound the situation, personnel at every level within DHS expressed strong dissatisfaction, if not outright hostility, toward the GMIS PM. This included severe concerns about both her technical and managerial skills, let alone her participation in improprieties. I even witnessed a Project Steering Committee meeting when she flatly denied any involvement with duplicate deliverable payments despite multiple paid invoices with her signature. Juan was also present and said nothing.

Oscar retold the awful story about the original department PM. The PM recently died of tongue cancer. His replacement, Sam Bali, was a technical expert lacking management skills. He was an affable character in one-on-one situations. Put him in charge of a team, as required by his new role, and he was awful. Managing people was just not his forte.

Oscar and I both saw the client/vendor relationship as exclusively competitive. Neither organization addressed the project-wide impact of the issues they faced. The GMIS PM did not invoke an escalation process with her superiors for issue resolution. Senior department management also appeared uninformed of the gravity of the situation, while front-line and middle management engaged in virtual vendor combat over the smallest issues.

After reviewing the resumes of GMIS project team members and speaking with them, none had large-scale system project experience. County counsel did not insist the GMIS contract include a clause requiring key project staff meet minimum qualifications. At most, each GMIS team member had one earlier project implementation in a small hospital. Oscar concurred and noted this just contributed to the lack of issue escalation and resolution with senior GMIS leadership. Oscar stated, "The GMIS team worked in a culture that concealed mistakes from their management and customers."

I noted Oscar did not comment on DHS project team comparable behavior, county counsel missteps, or the project leadership issue.

While Oscar explained he was not familiar with how to properly prepare requirements, he agreed with what I described. Specifically, project requirements management was so flawed, DHS could not rely on it. For example, about 75 DHS representatives took part in requirements definition, based on individual interviews conducted by GMIS. The GMIS analysts took this input and reconciled differences among themselves without verifying these updates with DHS users. There were similar examples in every imaginable functional area of the GMIS solution planned for DHS use.

Following our requirements definition discussion, I tried to find why the system implemented to date appeared to suffer from instability. Oscar mentioned fixes to defects only worked temporarily, if at all. Changes in one application area appeared to adversely affect other areas without explanation. I thought GMIS was not conducting adequate quality assurance (QA) to manage defect identification, resolution, and testing.

The outcome was terrible. The main billing module, dear to Oscar's expertise, was so defective it did not produce correct Medicaid claims. The county sent these claims to the state for health care services reimbursement, under Medi-Cal, the state's version of Medicaid. Medicaid is mostly federally funded insurance that states administer for U.S. citizens and qualified non-citizens who do not have the resources to pay for their health care. When Oscar discovered the Medi-Cal problem, there were $39 million in claims that previously passed their statute of limitations, preventing state reimbursement to the county. This was another crisis caused by the project that DHS assigned to Oscar for resolution. Oscar was amid negotiations with state officials and simultaneously preparing a potential lawsuit to resolve this issue favorably to the county.

Once Oscar found out the software was so unstable, he looked to revert to the old system. While extremely difficult to achieve, the county ran the old and new systems in parallel. Thankfully, this allowed them to restore the old system and leave the new GMIS solution behind.

We concluded our meeting with less-than-meaningful plans other than re-interviewing key individuals who represented the entire county and GMIS project. As I left, I did not say, but thought, the distinct lack of GMIS QA needed more investigation. I knew QA practices. Something was just not right. I decided to have Gustavo randomly select production source code and conduct a systematic examination to explain if there was something more than poor QA causing so many unresolved software defects.

During the next two days, I re-interviewed key project representatives. I did not find anything other than re-emphasis of previously found issues. While confirming, it did not supply insight for recommendations I hoped to deliver to the county for meaningful corrective action. I had nothing other than a treatise on how to manage a project. The county needed exact and actionable solutions, not general and amorphous management concepts. This would fall on deaf county ears. Meanwhile, GMIS would make millions more trying to correct their failure. The result would be an extremely long schedule, a huge budget overrun, and inferior quality. The county would be better off canceling the entire project now and staying with the old system.

SURPRISE

Gustavo was at GMIS's LA data center and randomly selecting application code from the program library. This took considerable time between accessing the information and reviewing the code. Gustavo planned to return to Seattle to document his findings, letting me know the outcome as soon as he finished it. Meanwhile, I started drafting the report for the BOS.

At 2:30 a.m., my telephone rang, waking me from deep sleep. I forgot I was in a hotel room and not in my bed at home. I barely spoke into the phone. Gustavo excitedly offered a quick, "Max, this is Gustavo." I thought something was horribly wrong. Why would an employee call me at this hour? "Gustavo, are you okay?" I was startled by the telephone ringing, and Gustavo's greeting shifted my adrenaline rush from surprise to fear.

Gustavo sounded scared. The cadence of his explanation for the call was as powerful as what he said. "Max, GMIS's main billing program is totally corrupt. Control within the program jumps all over the place. It's impossible to follow. No one can fix the defects, let alone enhance the software to meet the county's unique requirements.

"I randomly selected programs from the library at the data center, but I did not request this main billing program. It was in the stack delivered to me. It's as if Salvador, the programmer analyst I worked with at the GMIS data center, wanted me to find the source of the financial system's problems. People get killed for this type of nightmare!"

I was fully awake now. Auto-pilot took over. I heard my voice speak to Gustavo, but I had no idea where my thoughts originated. "Gustavo, take a deep breath. Copy everything you have and schedule a FedEx pick-up for first thing this morning. Send the copy to my friend Teri Amato. I'll call her now and leave her a voicemail message."

Teri and I went to graduate school together. Subsequently I worked as an IT consultant at an international accounting firm. Every year I had to perform IT audits for a couple of the firm's accounting clients. It was boring work. To make it interesting, I always selected clients with highly sophisticated IT shops like Boeing.

Teri worked in Boeing's internal auditor's office, responsible for the internal controls and risks to the company's networks. Eventually, Teri rose to the senior position of internal auditor.

We stayed connected, so contacting her was not unusual. Her second opinion would virtually end the possibility of GMIS, or anyone else, successfully challenging our findings.

Gustavo at once released a breath of relief I could hear on the phone. We had no facts as to why we received this program. It was imperative we had another opinion to back up our position before presenting it to the county.

Teri called me as soon as she got my message later that morning. I shared my plan for her second opinion. She said she would convey her position in an email, so I had it in writing. At 1:00 p.m., that afternoon, Teri thought it was worse than Gustavo said. The software was corrupt.

Teri explained, "It's incredibly old software, and now it's spaghetti code. When I reviewed the billing program, it was like unraveling a tangled, buggy mess, which looked like a bowl of linguine instead of a finely tuned piece of code.

"One individual file had more than ten thousand lines of code. Industry-proven practice would use five hundred separate files instead. GMIS's approach ignored the widely accepted computer science principle of *separation of concerns* from the early 1970s. This essential software design and architecture principle says that changing anything changes everything. This explains why Oscar kept finding new errors in the main billing program after GMIS tried to fix defects. Each fix introduced new defects."

PLAN

I scheduled a meeting with Oscar for later that afternoon and briefed him. He said it explained so much affecting the project. With his conclusion confirming mine, I met with Jane that evening. She was surprised at my findings and infuriated with GMIS.

During the following days, I wrote the draft CAP. I hit obstacles and worked my way through them, mostly discussing and resolving them in conversations with Oscar. In one case, I wanted to confirm Oscar agreed with the CAP recommendation on which software to implement first. When the GMIS financial system failed, DHS stopped all plans to implement remaining clinical and administrative modules. DHS needed to follow an entirely different sequence, starting with clinical software.

We both knew that since the county started with GMIS, EHR systems were now a U.S. requirement. The Centers for Medicare and Medicaid Services supplied financial incentives for health care providers and hospitals that implemented qualified EHRs. The Centers for Medicare and Medicaid Services planned to penalize those not complying after a forthcoming deadline.

Oscar explained DHS planned to replace its financial systems and then work on the clinical ones. He noted DHS currently used legacy clinical systems as a substitute for an EHR. This included cobbled-together systems for clinicians and their departments without interfaces, like radiology, pharmacy, and laboratory. Even in cases where interfaces existed, reporting and accreditation needs remained unmet, resulting in manual document preparation and potential errors affecting patients adversely.

We both agreed starting with the EHR made sense since it improved patient care. An EHR also integrated with DHS existing and planned systems and business processes. For example, using an EHR includes data coded at the point of care (POC), capturing billing codes that affect revenue cycle management (RCM) and revealing care patients receive for ongoing improvement.

At the end of our discussion, Oscar responded with, "The EHR is the most significant health IT investment of this department. To do the CAP project right, we must start with the EHR and maximize its benefits before financial system implementation."

I said, "Okay, which county hospital goes first?"

Oscar said we build a schedule to accommodate an inpatient EHR for the three hospitals that started implementing the GMIS solution. They were Martin Luther King, Jr/Drew Medical Center (KDMC), an acute care facility; RLANRC, a rehab facility for brain and spinal injuries; and High Desert Hospital (HDH), a small acute care and rehab facility. The other three hospitals could wait since they were just planning their GMIS implementation. More importantly, they were outside the scope of the CAP, as well as outpatient services at all six hospitals.

A week before the deadline, Dave scheduled my presentation on the BOS agenda. Four days before the BOS meeting, Oscar and I met in the evening to review my draft, finishing long after midnight. Two days later, I reviewed the updated draft with Jane. While she had few changes, she shared what the BOS was likely to do next. They would receive my report favorably but would not pass judgment on the CAP until the Technology Planning and Oversight Committee reviewed my final deliverable, met with me to answer questions, and issued its opinion. The Committee included CIOs from major Los Angeles companies like Toyota of America, Northrop Grumman, and Disney. I was ready, given the number of inputs, the software metrics I used for estimating the action plan schedule and cost, our company internal review, Oscar's extensive discussions with me, and my persistence. There's a fine line between persistence and insanity. I'd never succeed unless I was a little bit crazy.

What ensued was a whirlwind of fact checking, method review, and an excruciating session of test questions and answers that Dave drilled me on to prepare for the BOS and Technology Planning and Oversight Committee. In the end, the actual BOS and Technology Planning and Oversight Committee sessions included unanimous approval of the report and CAP, subject to one last step. Jane then told me DHS had its own plan the BOS wanted me to review before they mandated CAP execution.

She also said county counsel refused to pay my latest invoice given my draft report concluded they did not deliver skilled legal services for IT contract negotiations. In fact, county counsel was particularly outraged by my recommendation, which the BOS planned to approve, requiring all future IT contracts undergo review by attorneys with proven large-scale IT contract negotiation skills and experience. Jane smiled at me. I was not happy. Jane said, "Don't worry, Max, I'll make sure you receive prompt payment for all of your services."

The DHS plan was awful from the start, particularly since Juan authored it without input from anyone else. He proclaimed he expected BOS execution of his plan.

Oscar and I strategized on how to manage Juan's failed approach. Juan had a violent temper, throwing furniture and yelling at his subordinates. He was a tyrant. Oscar scheduled a meeting with Juan and key DHS staff involved in the GMIS project, who all had a stake in the CAP.

Oscar tried to start the meeting, but Juan interrupted at once, taking over. Everyone sat silently listening to his plan despite its absence of basic IT and project management fundamentals, sponsorship, requirements management, testing, and so forth. Juan wrote this as a high overview document without thought other than his desire to control the situation in the lead role and as an attempt to overcome his prior inappropriate actions with GMIS.

Finally, Juan talked himself out and silence prevailed. Oscar sat waiting. I explained that Jane, at the direction of the BOS, expected me to review DHS's plan before going ahead with any next steps. Juan, incensed, sprayed spit on me as he roared with quivering lips and stormed out of the room.

Everyone else stared at the tabletop in front of them and said nothing. Finally, JoAnn Graden, one of Juan's staff, spoke of how this was a classic example of a disagreement with Juan. I nodded, encouraged by her outspokenness, and asked her to open the door to our meeting room to see if we could find Juan and coax him back.

Juan eventually and begrudgingly joined us after a face-saving dance. He was a prisoner of his own making. But this was still an issue DHS needed to resolve. I stated the ground rules, explaining we would discuss and not argue about the two plans. I said no one was to leave until we all agreed upon the CAP. We started in earnest and continued for the next six hours without any major outbursts. While unbearable at times, we combined ideas from the DHS plan into the CAP for BOS-mandated execution. DHS additions were inconsequential, and the BOS would mandate continuing with these updates.

The following day at breakfast, I met with Oscar. I wanted a drink, but I knew this was not something Oscar would ever consider proper. Instead, we chatted for a while and sat in companionable silence relishing our success. I then told him he was my choice for managing CAP execution. He graciously understood that this derailed his CFO promotion. Oscar was a true professional. He offered only one requirement: I must supply project management QA to him and the county throughout DHS corrective action. By QA, Oscar meant regular interim checks on tasks to complete project deliverables. This ensured deliverables met pre-defined standards. This was not software development QA or testing. Oscar expected me to perform project quality management (QM). This role included QA, evaluating ongoing work on deliverable preparation and quality control, performing the final check at deliverable completion to assess compliance with pre-defined acceptance criteria. I preferred thinking of project QM as finding whether there was project adherence to proven practices. My interpretation avoided the academic view of QM, applying a more realistic approach.

I explained Oscar's position and offered my interpretation to Jane, and she agreed to my role. The BOS later passed a resolution approving the CAP. They also amended the contract with my firm to include QM and monthly progress reports about successful compliance with the CAP. While we all weathered a horrific storm, the future was far more daunting than anyone imagined.

2

Change

Oscar and I met in his office to prepare the foundation needed before we could even consider the details of the CAP. I started undauntedly with, "DHS is trying to do everything at once and not accomplishing anything beneficial!"

Oscar cringed before he responded with, "Our Executive Committee prepares a strategic plan every five years without an IT perspective. We never execute our plan, even though we update it annually. Multiple crises always thwart us. We have a reputation for failure. We live up to it."

I shook my head. "The current mess is a direct result of that thinking. When do you expect to try something sensible instead of running from one crisis to another?"

Oscar said, "How about now? The board just ordered us to implement the fix to this crisis."

"Oscar, that's not enough. As you know, as soon as the county approved using our services to implement the CAP, my staff conducted an organizational change stress test, evaluating priorities competing for DHS resources.[1] The results show that DHS continues to ignore the constant barrage of competing priorities that hijack strategic plans. We need to step back, think strategically, prioritize initiatives, and achieve value. DHS must first prepare a strategic plan while accommodating constant change. When I say *strategic*, I mean creating a vision that conceptualizes DHS's purpose and managing choices or priorities with a plan to achieve that concept of the future. DHS must do this for the CAP to succeed now and in the future."

DOI: 10.4324/9781003003809-2

DELTA FRAMEWORK

"This is an enormous change, and that scares DHS leadership!" confided Oscar.

"You're absolutely correct," I said. "It all comes down to change, and that can be frightening. Change is deeply human. DHS leadership keeps the status quo to help feel in control. Unfortunately, recurring IT failures don't support that. Despite continued failures, DHS leadership avoids doing IT projects differently because that's an unknown to them. They fear the unknown, which, to them, means total loss of control."

"You're right," confirmed Oscar.

"People change all the time without losing control," I argued. "They do this by learning new skills and behaviors safely while gaining greater control that result in successful outcomes, not more failures. Look at it this way: there's a solution for every problem DHS has. Others have solved them before. It's about knowing what works and applying it to the current situation."

"So, what methodology do you propose we use?" asked Oscar.

I said, "My company created the DELTA Framework. This is the integrator or holistic framework created to view a project as a whole, not the sum of the separate change, IT, and project management methodologies and Agile philosophy. Treating a project with one of these or applying them separately doesn't offer enough to deliver success in complex environments like DHS. For example, project management methodology includes a series of processes. These processes involve leading a team through an assumed predicable plan of tasks to achieve objectives within constraints. Software development methodology includes highly structured tasks for building a new or configuring an existing product to meet an organization's needs. The success of these methodologies depends on but omits synchronizing with organizational leadership at every level, as required by a change management methodology. Such leadership, based on the Agile philosophy, drives required tasks using an independent collaborative team and an iterative incremental execution approach. The philosophy and methodologies are intimately interconnected within DELTA and understood within the whole only. While DELTA is not a methodology, it improves the quality of what the individual parts offer by unifying them. This is a driving reason for the DELTA Framework."

Oscar said, "I understand what you said theoretically. What's an example that applies to our project?"

I offered, "The project management methodology begins with *initiating*, after preparation of a business case or the CAP.[2] The change management methodology improves on this by starting with the business case, the source justification for the project.[3] Agile take this one step further. It avoids handoffs to minimize miscommunication and mistakes. There's often a handoff between those preparing the business case and the individuals initiating the project. Employing the Agile management philosophy, in DHS's situation, suggests involving the same participants in business case preparation and project initiation. In this example, DELTA's combined approach puts DHS in an enviable position that increases understanding and enhances insights from the start."

"I got it," acknowledge Oscar.

I then went on, "This framework also draws on the principle of ongoing process improvement, not the goal of just completing a project. The DELTA Framework is about what needs to change and how to optimize it continually. While DELTA does not rigorously adhere to capability maturity model integration (CMMI), it draws on the concept of moving an organization through process maturity levels, completing at continuous optimization."[4]

I took out an ordered stack of diagrams from my portfolio and handed it to Oscar.

"The top diagram is an organization's processes fit in multiple levels. For example, previous DHS IT projects involved Levels 1 and 2 processes, with others at Levels 3 and 4 because of IT requirements. During CAP execution, applying methodologies included in DELTA will help DHS evolve processes to the highest level, continuously improving DHS IT and operations."

I asked Oscar to take the remaining items from the top of the stack and arrange the change, project, IT management, and Agile principle diagrams in a circle corresponding to their symbol on the DELTA Framework placed in the center. I then explained how the DELTA Framework works with these three methodologies and the one philosophy.

Change Management Methodology

I introduced change management as the core of the DELTA Framework not just because it unifies Agile IT and project management but to emphasize

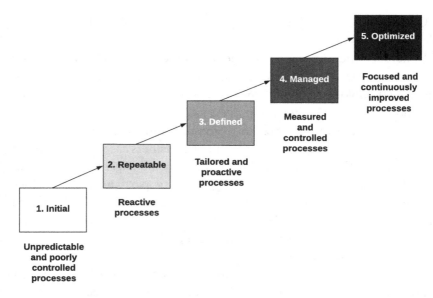

Capability Maturity Model Integration.[5]

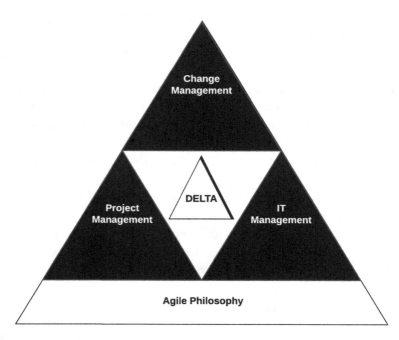

DELTA Framework.

that all human endeavors, including projects, involve change. In fact, nothing is stationary. DELTA uses the change management methodology from Implementation Management Associates' Accelerating Implementation Management methodology created by Don Harrison. AIM emphasizes rapid change to realize expected benefits and to minimize sticking to the status quo.

AIM includes a ten-part road map listed in the change management diagram. AIM also relies on assessments, such as climate, sponsorship, readiness, and risk, administered to evaluate organizational maturity. The assessment results show how to move through these ten components to the next level and eventually achieve and sustain change.[7]

As the county considers the aftermath of another IT fiasco, everyone involved is thinking about how to avoid failure. Failing again or canceling all future IT projects are not practical options. DHS must do something different to ensure project success. As DHS grapples with how to navigate success, it must change.

When done carefully, DHS can change and succeed. AIM starts by defining the change with a business case. The CAP is a business case, documenting reasons for initiating the project, estimating resources, and

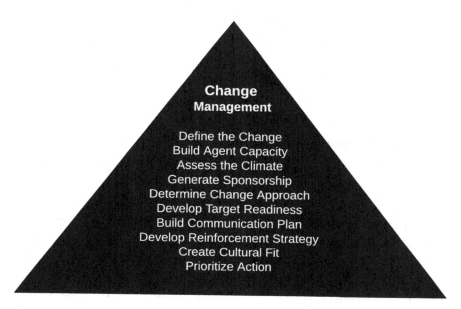

Change Management Road Map.[6]

specifying benefits realized from this investment. This is not enough on its own. Using AIM, the CAP fits within a larger context, a purpose-driven vision from DHS's top leadership to the frontline. This aligns the entire organization according to a defined purpose.

The business case is key, but it doesn't paint a picture of the future people can feel. It's an emotional thing. If everyone in the organization can explain to their family why the project is a great idea, then DHS has staff engagement. One of the best ways to do this is with visual depictions, displaying the vision, including where everyone is going and what it will look like when they get there. As they say, a picture is worth a thousand words.[8]

The AIM methodology is a mix of practical tools that establish and measure achievement of long-term change. After documenting the business case that specifies the change, AIM examines the organization's history or climate for change. It underscores the ultimate importance of leadership driving the change at all levels, not just the top of the organization, including how to manage inadequate leadership and maximize frontline input. AIM also includes communication and reinforcement strategies, plans, and specific tools required to execute the change. Critical to AIM's success are the tools for evaluating the current environment, methods for responding to it, and techniques that demonstrate progress of individuals and the organization achieving the benefits of change.

"I think I understand, but I want to confirm this is just a summary of each methodology and the philosophy combined by the DELTA Framework," interrupted Oscar.

"Yes, that's correct," I said.

Project Management Methodology

I then referred to the project management methodology included in DELTA. Project management relies on a traditional approach. The Project Management Institute documented this in its Project Management Body of Knowledge (PMBOK) Guide. Their traditional methodology includes 49 interrelated processes, categorized into a five-stage lifecycle of process groups: initiating, planning, executing, monitoring and controlling, and closing.[9]

Each process, also organized over the ten knowledge areas listed in the project management diagram, contain inputs and outputs. Application of tools and techniques executes individual processes and their interactions with other processes while applying expertise included in these knowledge areas. A skilled PM executes these processes while progressing from project initiation through closure.

"While I've never received formal project management certification, many DHS personnel have," Oscar said. "Unfortunately, despite certification, we have both poor and successful PMs. What do you attribute this to?"

"It's like any profession," I explained. "The degree, title, or certification is part of a larger package. An official certificate is an indicator of an individual's understanding of methodological theory. It's not a measure of their successful application of it in real-life situations with the challenging dynamics of people and organizations. Human Resources (HR) often requires a certification to minimize the number of job applicants. Once an applicant gets an interview, HR wants to know if the candidate can do the work. They determine this by focusing on experience, potential, and cultural fit, not certification. As it turns out, one of the most influential factors to consider is determining what any professional, including a PM, learns from their mistakes. If a PM claims they never fail, they don't have enough experience or they're dishonest. Bottom line, experience is the key to success because everyone makes mistakes, and, hopefully, this helps

Project Management Knowledge Areas.[10]

them learn how to perform better in the future no matter their certification status."

IT Management Methodology

Next, I told Oscar about the software development lifecycle methodology included in DELTA. In the mid-1980s, the waterfall methodology divided a software project into a manufacturing process with linear, sequential, and dependent phases, including requirements, design, implementation, verification, and maintenance. This involved completing each phase deliverable before continuing to the next.[11]

Originally, I applied waterfall to both commercial off-the-shelf (COTS) software configurations and new system development. My company then sought a formal software development methodology, which we derived from the Institute of Electrical and Electronics Engineers (IEEE) Guide to the Software Engineering Body of Knowledge (SWEBOK). I pointed to the diagram on Oscar's desk listing the 11 IT knowledge areas.

Oscar mentioned that while DHS relied on waterfall, it recently started sending IT staff to Agile software development training. This was fantastic

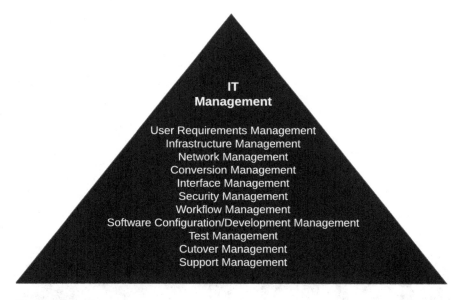

IT Knowledge Areas.

news. While I knew it was a daunting task to introduce Agile to DHS, this helped make it slightly easier.

Agile Philosophy

DELTA initially relied on the traditional PMBOK Guide and waterfall but then switched to Agile. In 2001, 17 software engineers met at a Utah ski resort and founded the Agile Alliance. They created a radical new management philosophy applied to software development. Now, Agile is a widely accepted problem-solving mindset applied to complex knowledge fields, including project management, based on four values and 12 principles.[12] I pointed to the last diagram on Oscar's desk, listing the Agile principles.

Project management and IT software development methodologies have crucial deficiencies resolved by Agile principles. Project management and software development depend on complete and long-term planning to minimize change. Project management documents precise plans handed off for execution, monitoring and controlling, and closing. Software development prepares detailed user requirements, handing them off to software developers for product creation, testing, and delivery. The intent is to complete an analysis that puts an end to any questions about the plans or product requirements. While there are adjustments, traditional project management and waterfall impose inflexibility, leaving little room to anticipate changing individual and organizational needs during both a long-term project lifecycle and software development, where change always happens. This type of long-term planning is artificial and results in dissatisfaction with the final product.

While DELTA embraces change management as the overriding methodology that combines IT and project management, Agile philosophy augments DELTA with an entirely unique way of thinking. This includes addressing the omissions of traditional project management and waterfall. Agile depends on a small independent team. The team collaborates, adapts, and constantly responds to change in short and repeated cycles. They build an improved and useable product in each short cycle, instead of spending considerable time and other resources to build the *perfect* product. Every cycle includes value based on priorities set by a product owner (PO) receiving customer input. Instead of long-term project plans and status reports, the PO shares a functioning product with customers to gauge progress at the end of every short development cycle. This promotes

Agile Principles

1. Our highest priority is to satisfy the customer through early and continuous delivery of valuable software.
2. Welcome changing requirements, even late in development. Agile processes harness change for the customer's competitive advantage.
3. Deliver working software frequently, from a couple of weeks to a couple of months, with a preference to the shorter timescale.
4. Business people and developers must work together daily throughout the project.
5. Build projects around motivated individuals. Give them the environment and support they need and trust them to get the job done.
6. The most efficient and effective method of conveying information to and within a development team is face-to-face conversation.
7. Working software is the primary measure of progress.
8. Agile processes promote sustainable development. The sponsors, developers, and users should be able to maintain a constant pace indefinitely.
9. Continuous attention to technical excellence and good design enhances agility.
10. Simplicity–the art of maximizing the amount of work not done–is essential.
11. The best architectures, requirements, and designs emerge from self-organizing teams. At regular intervals, the team reflects on how to become more effective, then tunes and adjusts its behavior accordingly.
12. At regular intervals, the team reflects on how to become more effective, then tunes and adjusts its behavior accordingly.

Agile Principles.[13]

customer collaboration to evaluate new product increments and include changes before moving to subsequent ones.

Finally, these short cycles set a predictable velocity or pace to complete prioritized work, which informs forecasting a product and project completion schedule. This schedule relies on actual repeated short production cycles, instead of less reliable long-term estimates found in traditional project management and waterfall.

Like change, IT, and project management methodologies, Agile philosophy has its own approaches. Scrum is an Agile approach that is now the most popular. DELTA relies on Scrum, in part because it involves small teams that break their prioritized work products into goals and repeatedly improve them during each fixed work period.[14]

"I hear you explaining," said Oscar. "On the one hand, we made a mistake with the GMIS project. Hopefully, our unwelcomed experience will teach us what we did wrong. But we have yet to learn how to do things right, especially when executing the CAP.

"On the other hand, others previously learned from mistakes like ours and fashioned proven solutions. Such hindsight is a gift because you integrated these lessons learned into the DELTA Framework, so you can show us what to do differently to succeed. You can help us improve, including repeatable new patterns. To do this, we must adopt the DELTA Framework that relies on organizational change to combine Agile IT project management."

"That's the essence of it." I said.

Reality

Oscar proposed, "While I understand the merits of what you are saying about DELTA, let's do a reality check involving working with DHS."

I welcomed Oscar's proposition.

Oscar then said, "Methodologies come and go. While they may include genuinely clever ideas, DHS wastes precious time and money on them when all we need is common sense."

I grinned and suggested, "There's a great quote, generally attributed to Voltaire, which says, *'Common sense is not so common.'* This viewpoint, which I embrace, stresses why it's important to delve into methodology deeply. Often those who are new to a methodology don't understand it well enough or lack sufficient experience to know when it's okay to deviate from it and simply apply common sense."

I chuckled and added, "In *Pirates of the Caribbean: The Curse of the Black Pearl*, Captain Barbossa says, 'The [pirate] code is more what you'd call "guidelines" than actual rules.'[15] I agree with this viewpoint. I'm not a purist when it comes to most methodologies because reality requires deviating from them. For example, a typical public sector procurement requires a contract, schedule, budget, and deliverable acceptance criteria built on an approved statement of work. Public agencies don't have the liberty to conduct procurements with much flexibility. Instead, they try to maintain accountability with absolutes. At the same time, there are plenty of ways to use change-driven methodologies within these constraints. For example, you can include prioritized requirements and schedule ranges when preparing a project time estimate, as commonly used in Agile to adapt to change. This approach is contrary to the highly structured change order process described and promoted in project management methodology.

"So, while we rely on organizational change combined with Agile IT project management, we adhere to them together in the DELTA Framework as guidelines, not dogma. If we don't do that, we'll never succeed when confronted with the reality of each project's political environment, different cultures, and other constraints and dependencies. Success requires having experience, maneuvering adeptly, solving problems, learning as you go to improve outcomes, and setting realistic expectations derived from proven methodologies."

Oscar then suggested, "The DELTA Framework is just a bunch of jargon that relies on fancy words from popular methodologies."

I countered, "Change, IT, and project management methodologies and Agile philosophy continue to evolve, using different elaborate terms. However, there are fundamentals that remain the same no matter what you call them. For example, stakeholder analysis, requirements management, collaboration, frequent and interim product reviews, and lessons learned assessments are key to product and project success no matter what the newest or updated methodology or philosophy calls them. We need a common language to communicate these and other fundamentals responsible for IT project success. I really don't care what people call these fundamentals, so long as everyone relies on the same terms to communicate and understand each other.

"What's also critical is that some people use methodologies deceptively. It's important to find and correct this dishonest behavior immediately, given so much is at risk in IT projects. For example, some vendors use terms from Agile as a sales pitch without knowing the philosophy or delivering the customer solution according to it. Agile terms like User Stories, Story Points, Sprints, and the like don't mean anything unless the vendor proves they understand and apply the intended meaning of these words.

"DHS must fully understand methodologies to manage the risk associated with vendor inappropriate practices. For example, suppose a vendor, using Agile, says they welcome customer change, but DHS introduced so many changes that it was responsible for project delay. Based on understanding the philosophy, DHS should expect the vendor to approach an increased volume of changed requirements by seeking a solution together instead of blaming the problem on the customer."

RESILIENCE

Oscar gazed out his office window, then looked at me and said, "We must be careful. There's only so much change DHS can absorb. I am not sure how we can overcome our history, digest our failures, tackle the CAP, and use DELTA with its different methodologies and the Agile mindset."

I could sense that while he understood what I meant, he needed help, given the required change was one of the most resource-intensive undertakings ever considered by DHS. I paused, then answered, "Everything you are about to do manages the volume of change DHS can expect to sustain. The current situation is unique, though. The project failure continues to traumatize the organization. The board demands DHS succeed. This means DHS must change. DHS is in an extremely uncomfortable position currently. It unfroze from the status quo because of its traumatic failure. It is now adrift and uncertain about how to continue. We have a rare opportunity to redefine how DHS works. This is about continuous improvement and learning.

"One of the most powerful things DHS leadership can do, in a situation like this, is to openly acknowledge their mistakes, explain what they learned, and define what will change. Leadership must admit its failures as an essential condition of building trust, instead of covering them up or shifting the blame. Such an admission gives DHS staff the confidence to move forward with the expectation of a different outcome, despite past failures. Once it's out in the open, education can begin. This includes DHS leadership instituting a structured mechanism, such as regular meetings, where leadership and staff openly assess what went wrong, identify how to minimize future failures, and discuss how to help each other understand what the trauma meant personally and organizationally. Connecting to each other individually and organizationally offers confidence-building strength to help reconnect the organization to its purpose without losing sight of the lessons learned from the past. Once DHS embraces this approach, it can move forward with resilience and set the CAP as a priority. AIM manages this process with the required identification of a desired future state, as defined in the CAP, and a process for getting there successfully."

NOTES

1. Don Harrison, *Introducing the Accelerating Implementation Methodology (AIM) A Practical Guide to Change Project Management* (Lakewood, CO: Implementation Management Associates, 2017), 30.
2. Project Management Institute, *A Guide to the Project Management Body of Knowledge (PMBOK Guide)*, PMBOK Guide, 6th ed. (Newton Square, PA: Project Management Institute, 2017), 25, 75.
3. Harrison, *Introducing the Accelerating Implementation Methodology (AIM) A Practical Guide to Change Project Management*, 10.
4. "Capability Maturity Model Integration," Wikipedia, 2021, https://en.wikipedia.org/wiki/Capability_Maturity_Model_Integration
5. Ibid.
6. Harrison, *Introducing the Accelerating Implementation Methodology (AIM) A Practical Guide to Change Project Management*, 1.
7. Ibid.
8. Claire McCarthy, Douglas Eastman, and David E. Garets, *Effective Strategies for CHANGE™, Effective Strategies for CHANGE™* (New York, NY: HIMSS Publishing, 2018), https://doi.org/10.4324/9780429055010. Chap. 2, Google Books.
9. Project Management Institute, *A Guide to the Project Management Body of Knowledge (PMBOK Guide)*, 556.
10. Ibid.
11. "Waterfall Model," Wikipedia, 2021, https://en.wikipedia.org/wiki/Waterfall_model
12. "Agile Software Development," Wikipedia, 2018, https://en.wikipedia.org/wiki/Agile_software_development
13. Kent Beck et al., "12 Principles Behind the Agile Manifesto," *Agile Alliance*, 2019, www.agilealliance.org/agile101/12-principles-behind-the-agile-manifesto/
14. "Scrum (Software Development)," Wikipedia, 2021, https://en.wikipedia.org/wiki/Scrum_(software_development)
15. "Pirates of the Caribbean: The Curse of the Black Pearl—Wikiquote," Wikiquote, 2021, https://en.wikiquote.org/wiki/Pirates_of_the_Caribbean:_The_Curse_of_the_Black_Pearl

3

Strategy

Meeting days later in Oscar's office, I learned the board requested the department director's resignation. While the GMIS project failure was not the sole reason, it was a key final ingredient. Most unexpectedly, within two weeks of Dr. Dice's resignation, the board announced DHS's new leader. The board appointed Dr. Gregory Zorn, the director of New York Health + Hospitals (NYHH), the nation's largest public health care system. The board had started a confidential executive search before requesting Dr. Dice's resignation.

Oscar briefed the new director about the CAP. This included ensuring DHS publicly reconciled its history of IT failures, prepared a viable strategic plan, and complied with the BOS mandate about my QM role and our application of the DELTA Framework. Oscar, at Dr. Zorn's request, started organizing the failure reconciliation and strategic planning processes. Dr. Zorn told Oscar he was familiar with AIM. Once DHS concluded the failure reconciliation process, Dr. Zorn wanted to begin with business strategic planning followed by preparing corresponding IT strategies.

I commented, "I'd start with IT integrated into the strategic planning process. Understanding DHS IT and business tight integration helps to define the initiatives and capacity available for the strategic plan. The phrase *digital transformation* says it all. IT offers useful input into business strategies, potentially shaping the very nature of DHS. For example, an EHR transforms how DHS patients and medical providers interact."

Oscar did not object. He simply agreed.

"Oscar," I said. "You're not complying just to avoid a disagreement, are you?"

"No!" he declared earnestly. "I'm learning. I made a mistake. I need to correct it and revise my thinking. We are changing our organization. You're advising us on how to do that, starting with the strategic plan."

DOI: 10.4324/9781003003809-3

PURPOSE

I welcomed Oscar's candor with an untroubled nod. "DHS is a conventional organization," I said. "It built a culture based on employee self-interest. Employees work to receive DHS payment that benefits them personally. If DHS leadership connects its employees to a vision or higher purpose, something greater than themselves, it will inspire and foster commitment, engagement, and creativity.[1] Everyone needs something that fulfills them. DHS is a health care organization that lost its purpose.

"Aligning employee interests with purpose drives ongoing change and success. Just look at examples from household names like Costco, Commerce Bank, and Amazon."[2]

"I agree with you, but I'm still not convinced we can save DHS from failing again," Oscar argued.

I asserted, "DHS had a crisis, challenging leadership to do things differently. To date, DHS's strategic planning defined a direction, guiding decision making for resource allocation without focusing on a purpose. Leadership needs to dedicate itself to identifying and aligning an organizational purpose with employees' personal desires for meaningful work and learning. This intersection is an energy source for change that DHS has yet to tap. Employees will commit, engage, and find the energy to work collectively on achieving project success, even adapting during disruption caused by this change initiative.[3]

"Whenever we interact with someone, we see, perceive, and remember. Each of these may differ, and they may not even match what happened. To discover DHS's purpose, each member of top leadership needs to invest two to three days watching, listening, and asking provocative questions of frontline employees to attain a better understanding of them. Leveraging leadership like this will identify a compelling purpose that DHS will translate into the foundation for the CAP project. I guarantee leadership won't have to invent a higher purpose. DHS already has one."[4]

I explained that while there was much more to do, this was the crux of the matter. DHS must change dramatically. It had the capacity and the ability. This was the perfect time to do it. In fact, the benefit of doing it now was that all future projects stood a much better chance of success. It would be an investment in the future. As DHS learned to execute an IT project successfully, it would create positive energy, favorably affecting staff and patients.[5]

RESOURCES

Sensing draining intensity, I suggested we walk to get coffee outside of DHS headquarters. With movement, we both found a renewed fluency about the topic, as I continued. "When formulating and executing a strategic plan, it is important to note DHS is like all organizations: it must devote itself to three different areas. The first is running the organization, or *keeping the lights on*, maintaining existing services. The second is growing, or *supporting organic evolution*, improving and enhancing those existing services. The third is transforming, or *seeking new ways of doing business better*, radically changing service delivery."[6]

I continued, "Transforming is the province of strategic planning. But it's particularly problematic because strategic projects must compete with running and growing the organization for resources. As a result, the challenge is to select strategic projects that answer three fundamental questions about adhering to DHS's purpose. *Are we doing the right thing? Are we doing it right the first time? Are we achieving the greatest value?*[7] If we do not answer *yes* to each question, the cost is vastly greater than the direct dollar expenditure for a chosen priority. It leads to repeated resource waste, if not outright failure. DHS cannot continue to focus on whatever new priority erupts. DHS needs a well-defined approach, yet it must also refocus the strategic plan as change occurs. This means continually targeting top priorities that support DHS's purpose. Those initiatives serving DHS's purpose are the top priorities that receive resources. Leadership is responsible for preventing other pressures from deviating from this position."

Oscar offered, "We can put together a plan according to this approach, but I fear we can't sustain it."

"I know," I said, "So let's start with building blocks that overcome obstacles to DHS's ongoing success."

STORYTELLING

"Storytelling is a powerful place to start," I stated.

"What makes storytelling so special?" asked Oscar.

To begin with, I pointed out, "While everyone learns in one of three different ways, storytelling delivers all three simultaneously. Visual learners picture the story. Audible learners hear it. Kinesthetic learners feel it. It's powerful. It connects people with each other and with ideas."[8]

"When leadership tells their individual stories about this organization, they unite people by conveying culture, history, and values. Let's take an example from Dr. Zorn's recent experience before joining DHS. Suppose he presents the number of undocumented individuals served before and after he was NYHH's director. Employees learn he increased the number. Now, suppose the director tells a story, explaining how the purpose of NYHH helped him convince employers to pay a new tax for a program successfully delivering health care to undocumented individuals. Employees come away learning about the power of purpose. Storytelling is a compelling tool the director used to influence, teach, and inspire them."[9]

"So how do we get started?" asked Oscar.

"DHS's purpose is a key ingredient to the strategic planning process. Once defined, there are structured ways to embed storytelling as a communication tool that fosters change. This requires senior management, middle management, and frontline leadership and employees joining in their commitment to DHS's purpose. DHS starts by training top leadership on storytelling. Top leadership then openly tells their personal stories about DHS's purpose to middle management leadership, encouraging their team to do the same. Finally, top and middle leadership can start engaging frontline leadership and employees by challenging them to a contest. For example, tell them they have three months to post 5,000 of their own inspirational stories on DHS's purpose on the DHS intranet. This collective purpose contest includes employees inserting their own picture with the posting, a tagline on how DHS's purpose inspires them, and a brief description of the details."[10]

PRIORITIES

Oscar looked less than satisfied. "I like what you're saying, but I'm not convinced this approach prevents DHS from changing priorities during the next crisis, despite a purpose-driven strategic plan."

I responded, "Currently, leadership sees health care planning and delivery as predictable. They review the past, see the present including a market scan and other influencing factors, and think this defines an unalterable forecast. They rely on rigid long-term goals, strategies, and projects. A crisis emerges, and DHS abandons the strategic plan, hastily bowing to new priorities. Even if DHS updates the plan annually, this is not the real world. Reality is in constant flux, disrupting leadership's inflexible outlook."

Oscar quipped, "I still don't believe DHS leadership will just shift from rigid to flexible thinking."

"There's more on how this works," I answered.

Oscar leaned back in his chair and listened.

I stated that leadership needed a reliable vehicle to help them. They could create a Project Management Office (PMO) responsible for *all* DHS strategic business and IT initiatives and their project adherence to DHS's purpose. A PMO provides an orderly mechanism for leadership adjustments to strategic projects and their resources in response to changing conditions.

Organizations often view reporting projects for approval to a PMO as bureaucratic compliance that obstructs getting work done. So instead of forcing adherence of each new imitative to DHS's purpose, the PMO adds value. For example, when the next crisis occurs, leadership meets with the PMO's director and portfolio manager, evaluates the DHS project portfolio, and adjusts priorities to quell the latest calamity without totally compromising the strategic plan and all its dependent projects. This immediate reinforcement of the PMO's value is a far better response than leadership's past performance of abandoning the strategic plan altogether.

The PMO also offers other benefits. The chief project manager runs a center for training and adhering to project proven practices. The PMO collects data and reports at strategic and individual project levels that measure and maintain ongoing improvement, like helping DHS adhere to priorities during and after projects.

"How in the world are we going to get any agreement on our priorities?" countered Oscar.

I advised, "This is a wonderful time to start introducing an Agile technique called relative value. Relative value determines the worth of something when compared to something similar. In contrast, absolute value ignores comparison entirely, examining the worth of something individually.

"To apply relative value, in this situation, assume we start by preparing a list of all products DHS expects to create by strategic initiatives. Identify and assign a PO responsible for each product. Ask each PO to confidentially record how they distribute 1,000 points across all strategic products based on support for DHS's purpose, cost, risk, and dependency between products. This approach demonstrates a specific priority assigned to each product and how they rank relative to one another. Initially, perform this activity confidentially, eliminating one PO's allocation from affecting how their peers distribute points. After confidential ranking, each PO shares, individually, their priorities and reasoning with their customer. The POs update their scored priorities based on customer input. The strategic planning leadership then collects each PO's revised worksheet and determines product priorities, and associated strategic initiatives, by calculating total points given to each product. This approach gathers widespread individual and group input in the final decision."

"I like this Agile technique," conceded Oscar.

"Good," I responded. "This is by no means the only way to prioritize strategic initiatives and their products. For now, it introduces DHS to Agile and how to set priorities using a technique from Scrum."

TEAM SIZE

While I addressed Oscar's immediate concerns, he thought of more.

"How do we determine the strategic planning team size?" he asked.

"Excluding a facilitator, the best approach is to limit the team to seven to nine participants. I find it useful to perform strategic planning sessions with an external facilitator. It is also helpful to conduct these sessions off site, away from distractions that provide easy opportunities to leave and not participate."

"What!" Oscar exclaimed. "How do you expect us to keep to that number? We have almost 35,000 employees, a budget of $4 billion, and responsibility for virtually every medical specialty in ambulatory and inpatient health care."

"Let me explain," I said. "You're right. DHS is too diverse an organization to limit yourselves, but not necessarily when you need a core team of knowledgeable people organized to tackle strategic planning. In my experience, a small team of seven to nine participants is better at collaboration, which is essential to getting the job done successfully."

Oscar frowned. "I get it, but I still cannot limit this team to seven to nine. There are just too many crucial differences to consider, like work shifts, geographic locations, collective bargaining requirements, and affinity groups of all kinds that we can't ignore."

I nodded understanding, then explained more about the team makeup. In the case of strategic planning, the core team might include the director, CFO, COO, CIO, CMIO, and chief nursing officer. Before this team begins strategic planning, they gather information from focus groups, providing pertinent internal and external organization perspectives. Focus group participants include senior tenured leadership, recent hires with a new perspective, patients, collective bargaining representatives, individuals from middle management, and frontline leadership and their staff. This accounts for the size and diversity of DHS.

Once this team starts strategic planning, they transmit and broaden organizational involvement. Each team meeting starts with a specific objective. At the end of each meeting, membership summarizes what they did to achieve the objective. Each team participant shares this information with two to three focus group recipients. This includes making sure each team member has different personnel on their list. To improve the effectiveness of this process, each team member reports how their recipients responded to team accomplishments. Often, this includes questions and follow-up for team discussion and resolution, for feedback to recipients after the meeting. This process continuously spreads the value of the evolving strategic plan throughout the organization, seeks input about it, and responds with feedback.

Oscar appeared more at ease for the first time during our meeting. "I can live with that," agreed Oscar.

"Great!" I said.

STRATEGIC PLAN

During the following months, Oscar and I met briefly to track DHS's progress. The DHS director dedicated himself to completing the IT failure reconciliation process and strategic planning. This made sense. The director is the highest-ranking DHS official, responsible for major enterprise decisions; operations and employees; and communication with the county CEO, board, and public.

After reconciling DHS's IT failure history, strategic planning started with an outline based on the previously ignored plan. The team, working with focus groups, gathered widespread input and created buy-in about the process. The team executed a series of collaborative meetings, resulting in a final strategic plan with organization-wide involvement and support.

This included a strong prospective approach. It offered employees a reason for being part of DHS. It required looking forward, taking stock in the broader environment in which they work, and assessing their potential impact on it. The idea was to make sense of the future and DHS employees driving the organization toward it.[11]

DHS developed its purpose as a singular message. The department created the vision statement: *Delivering the best health care to improve the lives of everyone in our community.* DHS focused its strategy as the foundation for investing in correcting health care delivery problems. The department selected the CAP as the top-priority clinical IT project to enable this strategy. Finally, DHS underscored it will make sure to translate its purpose into behaviors, so staff internalize what it looks like when they are doing it.[12]

Oscar stated, "DHS never had a chance without a workable strategic plan. We didn't even know there were three fundamental questions to ask, let alone how to answer them sustainably. Now, with a strategic plan, we can build and implement a PMO to focus on continually answering these three questions in a changing environment."

Oscar was excited. He then added, "We need to prepare DHS, starting by educating project participants about the DELTA Framework. This will help everyone recover from our recent failure. Starting training now will prepare us to implement the CAP. In fact, why don't we call this initiative the Recovery Project?"

I agreed.

At the final strategic planning meeting, Dr. Zorn said it all. As the top communicator for DHS, Dr. Zorn convened an audience of the department's leadership from top to bottom in an auditorium and online.

He announced, "I am responsible for the success of DHS. I cannot do it alone. I need your help. But I cannot expect you or anyone else at DHS to help me unless we all share a mutual understanding of our purpose. We all need connection and a purpose. Ask yourselves, *Do I want to commit to working here if I don't know DHS's purpose? Do I want to work here if no one bothers to understand my purpose?*[13] *Do DHS and I have a shared purpose?* We must uphold and connect DHS's newly defined purpose with those of our employees.

"We owe this to our employees and community. As DHS's leaders, we must align our employees with DHS's purpose and use this combined strength to drive our goals, strategies, and prioritized initiatives successfully. This requires your leadership and understanding employee needs.[14]

"Previously, DHS operated without a clear understanding of its purpose, lacked adherence to it, and failed to communicate and align it from the top to the frontline. Today I am launching a bold transformation, an alliance between our leadership and employees, to define, commit to, and deliver a purpose-driven approach to DHS success.

"This is a multi-year journey, in response to openly recognizing our past failures, building trust, and creating a future driven by ongoing improvement. As leaders, it is our responsibility to express, model, and reinforce this change. Join me in remaining undaunted and committed to a fundamental change in our culture.[15]

"We now have a new strategic plan. Today we begin implementing it by launching the top-priority initiative, the Recovery Project. My staff is going up and down the rows of this auditorium, distributing two documents, which are also available online. The first is the Recovery Project description. It summarizes our new strategic plan, followed by details about this change project, including an overview of the approach required for success. Second is a project overview assessment. Implementation success depends on a shared purpose. I want your first impression of that purpose, our strategic plan, and the outcome expected from the Recovery Project. Your collective response to this assessment reveals our current understanding of this shared purpose as the project begins. We will follow up with a series of communications about the assessment results. These findings give us the needed baseline about what we must do to achieve Recovery Project success.[16]

"Read the first document and then use the pencil supplied to complete the assessment please. My staff will collect your response, or you can submit it online for those of you participating virtually. We will post the results on a new DHS intranet page dedicated to this project. It will also include the Recovery Project description and our complete strategic plan. Look to this page and other communications from now on to maintain your understanding of our purpose-driven vision and to achieve Recovery Project success."

NOTES

1. Thomas W. Malnight, Ivy Buche, and Charles Dhanaraj, "Put Purpose at the Core of Your Strategy," *Harvard Business Review*, no. September–October (September 1, 2019), https://hbr.org/2019/09/put-purpose-at-the-core-of-your-strategy
2. Rajendra Sisodia, Jagdish N. Sheth, and David Wolfe, *Firms of Endearment: How World-Class Companies Profit from Passion and Purpose*, 2nd ed. (Upper Saddle River, NJ: Pearson FT Press, 2014), Chap. 1, Kindle.
3. Robert E. Quinn and Anjan V. Thakor, "How to Help Your Team Find Their Higher Purpose," *Harvard Business Review* July–Augus (2018): 78–85, https://hbr.org/2018/07/creating-a-purpose-driven-organization
4. Ibid.
5. McCarthy, Eastman, and Garets, *Effective Strategies for CHΔNGE™*.
6. Florence Chang, *Transforming Strategy into Operational Excellence* (Seattle, WA: Multicare Health System, 2011), 11–12.
7. Ibid.
8. Quinn and Thakor, "How to Help Your Team Find Their Higher Purpose."
9. Vanessa Boris, "What Makes Storytelling So Effective for Learning?," *Harvard Business Publishing*, 2017, www.harvardbusiness.org/what-makes-storytelling-so-effective-for-learning/
10. Quinn and Thakor, "How to Help Your Team Find Their Higher Purpose."
11. Fred P. Brooks, *The Mythical Man-Month, Essays on Software Engineerin*, vol. 10 (Reading, MA: Addison-Wesley, 1975), https://doi.org/https://doi.org/10.1145/800027.808439.
12. McCarthy, Eastman, and Garets, *Effective Strategies for CHΔNGE™*.
13. Malnight, Buche, and Dhanaraj, "Put Purpose at the Core of Your Strategy."
14. Ibid.
15. Ibid.
16. Harrison, *Introducing the Accelerating Implementation Methodology (AIM) A Practical Guide to Change Project Management*, 8–17.

4

Climate

The following day, the weight of the massive undertaking before us hit me. I arrived at Pacific Dining Car before Oscar. Sitting down in a booth, I opened the single button on my suit coat as my concession to informality.

I ruminated over a litany of disturbing thoughts. DHS had a terrible history of IT project failures. Even though they now had a purpose-driven vision and strategic plan, the Recovery Project had to succeed, and DHS didn't have any historical basis for that. All DHS seemed to do was pay attention to what they did wrong, relying on nothing more than hope to avoid repeating failure. They were part of an appalling county-wide IT structure, encouraging fiascos from the get-go. To top it off, DHS employees, in fact, the whole county, expected failure.

Despite these feelings, working with a client and talking through problems and solutions together was one of the best parts of my job. Sipping fresh hot coffee made my morning thoughts go down a bit easier. The white tablecloths, white-jacketed servers, and sterling coffee service, all in an elegant replica of a railroad dining car, gave me comfort. Built in the 1920s, Pacific Dining Car still offered 24-hour fine dining.

Oscar walked in and sat down. "What's cookin'?" he said.

"Good morning sunshine," I gibed.

"You can tell I'm worried," Oscar said.

"I am, too," I said, while nodding my head.

"Look Oscar, there's good news. We have DHS leadership, board, CEO, and county-wide support. DHS also has a solid strategic plan and way to manage changing priorities that fortify the Recovery Project and future initiatives."

Oscar did not react. There was something going on that he wasn't saying.

DOI: 10.4324/9781003003809-4

Oscar responded, "I'm not sure what anyone can do. The more I think about it, the more my anxiety increases. We have a byzantine county IT and DHS structure. Our health care system culture spends more time on power plays than on patient care. We've never had meaningful DHS leadership until now. The combination of these is enough to tear us apart and crush any hope of Recovery Project success."

I had no constructive response, nor did Oscar want one. Oscar sharing what he really thought about the county culture was alarming, yet beneficial.

I reassured him, "I appreciate you sharing your thoughts."

I volunteered that, at Oscar's direction, the county retained me and my firm to help him specifically. The county did this because they have faith in us. Cleary, that's both a compliment and daunting expectation. DHS must undergo monumental change despite its history.

If I had smoked, I would have taken out a cigarette then and lit up. Thankfully, the waiter arrived to take our breakfast orders. We both requested their famous omelets, sumptuous portions of yummy goodness to sustain our intrepid discussion.

We tried small talk for a while, and I held the coffee cup to disguise my shaking hands. We needed action, not anxious considerations of what could go wrong. I asked Oscar to go ahead and describe DHS's climate.

Just as he was about to begin, our breakfast arrived. We ate in silence.

Afterward, I suggested we have our waiter clear the table and bring a fresh pot of coffee while we talked.

Oscar agreed, adding, "I keep thinking about reasons for the original project failure. We must overcome the county's contribution." He then pulled out a sheet of paper with a list of specific areas he was about to discuss.

I interjected, "If you don't mind, I prefer commenting as you go along. If I wait, I won't remember what I wanted to say. Is that okay?"

"Sure," Oscar responded.

I then assured Oscar that after we completed his list, my staff planned to prepare and administer an implementation history or climate survey confirming that DHS's organizational maturity was Level 1 and 2. No one can expect to succeed with a project unless they understand its genesis and current maturity level. DHS's climate included a past, a present, and a context where we planned to implement the Recovery Project. Armed with Oscar's input and climate survey results, we could begin to understand DHS's setting, including both how and where to plan implementing change.[1]

Oscar acknowledged with a nod. I sipped coffee, ready to listen.

STRUCTURE

"I know you understand a lot about the county structure," began Oscar. "But there's more behind it, which currently shapes who's involved and what they want to do with our project."

Oscar went on to remind me that Jane was the Santa Clara County CEO before arriving here in Los Angeles. There she had budget control.

The LA County Board appoints the CEO to manage the county. The CEO keeps her job if she retains majority support of the five-member board. This is a delicate challenge. It is particularly difficult, in LA County, because the board controls the budget. This takes fiscal management and control away from the CEO. To make matters worse, the current board, and their young, arrogant, and often uninformed staff, favor re-election over solving critical public policy problems. For example, the directors of public works, health, mental health, public health, and others hold their positions based on board appointment. The board intrudes on these departments for re-election purposes. After setting strategic goals and authorizing funds, the board fails to let each department execute these imperatives and manage day-to-day operations. Appointed officials run their departments at the pleasure of the board with no other independent power source.

Since Jane can't do her job, she is in a tug-of-war with the board for fiscal control. Jane will eventually lose and leave.

Separately, elected officials like the DA, assessor, and others run county departments according to their own objectives. They answer to the voters, so the board has less control over them. This doesn't even begin to address the courts that function independently under constitutional separation of powers and the voters who elect their judges.

Funding dictates board control over all departments, except for the courts. However, it is not that simple. For example, most DHS funding comes from state and national sources, not the board. Other departments have similar outside funding sources. The DA even has asset forfeiture. This means the DA, if pushed, can charge a department with wrongdoing and seize assets.

The DA can then use these as financial resources to conduct activities outside of board control. While extreme, it's a threatening power source for the DA. He used it previously and could threaten to use it again to get his way.

The implications of this power structure are significant. For example, DHS sets priorities, but board funding control may change them for a multitude of political reasons. This applies to the Recovery Project. DHS is okay for now, but it could change at any time. DHS works under the shadow of political motivation. Frequently, this has little to do with delivering solutions to maximize patient value per DHS's newly defined purpose.

DHS and how it fits within the county just make it all messier. DHS has a director, chief medical officer (CMO), and CIO. Each hospital has its own CEO, CMO, and CIO. The county has its own CIO. There is also the county Information Services Department (ISD), responsible for enterprise shared services. County agencies cannot use outside services provided by ISD, like enterprise systems, supply chain, and fleet and procurement management.

Oscar concluded with, "Of course, the roles and responsibilities of these players overlap and compete. Bottom line, the power structure, organizational layers, and role and responsibility conflicts are not conducive to supporting this project."

Frowning and shaking my head, I confessed, "While I was aware of most of the power dynamics you described, I did not know about the prospect of Jane leaving. She is key to my county power base on this project."

Before moving on, I asked Oscar for more details about the medical facilities directly affected by the Recovery Project. Oscar reiterated that while the county had six hospitals, there were only three affected facilities. KMDC was a teaching, acute care hospital budgeted for 413 beds, 66 dedicated to psychiatric services. RLANRC was a teaching rehabilitation facility budgeted for 435 beds. Last, HDH was also an acute care and rehabilitation facility budgeted for 104 beds, supplying acute medical, surgical, and extended skilled nursing services.

ORGANIZATION STRESS

Oscar continued with his list. "DHS operates under constant stress. While this may sound typical for health care organizations, it is particularly challenging in LA County."

According to Oscar, the United States' immigration policy stresses DHS to the point where it cannot financially deliver health care to the growing number of undocumented patients. Providers can barely deliver medical care. They cannot consider any major organizational change initiatives. There is set funding not tied to the true volume of undocumented immigrants DHS cares for routinely. While *all* hospitals must deliver care to individuals in emergencies, even if patients can't pay, private hospitals closed their emergency departments (EDs) to avoid monetary losses. This just shifts the patients and financial problem to the county.

Oscar said, "Let me explain how this works. Not long ago, I sat in front of one of our IT analysts, who told me a story. Each year the IRS sends DHS an extensive list, in the thousands, of false Social Security numbers supplied by undocumented immigrants seeking care. She is supposed to follow up on this list and seek recompense. She doesn't because it's fruitless. Undocumented immigrants avoid deportation by supplying falsified identification. No one notices the false identities, and no one really expects follow-up.

"We care for these people, but we don't get funding for all of them. We function near a deficit annually, and each year we get a last-minute reprieve. For example, during his second-term presidential election bid, Bill Clinton campaigned in the county and met with key board members for their constituents' support. As he was leaving LA, he delivered last-minute funding to bridge our financial gap.

"This ongoing fiscal crisis destroys employee focus, as DHS teeters on the brink of layoffs to make ends meet. It's hard to focus on strategic initiatives like the Recovery Project. We don't have the resources to align with them. We may think so initially, but we always change our priorities to care for undocumented immigrants and stay alive as a department. We end each year in subsistence mode, incapable of focusing on other priorities."

All I could say was, "We can't allow the recurring fiscal crisis to distract us. It's a risk that always threatens but never occurs. While we must develop a fallback strategy driven by the new director, we should not expect or let this threatening situation stop us. The director appears ready to maintain strong leadership to protect project funding and focus on achieving success."

Oscar noted, "I agree. I know there are plans available if we fall short of our funding. For example, changing HDH to an outpatient clinic only will reduce expenses."

IMPLEMENTATION HISTORY

Oscar then said, "We struggle with any significant IT change initiative. Our IT implementation history tells it all. Apart from the current failure, DHS has a long history of badly defined, poorly procured or developed, and utterly dismal IT implementation failures.

"For example, we've had the never-ending Enterprise Master Patient Index (EMPI) project. It's a system for assigning a unique identifier to each individual DHS patient. It started over 16 years ago, and we are still working on it. We repeatedly start and stop the project.

"The project requires assigning a unique identifier to each patient. The same patients do not just go to a single medical facility. They may go to any of our six hospitals or 24 ambulatory centers. Patients may use a different identification at each encounter. This is significant given that so many are undocumented immigrants. There is no single identifier to track individual patients and their records. It is to the point now that no one expects success whenever we announce restarting and completing the EMPI project. No matter what happens, it is emblematic of how we never deliver IT projects on scope, time, or budget. That doesn't even address how poorly we perform on attaining project objectives."

I repeated, "The history is dismal. DHS used the same unsuccessful way of doing things, ending with the GMIS project failure. This time, the result was the CAP, a roadmap defining change. That's why you asked me for help. We built a new foundation with the strategic plan, defining and engaging employees in DHS's purpose. We introduced DHS to how we plan to do the Recovery Project, a way never considered before. This is the foundation for change. I know DHS hardly seems like a candidate ready for any of this. The only other choice is failure. Now, with the recent IT crisis and the response from new leadership, is a perfect time to change."

Oscar didn't react.

TARGET READINESS

Oscar just looked at his list and said, "I had a boss once tell me the captain and pilot house crew could run around topside, but no matter what, the engineers and below-deck mariners always moved the ship at the same slow speed.

"DHS leadership comes and goes. At the same time, our vast number of support personnel and frontline providers deliver care mostly oblivious of who's currently in charge and whatever they demand. The frontline and their patients are the Recovery Project Targets, the individuals most affected by the change, and neither are ready."[2]

I said, "Sponsors are the leadership responsible for initiating, backing, and promoting the project, so DHS must understand them before the project proceeds. They play the most influential role of helping Targets get the project done. After this discussion, my staff will administer a Sponsor assessment. This includes collecting information from DHS top, middle, and frontline leadership and their subordinates to identify what Sponsors need to express, model, and reinforce for Project change involving Targets."[3]

AGENT CAPACITY

Oscar appeared as if he wanted to prod me for more information. I decided to wait, instead of responding to unasked questions.

He started talking about the capacity of individuals responsible for implementing the Recovery Project, change agents (Agents).[4] "As the project director, I know there are many Agents DHS can rely on during the Recovery Project. The county recruited exceptionally talented individuals in the 80s and 90s, compensated them well, and promoted them throughout their careers. Today this team still is the backbone of DHS expertise. This is a trusted and respected group. They have a record of successfully driving DHS achievements. Frontline Targets rely on this middle management group. They share a common viewpoint of what it is like as a provider, delivering direct patient care or as personnel supporting these clinicians. Our biggest problem, though, is that DHS overtaxes these esteemed individuals."

I suggested, "We have two issues here. First, while DHS has Agents, they're too busy. They don't appear to have the capacity to do more, including the Recovery Project. That's a priority issue leadership must resolve to ensure the availability of these qualified individuals.

"Second, DHS may need more Agents, so we need to find them. There are a variety of methods for locating Agents, which I will share with you later. To start with, though, ask yourself and current Agents a series of questions. For example, who do Targets listen to and trust? Who feels the effects of the problems we want to resolve? Who are the peers of the Targets who want to make the change? Do any of these peers have formal or informal power to make this change happen? Who has the time, resources, and aspirations to make this change?"

"Good ideas," acknowledged Oscar. "In all the negative pressures we've talked about, at least we have trust between Targets and our overtaxed middle management team. We'll start by asking both parties about other available and trusted resources."

"There's more, though," I said. "Once identified, Agents need change management training and how their role strengthens the project. Project leadership must also understand the importance of Agents, particularly how to use them as a conduit for reaching Targets. Also, leadership must recognize Agents are frequently full-time participants in a project. This means leadership needs to backfill Agents and reinforce their success. This includes supporting Agents in their new full-time project role, especially as they leave their former positions behind."[5]

SPONSORSHIP

Oscar now appeared a bit more comfortable, continuing with, "Dr. Zorn has a reputation of owning and delivering change with management discipline at all organization levels. Given his massive implementation successes in New York, he is someone we sorely need. His arrival is at a point where DHS is ready to begin to revive and invigorate its leadership capabilities. His role in the strategic planning process, engaging and enabling leadership throughout DHS, was a stellar achievement. I hope this continues throughout the project."

I raised a hand and crossed my fingers in a gesture to wish us luck, and added, "Don't forget the Sponsor assessment. We will use this instrument's results to identify how to help Dr. Zorn improve all Sponsors' performance."[6]

CULTURAL FIT

Oscar considered the next subject on his list, cultural fit, saying it was about suitability. He explained the Recovery Project was appropriate, given DHS's current circumstances.

"We involved everyone in DHS to prepare the vision and strategic plan addressing business and IT perspectives. For the first time in my DHS career, we have an achievable list of priorities, with the Recovery Project as the top one, and a finite set of resources to complete it and the other priorities. So, our project is a cultural fit."

I said, "It's more than that. DHS is a collection of cultures. Each culture includes a group of individuals. Each of these cultures functions as a force, expressing similar values and beliefs, on everything DHS does. These diverse cultures interact, at varying success levels, in complex DHS networks in health care functions, technologies, geographic locations, and other areas. We need to understand how DHS cultures align with the project and affect achieving success."

To illustrate my point, I portrayed DHS's six hospitals as distinct cultures. HDH behaves like the youngest member of a large family, where everyone is too busy and out of resources to manage him or her. It's insignificant compared to all other facilities. It's geographically distant in the high desert and challenges DHS's ability to recruit and keep qualified resources at that location.

Harbor-UCLA Medical Center excels at everything: health care delivery, financial performance, IT innovation. It is the overachieving oldest child always trying to please management, mom and dad.

KDMC is the middle child, always getting into trouble, killing patients, losing accreditation, and so on.

Apart from individual hospitals, there are overlapping cultures within each. For example, there are doctors, patients, and the health care industry, each with their own expectations, beliefs, and conventions, shaping how they interact. Doctors are scientists, who must navigate these cultures delicately, balancing allegiance to science with emotional concerns of patients and the ever-changing financial, political, and technical demands of the health care industry.

I said, "I could go on, but you get it. We need to organize the project to fit the distinct cultures within each hospital. Each culture, like individual people, is unique and reacts to change differently, so we need to tailor our response accordingly. One size does not fit all.

"Similarly, we need to understand each culture's viewpoint. This happens not because we demand it or assume all DHS personnel and cultures are alike. It happens because we use perspective taking. This means we start interactions with others by first understanding individual and cultural diversity and then respond with tailored solutions to their different reactions to change. This can neutralize dissembling political subterfuge, taking care of *my department*, or defending *my turf*. Don't get me wrong, though, the maxim is right, *culture eats strategy for breakfast*. It is extremely difficult to do successfully."

Oscar remarked, "Now that you've explained cultures like this, the scale of their differences alarms me. We need to understand a vast number of entirely dissimilar cultures and Target viewpoints and then manage them together to achieve success."

I pushed my chair back from our table and said, "I know what you're saying, but I suspect there's something more. I'm not sure I am physically ready to consider it. It's after 1:00 and I'm starving again."

Oscar thankfully smiled, breaking the strain of the moment. He suggested we just order lunch here.

This was Oscar at his best. Etiquette all the way. We ate breakfast and then occupied a table for hours without generating restaurant revenue except for a pot of coffee. I knew Oscar's way of doing things. We'd stay for lunch and leave a generous tip, compensating the restaurant for lost revenue. It gave me comfort knowing how Oscar treated others.

He knew how tough it was to own and run a restaurant. His dad owned and ran a top-notch Turkish family restaurant in Los Angeles. Oscar's mom and dad raised him in their restaurant. Oscar continues to work on weekday nights and weekends. It is, without a doubt, a true family experience eating there. It's also my favorite Turkish food destination in the United States.

We ordered lunch, and with the prospect of satisfying my appetite, we continued our conversation. I brought us back to our cultural fit discussion and inquired, "What else is going on?"

Oscar gazed at me quizzically and said, "I have concerns about the organizational undertow, pulling leadership away from the strategic plan, specifically the Recovery Project. Given what I see and hear, there are disturbances afoot.

"To begin with, Mike Jen, DHS's public affairs director, just left to work for the Third District Board Office. He didn't just change jobs. As our public affairs director, he often responded to negative health care issues mistakenly attributed to our department when they were the responsibility of others, like Mental Health, Public Health, or the Sheriff's Jail Health. The public sees us as a single entity, County Health. We're painted with a single brush and find ourselves in the middle of crises that have nothing to do with us. The board knows better, but their constituents don't.

"Mike's employment with the Third District worries me. He's an ambitious Machiavellian. That District Office often floats the idea of centralizing all county health functions under our department. Mike always supported that position, too, saying we could avoid the problems created by others if we controlled all health functions county-wide. He also has allies in DHS supporting this same viewpoint, like DHS's CMO, Dr. Dan Brewster.

"If it happens, it's a massive merger. This is not the time, given the Recovery Project. DHS barely executes the scope of its current charge. I cannot imagine merging all health functions under DHS would improve anything. Implementing the new EHR at the three Recovery hospitals, the next three remaining hospitals, 24 ambulatory centers, Mental Health, Public Health, and Jail Health vastly increases complexity for all county and vendor participants.

"Any analysis of this centralization will look for cost justification, like a single-vendor EHR solution for everyone. It's a troubling concept few will consider in any depth but will push for financial reasons only. Think about the challenge. Mental and Jail Health have unique needs that no single EHR can serve well. Take AIDS as an example. DHS currently complies with the Health Insurance Portability and Accountability Act restricting disclosure of confidential patient information except under specific circumstances. In Jail Health, all the guards must know each inmate's AIDS status, as detainees can use this illness as a fatal weapon."

I cautioned, "While this is a monumental change, we have leadership's commitment to the Recovery Project. Also, we have a risk management plan that holds the Recovery Project to its current scope before expanding to other parts of DHS. Adhering to the Recovery Project is a test for DHS, whether the department stays the same size or expands significantly."

REINFORCEMENT

Oscar considered my comments without reacting and just continued, "As you know, DHS is a service organization. All we have are our people. Reinforcement is what lies behind motivating these people to do whatever DHS is trying to achieve.

"When I started in a leadership position, I encountered what every supervisor says, *managing people is the hardest part of my job*. So, I went back to school and audited behavioral psychology graduate courses at UCLA, focusing on reinforcement. I learned about the science and its application. Unfortunately, DHS does not know how to use reinforcement, diminishing leadership effectiveness.

"DHS leaders don't comprehend the basics about it. They do not grasp the powerful link between how acknowledging desired behavior encourages it. They virtually never tailor reinforcement to everyone's needs. Even worse, they don't understand how critical it is to provide it promptly, precisely, and routinely following desired behavior.

"Some DHS leaders think punishment is the same as reinforcement and use it, despite its questionable effectiveness.[7] Some try to dominate, keeping an upper hand, manipulating behavior with bullying to perpetuate a power imbalance in their favor.

"When DHS leaders do consider reinforcement, they mostly think about financial rewards, dropping it altogether because of HR and collective bargaining rules and restrictions. I understand how to use verbal encouragements, flexible work/life balance, learning opportunities, and so on. Regrettably, DHS leadership dosen't."

I sympathized. "This is disquieting. While I am prepared to help you and DHS, the growing number and nature of DHS obstacles concerns me, too."

Oscar agreed, adding, "We certainly have a negative theme going here."

COMMUNICATION

Oscar mentioned communication was next on his list. Before continuing, he wanted to know if I had more to say about reinforcement. I explained that it was important to hear about the entire DHS climate. Everything fit together. I noted the combination of his input about DHS's climate and the results of the upcoming assessments offered the picture I needed before I could provide additional meaningful suggestions.

Oscar nodded understanding and proceeded with, "We all know DHS's purpose is clear finally, and strategically the Recovery Project is DHS's highest priority. We failed, and the BOS mandated we now succeed. We've communicated that message, and we expect to continue that through implementation."

I said, "While you recognize some communication elements, there are numerous others. Managers must be sensitive to what they communicate, when they do it, and how they do it. This requires honest and frequent communication tailored to the audience with expected feedback. If managers do not include these key elements, underscoring the two-way dimension of communication, they will diminish trust and discourage dialogue about problem identification and resolution.

"Targets are generally not seeking more information. Like everyone else, they suffer from information overload. In fact, Targets do not feel empowered by more information. Empowerment comes from helping Targets achieve what they care about together with what DHS needs to accomplish. This requires a compelling argument about what personally benefits Targets who participate in the change, or *what's in it for me*. Communication must be about what motivates Targets and how to harness this to achieve project success."

It was clear Oscar was still troubled. He understood we must make the most of this situation. He again opted for silence while moving to the next topic.

INVOLVEMENT

Oscar said, "We are a command control organization that drives compliance. As I understand it, involvement means participation that spurs connection and buy-in. We don't look to engage or involve Targets. They don't feel heard as participants in a desired change.

"Given your previous comments about how small teams tend to collaborate successfully and increase involvement, we relied on this approach during strategic planning and will continue to use it in this project. Likewise, you just described perspective taking. Again, a highly effective technique we will use for Target engagement."

I said, "There's a tremendous difference between the person who sets the agenda versus the participants who must follow it. Group collaboration is a form of involvement that transitions positional power to a broader base of this force shared by team participants. Both collaborative teams and perspective-taking illustrate how to increase involvement in the change directly affecting individual Targets and cultures. There are innumerable ways of increasing involvement. I've just introduced a few at this point."

PERSONAL BELIEFS

I smiled and nodded slightly as Oscar said, "The last item on my list, assessing personal beliefs, troubles me more than anything we've talked about. Of course, I want commitment to this project, but I continue to fear few believe we will succeed. You must administer those surveys, so we can have a better understanding of what we need to do to gain personal commitment to help DHS.

"While success is hard fought and difficult to achieve, when it happens, it's sweet. That's why I'm here. It's why I get up in the morning and go to work here. While we do have infrequent success, those we have keep me going to the next one. This is especially satisfying since we are the designated county department delivering health care to the disadvantaged. This is a part of me, and I am a part of it.

"It hurts me when I hear about DHS and public sector bashing. It makes change so much harder when we work in an environment so many judge as not worthwhile. The public sector manages and even solves the most significant problems. The private sector leaves patients behind for our hospitals to care for and support without financial gain as a key driver. Our environment's dynamics are not comparable to the private sector. We need separate training and expertise. The public and private sectors are simply different. One is not better than the other. If we all understood this, instead of criticizing the public sector and cutting our resources, we could be far more successful supporting human needs and solving so many life-saving problems."

I told Oscar, "I've witnessed GMIS repeatedly and deliberately manipulate and damage public sector clients for financial gain, and they are not alone. I've had the displeasure of seeing the world's largest professional services firms, like Baluch & Stevens Consulting, Tobias & Sons Accountancy, and Ernie Tarblers Group, do the same, or worse.

"I've never understood why we can't work together on solving problems, like those DHS endures. The private sector has no basis for criticizing the public sector. They fear everyone will find out about all the mistakes commercial enterprises make and pass on to their customers while relying on tax breaks, subsidies, favorable industry tariffs, and government contracts to earn a profit."

Exhausted, we sat silently for a moment. We then settled our bill and got up to leave. As we walked to the exit, we arranged a date to meet. This included another meal at one of our favorite restaurants.

NOTES

1. Harrison, *Introducing the Accelerating Implementation Methodology (AIM) A Practical Guide to Change Project Management*, 30–39.
2. Ibid., 43.
3. Ibid., 62–71.
4. Ibid., 43.
5. Ibid., 20–23.
6. Ibid., 62–71.
7. B.F. Skinner, *Science and Human Behavior*, 1st ed. (New York, NY: Free Press, 2012), Chap. XII, Kindle.

5

Objectives

You know that feeling when you first wake up in the morning unsettled instead of ready to greet the day? Well, today I felt that way. I chalked it up to living in a hotel instead of home with my wife and two boys.

Truthfully, my hotel living situation was luxurious. I stayed at the Omni, one of the sumptuous hotels in downtown Los Angeles. When I arrived every Monday morning, the door attendant, Jorge Masis, always greeted me with, "Welcome home, Mr. McLellan!" Jorge shook my hand as I stepped out of a taxi, grabbed my luggage from the trunk, and ushered me to the front desk. The Omni Club agent, Miranda Clemens, handed me a key while Jorge waited at the elevator to take me to my room. I was always on the Club floor, even though I paid government rates. If the hotel had the presidential suite or another special room available, they always gave it to me. Not a bad investment on their part, given I stayed here about 200 nights a year. Hotel staff knew me. I was on a first-name basis with room service kitchen staff. I knew all about the bartender's children.

My frequent travel was hard on my family, especially my wife. She was the one who had reason for stress, raising two small boys while I was on the road. I traveled so much on Alaska Airlines, I always had first or premium class seats. Even with all the benefits, I felt unsettled away from my family.

FEAR

In addition to my travel malaise, I worried about the county and whether the project could succeed given everything Oscar told me. I knew this feeling. I always felt it at the beginning of fixing a failed project. Shortly after completing a failure assessment and defining a solution, I told exhausted clients this was the easy part. The hard part was solution implementation. The county expected us to deliver timely success. We had the option to focus our energy on resisting or welcoming it.

At some point, I heeded my own change mantra: *get comfortable with uncomfortable.* This is an immensely powerful message I learned while living overseas. Uncomfortable is not only okay but necessary. Our Western culture tries to eliminate all instances of discomfort in every way, physically and mentally. We have glamping now instead of camping.

While I'm not talking about abuse or violence, so many people in other cultures live their entire lives in the discomfort of sickness or injury they can't heal or medicate away. Hard labor for meager wages or too many family members crammed into a tiny, corrugated aluminum dwelling doesn't change the quality of their lives. They remain some of the most joy-filled, hospitable people I've ever known. So, I forget sometimes, but I try to embrace the uncomfortable and help others see organizational change as a gift to learn about what's important and how to grow from that lesson.

I left the hotel, after an overly abundant buffet breakfast, to meet with Oscar and share how to harness this energy for project success. Oscar looked at me pensively when I entered his office, exhaled a deep breath, and said, "I tossed and turned last night worrying about the project. How are we going to complete it successfully?"

"I have the same concerns as you do, but I also understand how to achieve success." I assured him.

I told Oscar everyone felt exhausted from the race to find the problem and define a solution. The board's undue schedule pressure made this especially grueling. We reported GMIS's role in the project failure and that DHS was not the primary reason for it. DHS even stopped GMIS from continuing their damage before we started our investigation. The challenge was ahead, implementing a complex IT solution, delivering a fully operational EHR for patient care in three hospitals, and constantly optimizing the benefits of this change.

This reminded me of an old joke my father used to tell.

I asked Oscar, "Do you know the definition of an optimist?"

"I don't," Oscar replied.

I grinned. "A man jumps out the 20th-story window of a building and yells, *okay so far,* at each story as he falls."

Oscar laughed and then stopped with a frown. "Is that what the project portends: a horrific end?" he asked.

"No!" I said. "Our fears are about the unknown future state and the process of getting there from the current failure. Most everyone on this project either feels this fear now, or they will. It's a constant that starts, escalates, and releases throughout the project. We let it go somehow and somewhere, constructively or otherwise."

I added details about fear coming from a variety of sources during organizational change. It's fear of the unknown or an ambiguous future. In this project, examples include job change and loss. So, employees may perceive the Recovery Project as a threat to their future livelihood. The biology of fear signals a survival alert to fight, flee, or freeze. While these are physical responses to fear, corresponding project behavior manifests itself as resistance. DHS can manage this behavior in diverse ways, helping Targets define beneficial practices to overcome it.[1]

All our thoughts happen within our own minds. When we think about our fear of this project, it's up to us to choose to share these thoughts. We undermine ourselves if we refuse to share. For example, we have only ourselves to find a solution, losing help from others. We ruminate when unshared thoughts dominate us. Ruminating can affect our well-being as well as others, including thinking poorly, making bad decisions, and behaving unprofessionally. This can be catastrophic when delivering health care.

I then stated, "I know we talked about perspective taking to a limited degree already. It's so important that I want to examine it further because it helps to reduce our fears in the face of change. It's critical to begin all interactions on a project by treating everyone as a Target of the change. This requires thinking in terms of their frame of reference (FOR). FOR is perspective taking.[2] It's our ability to understand the viewpoint of another person, which may be quite different from our own. It informs us about that other person's world, attitudes, background, experiences, and skills. Giving another person this opportunity reveals their vulnerabilities in a safe and trusting environment. The recipient of another person's disclosures who refrains from judgment, fosters an interpersonal connection. The Target feels heard, understood, trusted, and respected. Targets reveal information about themselves, informing others on how to help them and other Targets embrace and sustain change.[3]

"It all comes down to the fact that we have choices. We can choose to judge another person or not. It's difficult to refrain from judging instead of discerning who a person is or what the situation is that's affecting them without giving them the benefit of the doubt. This means engaging in perspective taking by gathering information as a watcher and listener. Otherwise, we make assumptions we believe are facts, which is when we make mistakes. We need to observe and ask questions focusing on the individual and their situation, like an impending major organizational change. We can engage and understand another person genuinely only after we gather information in this way."

Oscar suggested, "It's tough to avoid confirming our preexisting beliefs. This is more about unlearning judging others than learning objective consideration of different possibilities."

"This is an underlying AIM principle, which all of us need to learn and reinforce in this project and our lives," I responded.

I stopped and waited for Oscar.

"I understand, yet it's so easy to obscure this simple truth," affirmed Oscar.

I said, "AIM requires a lot of attention for all of us on the project. So, I plan to supply more staff to the project. My responsibility includes delivering the project and change management disciplines within DELTA. One of my employees, Renee Tarrel, is our Agile expert. Renee guides clients on how to apply the Agile philosophy to IT."

Oscar asked, "What's her background?"

"Renee started working for me as an employee 20 years ago. She designed, developed, and implemented software we use with clients as they apply the DELTA Framework and associated assessments. DHS could use her support."

Oscar appeared comfortable in his typical formal manner, mentioning he looked forward to meeting and including her as a new addition to the Recovery Project.

The meeting was getting long. I needed fuel. Oscar knew me well enough not to suggest going to the tenth-floor cafeteria for coffee. Oscar also understood my insatiable appetite. I am lean because my metabolism is off the charts. This required constant eating. Oscar was also very lean, but he just didn't eat. We both got regular exercise, but in my case, it just increased my appetite. So, I suggested we go, as planned, to another favorite restaurant for a long early lunch to continue our discussion. Thankfully, Oscar liked eating, too. Unlike me, though, he needed prodding.

After a remarkably brief time driving to Beverly Hills, we sat down to lunch at Nate 'n Al's, a famous Jewish deli.

I always marveled at the variety of great food choices on the menu. Opened in the mid-1940s, Nate 'n Al's was the best place for eating warm corned beef sandwiches. Served on fresh Jewish rye with caraway seeds and simple yellow mustard, it was a superb venue to watch celebrities come and go. It was also fun to go there with my wife, who introduced me to Nate 'n Al's when she joined me in LA some time ago. She was the only woman in the place whose red hair color did not come from a bottle.

I leaned forward and tucked into my corned beef on rye with immense pleasure, looking forward to eating a perfectly aged sour pickle.

SMART OBJECTIVES

I then said, "Let's begin with details about objectives. Do you know about SMART objectives?"

Oscar finished a mouthful of pastrami on rye and said, "Of course I do, but I haven't used them. Go ahead and give me a review."

I explained, "SMART is an acronym often used to guide setting specific, measurable, achievable, realistic, and time-bound objectives. SMART objectives supply precise clarity and direction about how to execute the department's vision for the Recovery Project. They are not vague notions."

I leaned back in my chair to let my food digest. After a moment, I started. It was easy to remember the components of an objective as defined by the SMART acronym. There are multiple versions of what the letters mean that change their definition. Also, following the acronym letter sequence was not the best way to explain them. Instead, I reordered them.

Measurable

I began with measurable, explaining it means providing a way to quantify achieving the objective. It's a good place to start because it establishes measuring value you expect a project to realize. In the Recovery Project, it should relate to realizing DHS's vision and goals. The *M* sometimes stands for motivator. I think measurable is a good motivator because it keeps those responsible for achieving an objective accountable.

No matter what, each project objective must be clearly measurable because if Targets don't or can't measure it, they can't determine if they're achieving it. Desired change will not happen unless DHS measures it.[4]

Often, measurable objectives rely on a pre-post analysis. For example, suppose DHS expects to decrease patient wait time by implementing patient scheduling software as part of the EHR. This means DHS must measure patient wait time before and after go-live. Comparing pre- and post-collected data measures whether DHS achieved the objective.

Oscar said, "We fail to document quantitative measures. Typically, we just start a project and proceed until we go live without driving toward a quantifiable benefit."

Achievable

I frowned and said, "Achievable is next because it links to measurable. Achievable means its attainable; DHS set a reachable objective. This includes considering challenging objectives that induce or compel commitment instead of just compliance. In fact, in some instances, the *A* stands for ambitious instead of achievable."

Oscar scowled this time, saying, "Once again, we fail to empower our people. We rarely receive their input on what's achievable. We just thrust the project on everyone and expect compliance. We don't promote involvement or consider obstacles to achieving objectives."

Realistic

"That's awful," I said. "The department's previous approach is unrealistic, which the next part of SMART objectives tries to avoid. While an objective may be achievable, it must be realistic or reasonable. While there are a variety of ways to define realistic, in this case, it means an objective requires leadership authorization and ongoing support, including the resources to achieve it successfully.

"This is particularly helpful because it can highlight resource limitations and help DHS understand what it must plan and overcome to attain an objective. It also explains why some people use *R* to mean resourced instead of realistic."

Oscar offered, "So, for example, suppose we set an objective of having all EHR users achieve a minimum user proficiency level by pre-live. Setting this objective is only reasonable if leadership funds and hires additional trainers and provides users with sufficient practice time to reinforce what they just learned."

"Yes, that's a *reasonable* example," I responded jokingly.

Oscar shook his head with a slight grin.

Specific

I drank my chocolate malt and pressed on with, "Specific, the next attribute, seems simple enough. The preceding definitions of the SMART acronym parts underscore specificity already. There are other considerations, though. For example, we want each objective to include an explicit definition of terms. This means defining acronyms and avoiding jargon, so we do not prevent or exclude understanding. Finally, specific means clarity, including those involved knowing an objective applies to them, knowing why, and understanding it."

Time Bound

"Okay," replied Oscar. "That leaves time bound as our final attribute. It's simple, so I understand it. But, before we conclude, I have a question. Is time bound like the term *time boxed*?"

"Yes," I confirmed. "Time boxed is an Agile term about dedicating a fixed time unit, including a start and end, to complete a prioritized scope of work.[5] Time bound, by itself, focuses on the duration for completing work by a deadline, such as by go-live, without necessarily establishing a start date.

"Time bound can also include a series. To illustrate, suppose you begin the series at go-live, setting patient wait time to ten minutes longer than pre-live, accommodating learning how to use the new EHR. About 30 days later, you require a post-live wait time equal to the standard experienced pre-live. Finally, after the project ends and transfers everything to operations, assume you expect users to start optimizing, where patient wait time decreases to five minutes less than pre-live."

QUANTITY

Oscar had another question. "How many objectives should we set?"

I noted, "There's no magic answer, but there are several factors to consider."

"Everyone on the project must contribute to at least one objective. I use the word *contribute* because, in many cases, DHS will assign objectives to groups or teams instead of an individual. For example, radiology includes doctors, technologists, nurses, and medical physicists. There may be objectives germane to all of radiology or one of the groups within it, depending on what's relevant to those responsible for achieving it. The Project Management Team (PMT) may be responsible for achieving stated scope, time, and budget objectives. Teams of IT personnel may be responsible for technical objectives. Caregivers may be responsible for clinical and patient objectives."

I added, "We need human objectives. Human objectives are primarily behavioral. For example, what are people going to do? What does the *right* behavior look like? It is these right behaviors that contribute to achievement of project success.[6] Human objectives must define skills and behaviors associated with the change and require training and reinforcement that encourage new ways of acting and discourage old ones.[7] For example, suppose DHS sets an objective to reduce clinician transcription cost 75%. In addition, this objective aims to decrease all patient safety errors attributed to handwriting illegibility by 90% in instances where the EHR captures data electronically. Training clinicians on EHR charting and speech-to-text software increases their skills. This alone will not change behaviors. The project needs to include reinforcement, where leadership holds their direct reports accountable during and after training with frequent meetings about progress. Leadership also removes obstacles, scheduling practice time and underscoring the value of increased patient safety. Finally, leadership sends the Targets a daily report, for example, indicating each clinician's transcription use rate to discourage this undesirable behavior.

"Overall, it's important not to have too many objectives. While there is no magic quantity, it's better to prepare a brief list of objectives. A short list is easier for Targets to remember and support. A long list fragments Targets' effort, diminishing the value of their project contribution."

Oscar offered, "That makes sense."

Sleepy from all the food we ate, we left the restaurant and drove to my hotel in silence. When Oscar dropped me off, he said, "I'm about to see firsthand that the easy part is over."

"This is where the fun begins," I said.

I went to my hotel room, feeling less distressed than when I started my day.

NOTES

1. Ann Marie Menting, "The Chill of Fear," *Harvard Medicine Magazine* (Boston, MA, 2011), https://hms.harvard.edu/magazine/science-emotion/chill-fear
2. Harrison, *Introducing the Accelerating Implementation Methodology (AIM) A Practical Guide to Change Project Management*, 21.
3. Menting, "The Chill of Fear."
4. Harrison, *Introducing the Accelerating Implementation Methodology (AIM) A Practical Guide to Change Project Management*, 10.
5. Andrew Stellman and Jennifer Greene, *Learning Agile: Understanding Scrum, XP, Lean, and Kanban*, 1st ed. (Sebastopol, CA: O'Reilly Media, 2013), Chap 2, Kindle. Republished with permission of O'Reilly Media, Inc., from *Learning Agile: Understanding Scrum, XP, Lean, and Kanban*, Andrew Stellman and Jennifer Greene, 2013; permission conveyed through Copyright Clearance Center, Inc.
6. McCarthy, Eastman, and Garets, *Effective Strategies for CHΔNGE™*.
7. Harrison, *Introducing the Accelerating Implementation Methodology (AIM) A Practical Guide to Change Project Management*.

6

Scope

I awoke in pain. I had a dull ache at the bottom of my neck, by the top of my sternum. Thankfully, I was home. I came home in time to celebrate our wedding anniversary. I expected to spend more time with my wife and to enjoy our two boys through the holidays, starting with Thanksgiving.

I looked forward to working from home instead of on the road. I could concentrate on analyzing the results from the climate and Sponsor assessments.

I also promised to help Oscar prepare the project charter, a first key project management document. We planned to follow with setting up and convening a kick-off Steering Committee meeting. Here Oscar expected DHS ratification of the charter.

Tonight, Jacqueline and I intended to celebrate our wedding anniversary. I took it easy, hoping my pain would subside so we could enjoy ourselves together. I decided a trip to my favorite hardware store was in order. Eli, our almost two-year-old, joined me. Carrying him increased my pain. I put Eli down on the store floor, keeping one eye on his whereabouts, while talking with Steve Adams, the owner of Island Hardware. It was a classic, family-owned-for-generations-type hardware store. It has everything you need, always.

Back home, Eli and I took a nap. I awoke in the late afternoon in greater pain. I told Jacqueline to ask a friend to join her instead of canceling dinner reservations.

While she was gone, the pain increased. I looked for painkiller prescriptions from earlier accidents or surgeries. Jacqueline must have discarded them when recovery was complete.

Jacqueline found me on the floor of our bedroom writhing in agony. She dialed 9–1–1.

DOI: 10.4324/9781003003809-6

A quick paramedic response team arrived. They thought I had a pinched nerve and decided to take me by ambulance to the hospital ED. Living on an island requires either medical transport by ferry, running roughly hourly, or by medivac helicopter. The paramedics thought I was stable enough for a ferry.

At the ED, the attending confirmed the paramedics' assessment. I couldn't remember the doctor's name, but she prescribed pain meds and a muscle relaxant. It was a slow night, so she let me sleep in the exam bay until the 5:30 a.m. ferry home.

The pain continued once the meds wore off. I went to my internist, Dr. Keith Price at Island Medical, that afternoon. He took one look at me and disagreed with the attending from the ED. He said, "You are a puzzle, and we need to send you to a specialist or two to figure this out."

Jacqueline drove me to each appointment during the early part of that week. A rheumatologist ordered a CT scan of the pain site. He took a fluid sample and, unbeknownst to me, searched for a mass.

I tried to manage the pain. My only relief came by lying on my back and barely raising my head. Car rides to specialists were excruciating. Massive doses of painkillers and cortisone, prescribed by one of the specialists, offered relief. Meanwhile, Sarah Wolff, our dear friend and babysitter, cared for our boys.

The call came at the end of that week. It was Jacqueline's sister, Georgia. Jacqueline's dad had esophageal cancer. We all thought of him as the healthy one, only 65, and recently retired. Jacqueline's mom, racked with aggressive Parkinson's disease, could not function without him.

Concerned about leaving me in my current condition, the doctor reassured Jacqueline there was no malignancy causing my pain and it would be okay for her to leave me in the capable hands of our friend, Sarah. Reassured, Jacqueline left early Saturday morning to help her family in Texas, taking Zach, our oldest, with her. Sarah stayed at our house to care for me and Eli.

Early Sunday, the rheumatologist called. "We figured it out. You have a systemic streptococcal infection. It's in your bloodstream. This is a severe, life-threatening illness. Come to the ED at once. We will admit you."

I told Sarah I needed to go to the hospital at once. I asked her to stay with Eli.

She asked, "How long will you be gone?"

"I have no idea," I said, as I kissed Eli on the forehead, and Sarah nodded in understanding.

I waited, lying on the hospital bed, with a penicillin IV drip in a port on my left arm. Meanwhile, the University of Washington lab worked on the best antibiotic mix necessary to stop my infection.

The painkillers and cortisone gave me comfort. Lying on my back helped more. Unfortunately, the course of high dosage cortisone weakened my body's immune system against the infection. It may have even hampered diagnosing it. I needed to stop taking it. I couldn't just cease abruptly. I had to taper off the drug. My body needed time to return to its normal chemical pattern.

While I waited for the lab, I had an echocardiogram. The doctor determined the infection had not damaged my heart.

Once I had the proper antibiotics, a home health nurse would instruct me on administering it for six weeks. I pressed everyone throughout the hospital to help me get those instructions quickly.

I wanted out. Hospitals are terrible places for sick people. I was in the infusion ward, a.k.a. oncology, with chemo patients dying around me. My doctor showed up. I told him I wanted to go home as soon as possible. Patients around me were horribly ill.

He paused and said, "Maybe they will supply perspective. You need to understand how sick you are."

That stung. Denial got me through this trauma until now.

It was the early evening, and my medical team surrounded my bed. They announced the lab confirmed my antibiotic formula, and the pharmacy had my prescription ready. But the home health agency nurse was not available until the following morning. I had to stay in the hospital overnight.

My telephone rang. It was Oscar. I took the call. I went to work.

The following morning, after a massive snowstorm, the hospital refused to discharge me after I received infusion instructions. Seattle's hilly streets were treacherous in the snow. The city shut down. My friend, Alec Johnson, planned to take me home. I explained my situation, with Eli at home and my wife in Texas with her dying father and seriously ill mother. The hospital resisted. Finally, I mentioned my driver, Alec, grew up in Vermont and could manage the snow. They relented.

Alec drove me expertly from the hospital and on to the ferry. We arrived on the snow-covered island, everything hushed and beautiful. Stillness was common as an aftermath of a major storm on the island. Trees fell and hit the utility lines, creating power outages. This was one of those storms. The outage was island-wide and could last a week.

As expected, my house was cold and dark because of the power outage. Alec delivered me home safely, expecting to return later that evening. He promised to pick up Jacqueline and Zac after their plane delivered them from Texas.

My welcome home included Sarah comforting me with hot tea from our propane-powered cooktop and Eli giving me hugs.

After what felt like an eternity, Alec returned with Jacqueline and Zac. The whole family stood in the doorway of our house hugging.

Jacqueline said, "Wow! I'm surprised the roof didn't collapse, and someone didn't run over our dog!"

I smiled and said, "Honey, we don't have a dog."

"Which is a good thing because it would have died!" she replied.

We all laughed.

Reality is awful. I knew I needed to keep my company and household afloat. I kept working virtually and relied on Renee to provide on-site services in my absence. I had no energy to do anything. I worked at about 50% capacity. DHS participants understood.

Two weeks later, Jacqueline's father died.

Calling upon every moment of her 20+ years of experience in the corporate world, Jacqueline went into overdrive, cared for me, her mother in Texas, and our boys. She found a Seattle-area care facility for her mom, prepared her family home of 40 years for sale, and sold it, along with a new car her father bought to drive himself to chemo. She just put one foot in front of the other. We followed.

My staff finished preparing and administering the climate and Sponsor surveys. The results confirmed much of what Oscar told me already. Further, his confidential insights about the county work environment and DHS leadership, together with the survey results, enhanced my project understanding significantly.

The climate survey asked respondents about their personal beliefs concerning the success of the Recovery Project. Respondents said overwhelmingly DHS would fall short, exceed the original scope, fail to deliver on time, and surpass the planned budget. Likewise, most responses emphasized DHS employees would not achieve their SMART objectives. Respondents also did not have direct reports, across DHS's hierarchy, who shared information and delivered consistent project support. The climate survey's critical conclusion: limited sponsorship will cause Recovery Project failure.

The Sponsor survey delivered similar findings and conclusions, once again confirming what Oscar told me. Targets maintained DHS's leadership had yet to commit to and communicate about the Recovery Project, including limited demonstration and reinforcement of their support.

I summarized the results from both assessments and shared them with Oscar during our next Webex meeting.

Oscar admitted, "I knew what was coming, but I didn't think it was this pervasive. I hoped there was some consistent belief in project success, which we could cultivate to foster widespread support."

I cautioned, "I don't see the results that way. The outcome of the assessment gave us the very information needed to cultivate broad approval. The results stand for opportunities to leverage sponsorship, build a communication plan, and develop Target reinforcement strategies. This is exactly the time when we need to know this information, while we initiate the project."

I let my comments sink in. Oscar hesitated and then said, "I know you're right. But I'm troubled by the size of the challenge ahead. I feel uncomfortable. I'm new to this project director role, the IT management responsibilities, and the DELTA Framework. I thought about how we arrived at where we are now. I know we already had success with preparing the strategic plan. While we are going in the right direction, it's kind of like your father's bad joke concerning the optimist."

I chuckled, "Okay, Oscar, so let's just build on our recent success and the latest information from the assessments.

"It's not like we don't know how to respond to this information successfully. In my 30+ years of client experiences, they all believe their situation is remarkably unique. That description is just not correct. Similar situations and problems occur in projects with considerable frequency. There are known proven practices available to solve them. So, while DHS faces these problems for the first time, we know what to do, and now it's time to do it. We are not desperately trying to identify unique problems and practical solutions no one has considered previously."

Oscar let out a desperate breath, "Okay, I'll listen."

I responded, "Thanks, Oscar. Let's start with the project scope."

DEFINITION

I said, "Project scope refers to the breadth, pinpointing who and what's affected by the change. It may be easier to think of who and what's inside and outside the project. Another useful approach includes looking at an organization chart and finding the functions within the project and their associated supervisors and subordinates."

I shared, via Webex, the DHS organization chart, indicating it was DHS's published lines of authority by function. I explained all directives flow down from superior to subordinate, following a nested chain of command, to those who execute them on the frontline and underscored that feedback from the frontline is equally, if not more, essential. Feedback flows up the chain of command, informing leadership about frontline reactions to directives and task performance that serve as the basis for ongoing improvement. It also reveals the organizational parameters of the project scope, including the directors of functional areas, subordinate functions, and implied positional roles and responsibilities.

Key Role Map

I said, "Let's continue by changing this DHS organization chart into a key role map."

Oscar asked, "Is this where we visually overlay, on the organization chart, project roles and responsibilities for Champions, Agents, Sponsors, and Targets (CAST)?"[1]

I had no idea Oscar was learning independently about change management. I responded, "Exactly!" and elaborated by explaining CAST was a great acronym but not meant to imply hierarchy. However, it helped illustrate that projects, like plays, required a script or plan and a *cast* performing specific roles.

Champions

I continued, "A Champion is an advocate, passionate about the change. I once heard the definition of passion as something someone keeps talking about long after everyone stops listening. Passion, in this context, is the ultimate alignment of personal and organizational purpose. Look for

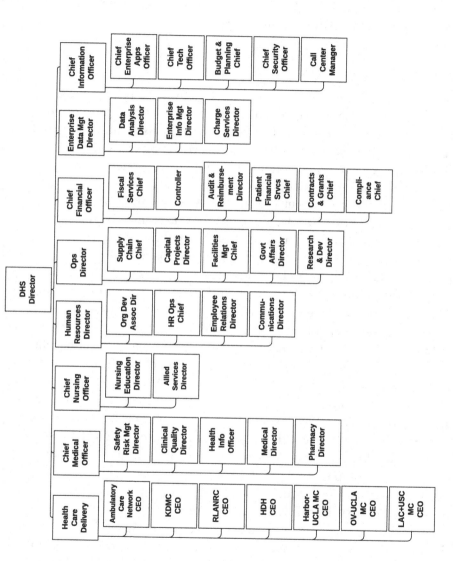

DHS Organization Chart.

passion when trying to identify Champions. Champions are often innovators, early adopters, or opinion leaders, who *may* not hold positional power or authority.[2] Champions also include successful Agents and Sponsors doing what they can to make change happen."[3]

Agents

I continued by pointing out an Agent works actively on behalf of another to help make something happen, like a gate agent, talent agent, or press agent. In AIM, an Agent works on behalf of a Sponsor, addressing and aligning organization and Targets' needs to achieve project success.

To do this, Agents have credibility because they are often trusted peer of Targets. In this influential position, Agents understand their Targets' problems and concerns about the change. Agents start to interact with Targets with a question like *Are you okay?* Or statements like *Something's not right.* Agents come from a place of understanding. By starting in this way, Agents invite Targets to begin a difficult conversation about *why* they have concerns, fears, and obstacles preventing them from achieving change before defining *what* to do about it. Targets' trust in the change increases as they collaborate with Agents to overcome what prevents change adoption. It is only after this type of interaction that Agents can reinforce the organization's change initiative to align with what benefits Targets, or *What's in it for me*, to increase change likelihood. This includes Agents helping Targets achieve SMART objectives.[4]

Agents perform in a formally assigned role, linking their Sponsor's authority to their Targets' change. While Agents do not necessarily have their Sponsor's authority, they execute change on their Sponsor's behalf. To do this effectively, Agents keep and regularly update a contract with their Sponsor to execute specific actions or achieve certain outcomes. This maximizes Sponsor focus on the change and minimizes use of their limited resources, such as time, power, and funds.[5]

Oscar asked, "What are the notable attributes of an Agent?"

I explained, "Agent traits tend to include a combination of problem-solving, persistence, team-building, and listening skills. I could go on with a longer list, but Agents are innately comfortable with change instead of just having a specific set of a skills.

"Agents and their pivotal Project role include many factors involving their Targets and Sponsor. For example, DHS's Agents are clear about their Sponsor's role in Target skill development and behavioral change required to achieve the organization's imperatives, like, vision, strategy, goals, and SMART objectives. An Agent helps Targets receive training and reinforcement, embracing and aligning a collective understanding of these imperatives.

"Sponsors are effective leaders because they take care of those they lead. However, just because an individual holds a leadership position, which means they have authority over others, doesn't mean they know how to lead. So, there are instances where an Agent works with a problematic Sponsor. While having a conversation with a Sponsor about this is never easy, it's necessary. This requires preparation before this meeting, including clarity about what an Agent needs from the Sponsor described in safe language. It is not unusual for a Sponsor to have little idea of what sponsorship means. So, an Agent must start by treating the Sponsor as a Target, taking time to understand their viewpoint, particularly about their role and *What's in it for me.* This input and an Agent's response may help the Sponsor grasp the importance of their role and improve their performance. When it doesn't, the Agent must seek other options. This can include assessing the Sponsor's performance and providing feedback. Sometimes it also helps to enlist an effective Sponsor peer in the problematic Sponsor's development process. In severe cases, the Agent may need to take steps to replace the Sponsor, since an underperforming Sponsor can derail a project."[6]

Sponsors

I told Oscar that I previously defined Sponsors in a general sense as initiating, backing, and promoting a project. I explained now that AIM includes two kinds of Sponsors. An Authorizing Sponsor is like a patron, who blesses a project on behalf of their organization. They hold a leadership position, such as a hospital's chief financial officer. The CFO, as an Authorizing Sponsor, has formal and informal power legitimizing their organization's undertaking by approving funding and executing a RCM system project. The direct subordinates of this Authorizing Sponsor may include patient billing, insurance, collections, cash posting, account management, and contract analysis managers. These managers are Reinforcing Sponsors, or subordinate leaders, strengthening and upholding their superior or Authorizing Sponsor. Reinforcing Sponsors support the RCM system with their direct reports on the frontline on behalf of the Authorizing Sponsor.[7]

Each Sponsor is a servant leader. Their role is to serve all Targets in reaching the project objectives instead of Targets existing to serve their Sponsor.[8] Both Authorizing and Reinforcing Sponsors' personal actions must express, model, and reinforce their change commitment throughout the chain of sponsorship. This means what an Authorizing Sponsor says and does, in their role at the top of a key role map, cascades down the hierarchical chain of command of Reinforcing Sponsors to frontline Targets.[9] In the RCM example, Targets are frontline individuals, like medical billing specialists, who experience the change when working with medical professionals, insurance companies, and patients.

AIM depends on sponsorship as *the key* project success ingredient. AIM includes at least one Authorizing Sponsor and a chain of Reinforcing Sponsors in each change initiative.[10] AIM expands project leadership beyond the single Executive Sponsor found typically in the project management methodology. This distinction is particularly important because it promotes collaboration. As leadership consistently shares the power of their authority through the chain of sponsorship to the frontline, they increase organization-wide involvement in the change.

Targets

Before I defined Targets, I explored the different types of project participants and their relationships. Stakeholders are all types of participants: anyone affected by the project. This includes, Targets, users, and customers, who each have differentiating characteristics. Targets include anyone affected by the change. Users have an account on the system that is the primary focus of an IT project. Customers are consumers of the product or service created by the project. Each stakeholder type can overlap one or more types. For example, a Target can be a system user.

Stakeholder types are also a collection of many people with different needs, not a group of identical individuals assigned a role or label. Surfacing these differences helps project leadership understand how to constructively communicate, involve, and reinforce desired change; govern the project; define success; and track progress toward that goal.

From a change management perspective, Targets currently experience the problems that the project expects to fix. They contribute to current problems through their actions or inactions. They also must adapt because of the change.[11]

As a project progresses, some Targets may stay in this position, while others evolve into one or more CAST roles as they gain understanding and begin to actively support the effort. It is also common for people to return to a Target role temporarily if they become disillusioned or fearful. When they resolve their concerns, they move back into another CAST role.[12]

"This all makes sense," acknowledged Oscar. "I want to see if I can prepare an initial project key role map with you now. Is that okay?"

"Actually, that sounds like fun, and it would help me understand the project chain of sponsorship," I said. While I wanted to say, *Let's do it*, I had to add, "I'm totally wiped out."

We decided to pick up where we left off tomorrow with a late afternoon meeting time. But our Webex video call, the next afternoon, did not start well.

Oscar said, "I have unwelcome news. Jane notified the board today that she is resigning and taking the Monterrey County CEO position in two weeks."

"That's dreadful," I said. It was no surprise, though. Jane's battle with the board for budget control was a huge power shift she could not win. Jane saw she no longer had board support. It was time to leave.

"What's the board doing to replace her?" I asked.

Oscar said, "They say publicly the county will conduct a national search for a new CEO. The politics are thick, though. The board appointed Mike as the acting CEO while he manages the executive search. He always has an agenda, so it's not clear what will happen."

"Interesting. Could the board select Mike as the CEO?" I inquired.

Oscar responded, "Technically, he is conducting the search, so the board cannot select him."

"It's a relief to know he can't consolidate health care under DHS and disrupt the Recovery Project," I noted. "Unfortunately, though, the board has a tendency for politically motivated actions, not necessarily in the best interest of the county. We need to define how to prevent the unexpected from adversely affecting the Recovery Project."

Oscar replied, "How do we that?"

"I know it sounds impossible to plan for the unexpected," I conceded. "This is a classic case of preparing for uncertainty instead of risk."

"What does that mean?" wondered Oscar.

I explained, "Risk is where we know the probability of occurrence and possible outcome. Uncertainty is a situation where we don't know one or both, making it exceedingly difficult to prepare a plan that mitigates the adverse impact.

"This may sound odd, but in situations like this, I rely on my off-shore sailboat racing experience. When racing, we put every conceivable safety measure in place before leaving the dock, given the uncertainty of Mother Nature. If the unexpected occurred, we had those resources at our disposal and didn't have to waste time assembling them. This *extra* time preparing helped the crew understand and respond to the unexpected. Believe me, the unexpected happened, and often ferociously. We were ready for it with all we had and always survived. Despite all of the preparation, the most important factor was that every crew member knew they could rely on one another.

"From a project uncertainty standpoint, we don't know what the BOS will do. So, we prepare by finding and setting up all possible responses to this situation and all other project uncertainties routinely. This vigilance helps us work together while we manage and minimize the full impact of adversity, but it's the team ready and available to help each other that matters more than anything else.

"So, in keeping with your uncertainty and risk management comments, let's talk about how we will manage responding to a new CEO disrupting the Recovery Project," Oscar offered.

I noted, "We planned to implement the EHR at each of the three Recovery Project hospitals. The CAP recommended starting with the Recovery hospital using a common technique called fast-tracking to shorten the schedule. This meant the schedule assumed some tasks could occur simultaneously across the Recovery hospitals, instead completing each task and hospital separately.

"Let's assume the board appoints a new CEO, who consolidates all county health care under DHS and requires EHR implementation at additional facilities. Instead of using a single fast-track schedule during consolidation, I recommend we replace it with three separate schedules, one for each hospital. Each hospital starts its implementation sequentially without overlap. This dedicates all resources to individual facilities, minimizes inherent resource sharing risks, and helps each hospital stay a self-contained part of the EHR implementation. Implementation starts at other facilities that join DHS because of the consolation only after DHS completes sequential EHR inpatient and ambulatory implementations at all six Recovery and non-Recovery hospitals."

Oscar confirmed, "That's a wonderful idea that relieves some of my concerns. I like knowing KDMC has more resources to finish the EHR implementation, given there is no overlap with RLANRC or HDH. I also don't think implementation delay involving all the remaining five hospitals is a problem, especially since success is more important than a longer schedule."

I clarified, "Can you meet with Dr. Zorn ASAP and confirm he agrees?"

"Definitely," Oscar said. "I have one outstanding concern, though. We have six separate EHR implementation projects, one for each hospital. Isolating them in this manner makes sense, but we need a mechanism where all six hospitals make decisions during one facility implementation that affects all the others."

I said, "You're right. The project governance organization, something we will discuss later, includes leadership from all six hospitals, who will tackle and resolve these issues."

Via Webex, I could see that Oscar had the printed version of the DHS organization chart in front of him on his desk. He had notes on it. I also had that chart and one for KDMC open on my computer.

"Okay, let's start talking about my version of DHS's key role map," Oscar said.

"Sure," I replied. "I'll update the DHS and KDMC organization charts to create a key role map online as you walk me through."

Oscar began with, "Dr. Zorn is the Authorizing Sponsor, each hospital CEO is an Authorizing Sponsor, and their subordinate managers are Reinforcing Sponsors cascading to their frontline Targets."

I explained, "The DHS CEO is an Authorizing Sponsor. However, each hospital CEO doesn't need to be an Authorizing Sponsor, too. In fact, Authorizing Sponsors may communicate with each other, but they never *report* to one another. An Authorizing Sponsor has *full* organizational authority or influence to legitimize the change and commit resources to it. If one Authorizing Sponsor reports to another, that implies the subordinate Authorizing Sponsor does not have complete authority needed to fulfill their role."

Oscar conceded, "I didn't know that, but it makes sense. So then, each hospital CEO is a Reinforcing Sponsor."

I clarified, "That approach works. Does each facility CMO report as a Reinforcing Sponsor to their hospital CEO or to the DHS CMO?"

Oscar reasoned, "Each hospital CMO, COO, and CIO reports to their facility CEO."

I agreed and then asked, "Let's suppose KDMC's CMO needs to resolve an issue with the DHS CMO. What is the chain of sponsorship?"

Oscar explained, "The facility CMO reports up his chain of sponsorship to the KDMC CEO. The KDMC CEO communicates with the DHS CMO to resolve the issue."

"That's correct, but why?" I challenged.

Oscar puzzled ever so briefly and suggested, "KDMC's CMO does not have project authority to go directly to DHS's CMO. The KDMC CEO is the only person within his hospital with the same positional authority as the DHS CMO."

"That's a fine start," I offered. "You've addressed Reinforcing Sponsors reporting through their chain of sponsorship. I should add that there must be a Reinforcing Sponsor at each level below the Authorizing Sponsor. This means there are no breaks in any cascading sponsorship chain. If a key role map omits that, there's no way to reinforce accountability at each level within the project scope."[13]

"I understand how to prepare a key role map. I don't think I need to do any more right now," said Oscar.

"There's a bit more. You must include all other entities affected by the project, even those outside DHS," I added.

"For example, within DHS, there's the departmental CIO. KDMC also has its CIO responsible for working within the hospital on the EHR. Externally, ISD's director, Eloisa Zarifian, is an Authorizing Sponsor responsible for all county shared services. Each of these organizations has a role in the project. So, it gets complicated, with multiple roles across DHS and external independent organizations."

Oscar nodded and added, "How does the chain of sponsorship work between DHS and external organizations?"

I explained, "DHS's CIO serves as a project Reinforcing Sponsor and reports to the Authorizing Sponsor, the department CEO. KDMC's CIO, Tina Green, is a Reinforcing Sponsor, who reports to KDMC's CEO. Tina, in her Reinforcing Sponsor role, cannot direct ISD's Authorizing Sponsor to support enterprise system interfaces with the EHR. Tina needs to follow the chain of sponsorship. She must go to her hospital CEO and Reinforcing Sponsor, who communicates with DHS's Authorizing Sponsor. Dr. Zorn contacts ISD's Authorizing Sponsor, and Eloisa identifies a Reinforcing Sponsor within ISD to work with Tina."

"That makes sense, I think," said Oscar.

I then shared the DHS Key Role Map with Oscar, via Webex.

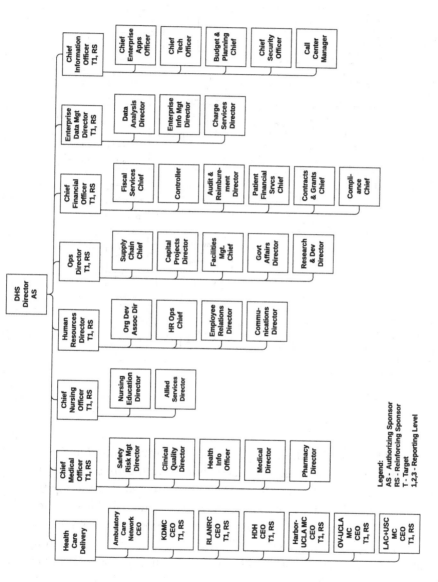

DHS Key Role Map.

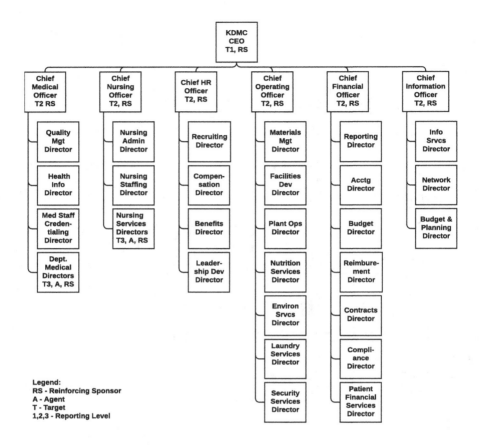

KDMC Key Role Map.

I explained the legend in the chart identified Authorizing and Reinforcing Sponsors and Targets. The Targets included a number, indicating their reporting level. I then shared the KDMC key role map. I noted that the top-tier KDMC Target numbers appeared in the DHS key role map to illustrate how the two maps worked together, including an uninterrupted chain of sponsorship. I also included Agents in KDMC's legend. I took the liberty of assigning medical department directors as Agents and Reinforcing Sponsors. Examples include the oncology, emergency, and surgery departments. Similarly, I identified nursing service directors as Agents and Reinforcing Sponsors. The project could assign the Agent and Reinforcing Sponsor position to directors of, for example, medical surgery, critical care, and post-anesthesia.

I followed with, "We've identified some *rules* as you started building a key role map. These rules refine the script for the CAST in this play we're calling the Recovery Project. As you can see, there is a foundation created by the key role map. It precisely defines the Recovery Project's scope, resources, and roles and responsibilities. To retain this clarity, you must update the key role map as DHS changes throughout the Project."

"I like this," Oscar announced. "While I still have reservations about the Project, this helps reduce some of my worries."

Social Network Map

"Good," I said.

"While what we are doing now helps define Project scope, it also contributes to our understanding of information sharing. Information is a contagion. It spreads from one person to another, especially when they are in close contact. Think about catching a cold or participating in a new trend. Whether or not you know the source you may get *it* willingly or otherwise. Bottom line, we must use this scope analysis to manage the contents of Project information and the conduits available to share it.

"We've examined DHS's formal organization already. Formal organizations are what we all can see, like the organization chart. Now let's tackle the informal organization. An informal organization is not visible but certainly no less powerful than a formal one. Examining an informal organization requires delving into DHS's cultures, norms, customs, and unwritten rules. The Recovery Project needs to fit with these DHS collective cultures to succeed.[14]

"During development of DELTA, before including AIM, we examined social networks for key attributes of an organization's cultures. A social network, not to be confused with social media applications like Facebook, Instagram, and Twitter, is a group's structure and the participants' interconnected relationships.[15] Culture and social networks intertwine and shape each other."

I stopped here to asked Oscar for an example of DHS social network communication.

It didn't take long. Oscar ventured, "It's culturally customary for men to wear a shirt and tie while working here. I don't remember anyone telling me that I must wear certain clothing. Our social network communicates this standard. It sets a nonverbal tone about our professionalism and competence.

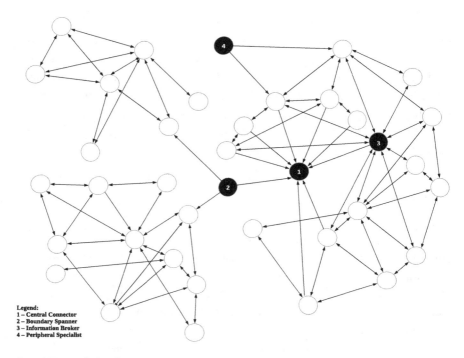

Legend:
1 – Central Connector
2 – Boundary Spanner
3 – Information Broker
4 – Peripheral Specialist

Social Network Analysis.

"Right!" I confirmed.

I then explained that the formal organization complements the informal. Mapping and using the results of both formal and informal organizations broadens our understanding of project scope and information sharing included in it.

I noted, "Unfortunately, because cultures are about unwritten rules, there is no documented organization chart to build a social network map. However, with a survey and social network analysis, we can prepare one.

"My staff will administer a confidential social network survey for the Recovery Project. We only use the information collected to manage this project. When we developed DELTA, our original survey had a single question. *Who do you trust?* We now have a modified version of *Who do you trust* . . . with variations including . . . *to share confidential information,* . . . *to get information about what is really happening,* . . . *to reach the right person that gets something done.* Each response requires a specific name. The results most often cluster around one or a couple of names among all other members of a particular group."[16]

I shared an example of a social network analysis with Oscar via Webex and said, "Social network analysis offers a window into an organization's cultures, including roles and responsibilities that affect change. It reveals clusters of non-hierarchical interconnected actors. Each cluster includes direction of information flows, the number of inflows and outflows, and proximity of key individuals to others. The survey results find possible key network actors. We follow up by interviewing potential key actors to confirm their role. This includes determining whether they could use their role to affect the project positively or negatively."[17]

Central Connectors

I continued with examples, starting with the Central Connector. This is the person in a network map to whom everyone in the group talks the most. Information flows go to this person from others in the network. This person is an essential information source in the network who should take part in the project with other formal members, potentially as an Agent.[18]

Boundary Spanners

The Boundary Spanner is a member of one network who crosses borders and connects with other networks. They function as a conduit between networks internal and external to an organization.[19]

"Do you have an example of a Boundary Spanner?" I asked Oscar.

He responded immediately with, "Recovery Project dependence on other organizations, like ISD, is really significant. For example, the project has boundary spanners that connect DHS and ISD procurement to acquire the EHR product."

"Perfect!" I said.

Oscar said, "Honestly, this is fun."

Information Brokers

The Information Broker ties groups within their own network together. They receive and send information between these groups, or subnetworks. While a Boundary Spanner connects their own network to an external one, an Information Broker connects separate groups that exist within their own network.[20] For example, an Information Broker could be a member of the KDMC CMO's staff, who connects with their counterpart in the chief nursing officer's department.

Peripheral Specialists

Last, the Peripheral Specialist tends to function on the edge of the network. They interact with their network, offering expertise as needed.[21] For example, a technically gifted IT staff member of KDMC may not interact with others much, but they offer tremendous value when called upon to deliver their expertise.

"That's really cool," Oscar said.

INTEGRATION

"It is," I concurred, "It also helps if I explain how to integrate formal and informal organizations to effect positive change. For example, you can strengthen formal Sponsors based on how you manage and share information with informal social network actors. It may prove useful to pair a strong Central Connector with an ineffective Reinforcing Sponsor. Conversely, it's better for a Reinforcing Sponsor to share information widely with multiple social network participants to overcome a Central Connector who deliberately withholds information as a power play."[22]

"One final note," I said. "External organizations, like ISD, take part in the project and still require mapping and analysis. DHS cannot direct us to administer assessments in other county departments to create a key role map and a social network analysis. DHS may still know enough to identify the CAST and prepare a key role map for external departments. For example, you can map DHS's chain of sponsorship that communicates with counterparts at ISD. You already know DHS network connectors who work with their ISD counterparts without a social network analysis."

"That's clever," responded Oscar. "This is powerful. I can see how examining formal and informal roles identifies the individuals who fill them, the project scope, and the facets of information sharing. This is entertaining, too. I'm excited about putting it together and starting to use it for project governance once you administer the social network survey."

I confirmed that my staff would administer that survey immediately.

Oscar had another meeting. Our Webex session ended just as my cell phone rang.

It was the county CIO. I felt even more sick that I was already. I imagined the CIO in his office. He often stood at his desk while on the telephone. He was short and built to last. His hair was black and gray. His face had a pallor from avoiding the LA sun. His eyes never focused on anything. They constantly darted about as if they were searching for the next victim. They made me nervous. I was thankful this was not a virtual or in-person meeting.

Clarence didn't seem too pleased when he spoke, but he never did. "I haven't seen you for quite a while. Where have you been?"

I ignored his question, responding cheerfully, "So nice of you to call, Clarence. What can I do for you?"

"DHS has a new CIO," Clarence explained. "We are meeting next Tuesday, and I expect you to be there. We pay you enough so you can certainly fit us into your schedule."

Clarence always tried to irritate me. Typically, he accused me and my firm of making too much money from the county. I simply refused to display an emotion in response to his constant needling. It was a successful practice I used with all bullies.

"Renee, our chief technology officer, will definitely attend. I am not available," I shared.

I saw no benefit in giving a reason for my absence. If I did, Clarence would simply say his reason for my presence was far more important. Clarence always focused on his purpose. He was brilliant and unstoppable. It was as if he didn't notice anything else except what he wanted.

"You need to be there," Clarence responded forcefully.

A client fight was never a choice. So, I said, "I will join you via Webex." Clarence's offices had a full videoconferencing center. My virtual attendance was hardly an anomaly.

"Be there at 2:00." He rang off without so much as a good-bye.

NOTES

1. Harrison, *Introducing the Accelerating Implementation Methodology (AIM) A Practical Guide to Change Project Management*, 43.
2. Everett M. Rogers, *Diffusion of Innovations*, 5th ed. (NewYork, NY: Free Press, 2003), 414–417.

3. Harrison, *Introducing the Accelerating Implementation Methodology (AIM) A Practical Guide to Change Project Management*, 43.
4. Ibid., 21–23.
5. Ibid., 61–71.
6. McCarthy, Eastman, and Garets, *Effective Strategies for CHΔNGE™*. Chap. 3, Google Books.
7. Harrison, *Introducing the Accelerating Implementation Methodology (AIM) A Practical Guide to Change Project Management*, 43.
8. "Servant Leadership," Wikipedia, 2021, https://en.wikipedia.org/wiki/Servant_leadership
9. Harrison, *Introducing the Accelerating Implementation Methodology (AIM) A Practical Guide to Change Project Management*, 61–71.
10. Ibid., 43–59.
11. Ibid.
12. Ibid., 43, 45.
13. Ibid., 47.
14. Ibid., 123–126.
15. Laurence Cross, and Rob Prusak, "The People Who Make Organizations Work," *Harvard Business Review* June (2002), https://doi.org/10.1093/oso/9780195159509.003.0017. Concepts adapted and reprinted with permission from "People Who Make Organizations Go—Or Stop" by Rob Cross and Laurence Prusak. Harvard Business Review, June 2002.
16. Ibid.
17. Ibid.
18. Ibid.
19. Ibid.
20. Ibid.
21. Ibid.
22. Ibid.

7

Governance

Renee was a perfect match for Clarence. Like Clarence, she had previously worked for SpaceRock International. She also impressed him straightaway with her confident demeanor and intelligence.

Renee and I grew up together, meeting for the first time when we were about five. We lived a block apart in our Chicago neighborhood until we left for college. Renee never fit in with anyone because she was a geek.

In middle school, we started model rocketry. Renee began taking the metabolic rate of mice before and after sending them into flight. She wrote her middle school 90-page paper on the results of her experiments the night before the due date. Of course, Renee typed about 100 words per minute, error free. All of this foreshadowed her MIT and SpaceRock future.

Renee never slept, getting into everything imaginable at all hours. She finally met her peers at MIT, where she received astrophysics and aerospace degrees.

It took Renee six years to finish her degrees because she worked for SpaceRock while attending MIT, testing space shuttle engines. She'd often call me in the middle of the night to tell me all about the test results.

After college, Renee received her flight instructor certification, adding to her previously attained commercial pilot license. She made money training others to fly to feed her parachuting and downhill ski-racing habits. During this time, Renee learned all about Agile software development. That's when we joined forces at my firm.

People may think Renee is larger than life. Like everyone else, she's far from perfect. She admitted to me more than once that she doesn't suffer fools gladly. It was easy to understand why. Men don't like her. She threatens

DOI: 10.4324/9781003003809-7

them as a woman. Her intelligence makes it worse. What little intellect those men have, they waste on misogyny, unable to keep up with her.

DHS IT

I jumped on Webex early. Our meeting with Clarence began at 2:00. He started the meeting just as DHS's new CIO, Zelda Wilkey, was sitting down at the conference room. Clarence introduced everyone, including Renee, whom he never met before this meeting.

You could tell at once how Zelda viewed LA county the moment she arrived. There are 10 million people living in one of two perpetual neighborhoods: poverty and wealth. Her finely coiffed white shag haircut screamed: make no exception about where I live. She deliberately clothed herself in an expertly tailored black suit, with a cream silk blouse, to accentuate her hair and meticulously tanned face.

She made an unsuccessful attempt at friendliness with, "Hello, Max. I don't bite." Meanwhile, I could see her, even on the Webex, furiously tapping a Mont Blanc pen against a Gucci leather portfolio on the conference table.

While I acknowledged Zelda's greeting with a genial hello, I refused to surrender to my first thoughts about her. It was too early to tell if she was an improvement over her recently fired predecessor, Juan Luis.

Always in charge, Clarence explained how he managed DHS's CIO recruitment, given the earlier director's recent departure. He noted Zelda was his top choice. He continued to account for our role and the execution of the Recovery Project. He offered little room for my input.

Renee interrupted him, underscoring we worked on behalf of the county CEO and board. Further, we completed our charge, investigating the reasons for project failure and defining a recovery solution. She concluded, noting the board mandated we supply ongoing QM, including monthly status reports to the county CEO. Her comments plainly showed we were independent of DHS and the county CIO.

Clarence responded with the usual snide comment that our contract afforded me an opportunity to buy the island where I currently lived.

Unabashed, I offered, "We helped DHS remove itself from a troublesome situation, and the county now expects us to assist DHS on the Recovery Project through completion."

Before I could offer a copy of the CAP to Zelda, she interrupted offi-ciously. She made it clear DHS would, of course, abide by the board's man-date. While she had not yet reviewed the plan, she mentioned Oscar had given her a copy previously.

I concluded, "Renee is our on-site resource. I am also available. I look forward to meeting face-to-face to help in any way we can."

Clarence ended the call with, "Max, I expect to see you soon as well."

Renee called me from her cell phone moments later. "That was weird. Clarence doesn't like us, and Zelda appears well on her way to the same opinion."

"I don't agree," I said. "The county CIO is not the friend of any depart-ment. Individual departments prefer to work unnoticed by the county CIO. Departments engage with him only if required and with a well-rehearsed plan when needing his support.

"The county CIO has his own agenda which, hopefully, only requires individual department compliance reporting during annual budgeting. Sparring begins when the county CIO has an agenda involving one or more county departments. That is what you need to watch for carefully. We also need to nurture a positive relationship with Zelda. She needs help, and she knows it. We can provide that help, which will only improve her situation. Remember, the DHS CIO is in a weak position. The hospital CIOs control the technology that really matters to DHS.

"I must confess I am skeptical of Clarence. During our investigation, we never found anything worth reporting about an inappropriate GMIS relationship. Clarence is a very smart person in a newly defined county position. If anything, he is behaving as a bully until he figures out what he needs to do as the county's first CIO. Right now, we need each other as allies ensuring Recovery Project success."

Renee added, "I left a message already with Zelda's office to schedule a meeting about the Recovery Project. I will let you know when I hear from her so we can include you in that meeting."

It took Zelda a month to schedule that meeting with Renee. I assumed Zelda took time to settle at DHS, understand the Recovery Project, and appreciate all other IT priorities.

Zelda's delay worked to our advantage. It supplied time for my staff to administer the social network survey. Oscar conducted follow-up inter-views based on the survey results. Together, my staff and Oscar built a social network map. Separately, Oscar built a key role map. Oscar assem-bled these two maps and the conclusions from the climate and Sponsor assessments so he and I could meet and build the governance or project organization together.

Zelda's delayed appointment also allowed me to recover. I could attend LA meetings on site. Resuming travel was tricky, though. I continued injections for my antibiotics and to keep the port open. This meant ensuring I had refrigeration in my hotel room for the antibiotics. It also meant explaining to clients that I was an infusion therapy patient and not a drug addict. It sure looked sketchy, at best. Mid-day injections made for occasional awkward encounters. I tried to avoid surprises by letting my clients know, but it was impossible to provide advance warning to anyone entering a restroom while I cleared my implanted venous port and administered antibiotics with a syringe. This included arranging intravenous tubing, medicine vials, gauze, and tape by a sink.

At the same time, Jacqueline had her hands full caring for her mom and our two boys. The boys were okay, but I was gone again. This made life harder for my family and for me.

Finally, we met with Zelda. She appeared relaxed. Good naturedly, she offered quips from *Poor Richard's Almanac*. I was a fan, thanks to my mom, who introduced me to the book. We exchanged witty remarks from it often.

I had an immediate response when she said, "He that lies down with dogs shall rise up with fleas."[1]

I supplied, "The honest man takes pains and then enjoys pleasures; the knave takes pleasures and then suffers pains."[2] This little repartee offered a glimpse into a real person. There was much to explore about Zelda. I made a note to send her a copy of *Poor Richard's Almanac* as a friendly gesture.

Zelda started with an introduction to her senior programmer analyst, Nolan Hursey. Nolan received his Ph.D. from the University of Chicago's Divinity School. Nolan was from Marquette, located on the Upper Peninsula (UP) of Michigan. He appeared genuinely bright, agreeable, and conscientious. How refreshing, especially given project demands. Working with Renee and helping DHS use Agile on their first project looked good.

I explained how DELTA relies on Agile. Zelda at once turned to Nolan and said that it was up to him to make that work for the Recovery Project.

I pointed out a few cautionary items, "Agile mindset is a profoundly unique way of thinking about work. For example, Agile thrives on embracing uncertainty. This may be challenging for DHS's management. DHS tries to control uncertainty broadly by keeping a hierarchy of supervisors and directors, where bosses boss by restricting who works for whom and knowing what everyone is doing exactly.

"We need to avoid clashing between this DHS management style and the Agile philosophy. We know Agile can work in DHS, based on our success with similar organizations. Most organizations fail when they try to graft Agile onto their existing cultures. They return to the status quo. In response, we suggest creating an entirely separate Agile team within the department, assigned exclusively to the Recovery Project. This includes isolating seven to nine individuals in a dedicated office, giving them full project ownership, separate from the rest of DHS. Our approach is an experiment where we create and nurture a new culture within DHS. When our experiment succeeds, by delivering Recovery Project success, DHS can then gradually expand this Agile culture to the rest of IT and other parts of the department."

Zelda gave Nolan an encouraging look. Nolan responded with, "I'll make this happen, assuming you support what Renee recommends."

Zelda smiled. "Leave this to me. I'm new to DHS. I don't know how the department works yet. I can continue with Renee's recommendations, with one proviso. I won't necessarily have the authority to challenge supervisors who want to take our dedicated team members away."

I jumped in here with assurance. "Oscar and I plan on preparing a draft project organization at an upcoming meeting. He is assembling information on Authorizing and Reinforcing Sponsors, who are responsible for Recovery Project success. While this may be your first time hearing about these concepts, we will share more about them in detail as we work together on change management, a vital part of this project. This includes constant vigilance, making sure Sponsors fulfill their pivotal role in driving project success, like maintaining a dedicated Agile team."

We concluded with Renee and Nolan arranging a meeting about Agile, followed by an introduction to DELTA.

Zelda plainly wanted to make sure she helped us. She even suggested Nolan was her best resource on the Recovery Project. She needed him to work with IT in each of the three Recovery hospitals. She planned to rely on him as her internal conduit about all things Recovery Project.

PROJECT ORGANIZATION

Oscar and I reviewed the draft project organization, which he and I prepared with my staff. We needed to confirm it made sense before distributing it for review. After completing the draft, Oscar planned to meet with DHS's HR director and other staff for their input. He also expected to use this time to tell them about the demands governance places on project participants. Overall, the impact could average 50% of their time during the project. In most instances, these project participants must offload 50% of their current responsibilities to others. They also must receive rewards for their governance activities that achieve project success.

Membership

We agreed to discuss the organization at every level, including the membership. Membership varies. Permanent members are mostly individuals

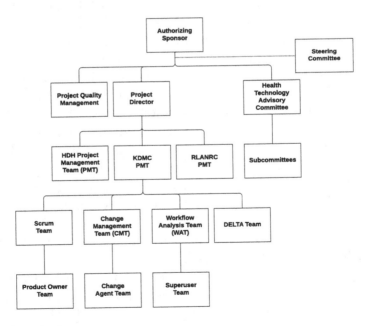

Project Organization.

in charge of a particular committee or team. Temporary members tend to work at specific hospitals and take part in a committee or team depending on the aspect of the EHR and hospital department involved at a particular time.

Director and Steering Committee

Oscar started with, "The DHS Director, an Authorizing Sponsor, chairs the Steering Committee and is responsible for EHR implementation success in all six county hospitals. The Steering Committee permanent membership includes the CEOs from all six hospitals, the department's CMO and CIO, and the selected vendor's project director. Including all DHS hospitals and departmental executive leadership helps ensure EHR and project continuity enterprise-wide. For example, KDMC is the first acute care hospital to take part in the Recovery Project. Continuity occurs when KDMC engages HDH and all three non-Recovery acute care hospitals in key EHR and project decisions. RLANRC is unique, as a rehabilitation facility, but it is still useful to include them as well.

"Separately, departmental executives, as members of the Steering Committee, instill strategic leadership into the project. Including the department's CMO and CIO helps communicate and reinforce the DHS vision in operational decisions made during the project."

"That make perfect sense," I said. "The Steering Committee is the place to raise issues found during the EHR implementation at one hospital that affects all other facilities. The Steering Committee can resolve the issue on its own or assign it for resolution by others."

Quality Manager and Project Director

Oscar continued, "You are the quality manager, supplying QA and quality control. I am the project director, responsible for successful EHR implementation in all three Recovery hospitals. We serve the Recovery hospitals only and report to the Steering Committee. You report also to the county CEO, on behalf of the board."

I nodded concurrence and motioned that Oscar continue to the next part of the governance structure.

Health Technology Advisory Committee

Oscar explained, "The Health Technology Advisory Committee (HTAC) oversees policies, standards, specifications, and compliance for implementation of health care IT in all six hospitals. HTAC informs the project about clinical service delivery. HTAC's decisions have significant EHR impact on ongoing hospital operations during and after the project. Examples of affected areas include training, workflow analysis, chart abstracting, and clinical documentation.

"Co-chairing HTAC are DHS's CMO and chief nursing officer. All HTAC members are permanent, representing DHS leadership responsible for individual professions: physicians, nurses, health information management (HIM), health care informatics, quality improvement, revenue management, and compliance. Each profession has its own subcommittee, reporting to the HTAC. HTAC increases crucial involvement, unifying individual professions and departments that share responsibility for DHS patient care delivery."

I noted, "HTAC is a terrific complement of professions key to project success."

Oscar responded, "We built the chart together; I'm just filling in the details. And at this point, I need you to take the lead."

Project Management Team

As Oscar requested, I offered, "The PMT centralizes and manages execution of the project. As I understand it, DHS's Director recently approved implementing the EHR in each of the six department hospitals sequentially, starting with KDMC. PMT membership varies by hospital except for selected Scrum Team participants. KDMC's PMT includes their hospital's PM, selected vendor's PM, change manager from the Change Management Team (CMT), workflow analysis manager (WAM) from the Workflow Analysis Team (WAT), Scrum Master (SM) from the Scrum Team, chief product owner (CPO) selected by all POs on the Product Owner Team, chief superuser (CSU) chosen by their peers on the Superuser Team, and a senior systems engineer to supply infrastructure support."

Scrum Team

With Oscar's consent, I went ahead, noting the Scrum Team works on the selected vendor's EHR. This includes changing the EHR configuration and supporting vendor software modifications required by LA County's 1115 Waiver. LA County applied to the Centers for Medicare and Medicaid Services and received a Medi-Cal waiver under Section 1115 of the Social Security Act to help stabilize funding and increase health care access by the uninsured.

The SM is responsible for team adherence to Agile. The Scrum Team permanent members work with all six DHS hospitals, including Nolan as SM, one software engineer, one systems engineer, one tester, and a database analyst.

Temporary team participants include the PO, Workflow Analyst, Agent, and Superuser. Superuser team members are mostly clinical informaticist or health care IT specialists. These temporary Scrum Team members rotate as configuring changes to specific parts the EHR. For example, the PO, Workflow Analyst, and Agent from the ED join the Scrum Team to configure that part of the EHR. A different PO, Workflow Analyst, and Agent replace their ED counterparts when the Scrum Team works on neurology. Also, POs, Workflow Analysts, Agents, and Superusers each have their own teams, sharing ideas on customer needs management and EHR support.

I said, "Should I continue?"

"Yes, I understand and agree so far," said Oscar. "My concerns are with the occupants filling these positions and how we manage them, not the roles we've just defined."

I agreed and emphasized, "To start, the answer lies with leadership. The chain of sponsorship, including the Authorizing Sponsor and cascading through Reinforcing Sponsors, is what keeps the project organization and the individuals that fill it aligned with DHS's purpose. There's more, and we will get to it shortly."

Change Management Team

I noted how the CMT is responsible for the people aspect of change, including workflow, IT, job changes, and other organizational implications. The CMT membership includes the change manager; senior leadership from DHS Training, Communications, and HR; the WAM; and a Chief Change Agent, selected by their peers; CSU; and CPO.

When an Agent works with the Scrum Team, they find Target job changes, including both modification and elimination of positions. Agents work with and on behalf of their Targets. The CMT is where agents go to ensure Targets receive training for these job changes. Combined with this support, Agents also help specify how their Sponsors can reinforce changes affecting these Targets as they transition to the EHR.

Agents have their own team as well. All Agents are members of the Change Agent Team. This team offers a venue where Agents share their experiences and ideas to maximize continuity and uniformity across the work of Targets and Sponsors.

Workflow Analysis Team

The WAT examines operational procedures, and how they dovetail with the EHR, to identify and implement improvements. The WAT includes Workflow Analysts, Superusers, and individual Targets. The WAM and Workflow Analysts are permanent team members, serving all six hospitals. Targets, who are subject matter experts (SMEs), and Superusers are temporary members, varying by the workflow under analysis and associated EHR feature requiring configuration.

I concluded, "The project organization is a network of relationships among diverse teams and their members. The organization roles and responsibilities draw on varied expertise that drives cooperation to complete tasks and their outcomes successfully."

Oscar paused and stared at the organization chart. He then said, "There's no such thing as a perfect Project Team. However, despite recent survey results, the project still has the potential for skilled individuals to fill the positions we've defined. I agree, the chain of sponsorship is also a powerful factor that will maintain alignment of these individuals to the strong foundation in DHS's vision and strategic plan. What remains is whether the PM has the fortitude to bring change throughout the project and its team to achieve a positive outcome for DHS."

I said that I agreed and that we would explore this topic even further in a moment.

DELTA Team

"There's one more piece to this puzzle," I offered. "My take on change management involves a special force. I'm talking about DELTA Team, a crack team assembled in the project that continues afterward as a new operational part of DHS. The DELTA Team is the group that checks in with frontline Targets to proactively deliver support. Silence from Targets may not necessarily mean everything is okay. To avoid this trap, DELTA Team resolves issues before they grow into significant problems. Its membership includes DHS's foremost technical support representative, Workflow Analyst, Change Agent, and trainer. Frequent participation by the Authorizing and Reinforcing Sponsors stresses the importance of this team to Targets and DHS's willingness to support them. DELTA Team, set up early on, helps DHS launch the EHR, realize its benefits, and improve patient services continuously long after project completion.

"DELTA Team conveys what is happening on the project, supplementing other communications. DELTA Team receives feedback from Targets about project well-being. The team shares this feedback immediately with IT specialists, trainers, Workflow Analysts, Agents, and project governance entities, often highlighting and resolving previously unidentified issues.

"DELTA Team is the resource deployed to support Targets before they contact the Service Desk, reducing its workload. This initiative-taking change management is a constant presence on the frontline, delivering support Targets rely on as they gain confidence, learn about the change, and continue with ongoing improvements."

Oscar suggested, "So is this your way of introducing, at project start, a component to help structure and later sustain change?"

"You got it," I said.

Reporting

Oscar announced, "Now that we're in agreement on the structure, let's talk about reporting to the Steering Committee briefly."

"Okay," I responded.

I explained that every month, the vendor PM, hospital PM, project director, and QM update the Steering Committee. This includes my report on schedule status, issues, and risks, which I prepare in advance for review by you and Dr. Zorn. There are attached added details, prepared by the hospital PM, with input from the SM, Change Manager, and WAM. Also, the Steering Committee receives demonstrations, where possible, related to vendor deliverables to support contract acceptance recommendations. Borrowing from Agile, this focuses on product delivery instead of status reporting.

Communication

I then offered, "Let's discuss communication next because so much of any project is about it. Communication suggests scores of questions. For example, how will communication occur? What are the topics to include in communication? What communication methods are best for different CAST members in terms of capturing their time and attention?"

Oscar responded, "I thought about it and met with Dr. Zorn. Based on his input, we must understand how he expects communication to occur within the project. To start, Dr. Zorn asked DHS Communications to conduct an audit, examining current DHS communication practices, including processes and their contents. Based on the audit results, he suggested preparing a project communication plan combining current practices that support AIM. Communications assembled this plan, which they will execute, evaluate with another audit, update based on the audit results, and implement with more changes from ongoing feedback. For example, all Sponsors will conduct weekly face-to-face sessions with their direct reports, emphasizing the vision link to the Recovery Project and supporting SMART objectives. He already enlisted DHS's Communications to distribute bulletins to all employees about upcoming project milestones, delays, and achievements. The director also expects to hold monthly town hall meetings focusing on Q&A for employee feedback. DHS intranet postings will include document libraries on past and current Project Steering Committee meetings, reports, key decisions, and recorded town hall meetings. The key here is he expects vigilant focus on communication channels that have the most FOR impact. Not surprisingly, this includes one-on-one and small groups whenever possible.[3] The follow-up audit will assess effectiveness of the plan and improve it, as needed. Dr. Zorn said he will mix it up, changing both the channels and the messages to customize reaching different Target groups. Finally, he believes persuading people to change is not a one-time sales event. As a result, he expects ongoing dialogue with frontline Targets. He sees these Targets as the most important participants responsible for project success."

"Great start," I said. "It's critical for Project Sponsors to control the narrative. This means Sponsors must communicate genuinely and transparently to build trust. It's important that Targets rely on their leadership for information about the project. To encourage this, project Sponsors must communicate their knowledge or *why*, not just what. Knowledge makes the message far more compelling. It's a way of connecting with each Target audience, supplying full disclosure about the project."

Reinforcement

Oscar nodded his understanding, and I asked, "Have you considered preparing a list of reinforcement strategies like assignment of preferred duties, professional recognition, or relief from unpleasant tasks?"[4]

"No, but I know what you're getting at," answered Oscar.

I followed with, "Reinforcement is the most powerful tool available for changing behavior. Once you and other DHS top leadership identify everyone in the project organization or governance structure, it's important to assess the assigned participants. The membership of the governance structure supplies vital project services, whether part of the formal or informal organization. As key Recovery Project players, they need to use reinforcements to encourage positive and discourage negative behavior. My staff plans to administer a readiness assessment of Sponsors, Champions, Agents, randomly selected Targets, and all other members of the project organization. The assessment measures the FOR of each group, including their ability and willingness to support the project. From an ability standpoint, the assessment results will find training requirements. The assessment outcomes on willingness help DHS prepare a reinforcement index or options to manage change from participants' FOR.[5]

"Separately, my staff will administer an Agent assessment. It examines their characteristics, performance, relationships, and ability. I will provide you with our findings and conclusions from this and the readiness assessment.[6]

"Regarding specific reinforcement strategies, gratitude is the most powerful. Gratitude helps the recipient feel valued. Someone sacrificed something for this recipient. It doesn't have to be complicated or financial. It can be something as simple as a Reinforcing Sponsor taking time to genuinely express personal thanks for their Target's contribution. This can motivate that Target to deliver even more effort, including achieving previously unattainable heights for themselves and DHS."

Oscar pointed out, "It's so darn simple, yet people don't realize the power of gratitude and the diverse and simple ways to express it."

I agreed and stressed, "Reinforcement is about rewarding desired and discouraging negative behavior. For example, the WAT finds a scheduling process DHS can introduce now, before EHR implementation. A scheduling representative starts using it at once. The scheduling manager promptly thanks and praises this individual.

"Negative reinforcement removes or stops an adverse outcome in response to a desirable behavior. For example, the same scheduling manager announces if everyone follows the new scheduling process during the next week, he will cancel the boring Friday afternoon staff meeting. Targets associate following the new scheduling process with avoiding an undesirable result.

"Reinforcement includes key ingredients. It must occur at once after, and relate directly to, the behavior the project needs to affect.

"Targets must also know positive reinforcement will occur when they at least try to achieve desired behavior.[7] Failure is helpful in this situation. Everyone has a first time doing something new. So, it's ridiculous to assume everyone will get it right the first time. Mistakes happen, and we learn from them. Establishing rewards for attempting to achieve something new motivates learning. If, because of change, new work is tough to do, managers must also allocate time where Targets develop and practice their new skills and responsibilities."

Oscar contributed, "So, for example, if DHS has an obligation to set challenging objectives, we must create a safe environment where Targets try and fail without fear of adverse consequences."

"Absolutely correct," I said.

I added, "One of the greatest difficulties concerning change facing all participants is uncertainty about the future or ambiguity. To reduce anxiety, and the resistance that comes with it, the project must keep and invoke a menu of reinforcements that positively adds or negatively removes something to motivate change. This includes making the new way of doing things easier than keeping the status quo, benefiting Targets directly, or *What's in it for me*. Offering Targets this structured method helps minimize uncertainties and encourages achieving the desired change.[8]

"Before moving to the next topic, there's a specific reinforcement issue that we need to address. All healthy relationships have boundaries or limits. Communicating boundaries is about clarifying what the project and DHS value as important. Articulating those values improves working relationships because everyone knows the same basic principles guiding the project. When a project participant crosses a boundary, it may require punishment. Punishment penalizes undesirable behavior but doesn't necessarily cause favorable conduct. For example, an employee who repeatedly does not follow new patient safety workflow requirements disregards a non-negotiable or boundary. This situation requires punishment, like removing the employee from their patient care role or employment."

Oscar volunteered, "I agree entirely. I'm beginning to appreciate how the application of the DELTA Framework on change, strategy, climate, objectives, scope, and governance structure will help the project succeed, especially if we continue the kind of work we've done to date."

I smiled and proposed, "Now let's consider reporting routinely about governing the project."

Oscar concurred, and I offered my perspective.

Results-Based Management

We began this project with assessments administered to evaluate DHS climate, organizational stress, social networks, and so on. The results measured project technical and operational conditions and how best to respond, including required performance changes.

DHS needs to continue this approach to ensure ongoing process improvement by using results-based management (RBM) during *and* after the project. RBM is about collecting, analyzing, and reporting on tasks and resources achieving clearly defined and verifiable outcomes. RBM increases transparency, allowing complementary interventions by members of the governance structure. RBM examples include information about Target progress toward milestones or achievement of SMART objectives, lessons learned from Scrum Team retrospective meetings on completed product work, EHR user techniques learned by trainers and Superusers, DELTA Team improvements identified when working with users, IT Service Desk solutions gathered from issue reporting trends, and so on.

Members of the governance structure can start using these data now. Reinforcing Sponsors and their Agents meet with Targets routinely to evaluate performance, tailor their training, supply time for practice, and maintain accountability.

Training

Training offers an example of effective use of RBM and how it works with governing the project. Training is about education for skill development. Most Targets have had bad prior training experiences that the project must avoid entirely and overcome for EHR education to succeed. This requires sponsorship commitment to delivering education relevant to each Target's needs, found in a training assessment. It is important to remember that software training alone is seldom enough to prepare staff for success. Training must concentrate on job training based on changes introduced by the EHR. Are there new performance expectations? What behavioral expectations are there? Are teams staying intact?[9]

To begin, project instructional designers, skilled in the selected EHR, administer a training assessment and plan driven by evaluation results defining Target needs. This means the Authorizing Sponsor must distribute sufficient funds to support Target training needs, including trainers qualified to deliver education before, during, and after go-live.

Training modalities vary widely, so the assessment should answer questions about learning styles and trainee schedule needs so trainers deliver what is best suited for each group of trainees. For example: in-class, online, Just-in-Time (JIT), at-the-elbow, and so on. Trainers who make this content engaging are especially helpful. To achieve this, the HR representative on the CMT must make sure DHS hires and assigns trainers based on video examples of their prior experience. Also, DHS must make sure trainers have enough knowledge of the KDMC or similar environments so their education delivery and supporting materials include typical situations relevant to each Target's role.

Training sessions work within the limited time trainees have available given their day-to-day work demands. As a result, trainers customizing training to Target groups must concentrate on the parts of the EHR these trainees use most. This means training focuses on the core 20% of functions Targets use 80% of the time. However, trainers also must deliver other modalities to support EHR areas used infrequently, for example, readily available checklists or quick reference guides that don't necessarily require classroom training time.

During and after training, Targets must practice their new skills, using multiple modalities that fit individual learning styles. To do this, Reinforcing Sponsors schedule time for frontline Targets to practice in a variety of ways, like peer coaching, rehearsals, and time using the EHR in a sandbox. A sandbox is an isolated safe system environment where Targets use or even *play* with the EHR and see how it fits and supports their role. It's worth noting that the sandbox must be stable and updated often to reflect EHR configuration changes. Otherwise, the project wastes valuable Target time.

To reinforce EHR training, the Authorizing and Reinforcing Sponsors attend too. They also communicate major software updates and share how these changes relate to the DHS vision. Other techniques include impact sheets. These are a two-column sheet with the current state steps on the left-hand side and the future state on the right-hand side. It clarifies change by reading across the page to see what starts, stops, or stays the same for each integrated workflow and EHR task. Making this available by role to each Target focuses them on what's important as they perform their job.

Finally, training timing is particularly important. Training should occur early enough to allow for practice. Training should also not happen so far in advance of cutover that users lose their passion and new skills before they have an opportunity to apply them.

Support

"I think we have one more topic to discuss," I concluded.

Oscar affirmed I should continue, so I explained technical and operational support occurs before, during, and after cutover. Given its enduring role, the Authorizing Sponsor must distribute sufficient project and operational funds to reinforce support's change management role. For example, the IT Service Desk performs a central data collection position for issue identification that helps to improve EHR use in the short and long term. During the project and afterward, Service Desk RBM reporting captures information used in training and associated materials on how to improve Target and EHR performance. Used correctly, a quick training or JIT response from this data shows Sponsors understand Target needs and diminishes user frustration. Feeling supported, Targets know they can safely learn, thrive, and improve their EHR use.

Reinforcing Sponsors also aid their Targets by creating departmental user groups, led by a PO. User groups meet regularly with these Sponsors and their Agents. These meetings reinforce Target performance in several ways. For example, suppose a user group meets with their Agent about

Targets getting help to fully understand how to use a specific function in the EHR. Afterward, the Agent notifies their Reinforcing Sponsor, who contacts training for required resources to ensure they educate Targets as asked. Such user group meetings occur daily during go-live, weekly during post-live, and monthly afterward.

After the project, the EHR continues to include technical and operational changes. Ongoing funding and support for Target participation in departmental and vendor user groups reinforces learning how to support those changes beneficially to DHS. For example, when the vendor releases periodic EHR enhancements, relevant POs from departmental user groups work with the Scrum Team to evaluate these changes, including workflow implications. Targets taking part in the EHR vendor's user group events and communications collect valuable input about such upgrades as well.

"Does this help?" I asked.

Oscar said it did, immensely. He then invited me to join him for dinner, which was particularly kind.

After a walk from DHS, we sat down at the Water Grill, a classic downtown LA restaurant that boasted fresh seafood. It was a bit clubby, but the aroma was tempting and pleasing.

Oscar ordered a glass of house red wine. Astonished, I joined him happily. While taking time to enjoy our robust Argentinean malbec, I suggested, "We cannot discuss the project tonight. The first one who fails buys dinner."

Oscar accepted.

I didn't want Oscar to lose. If he did, he could not expense our high-priced dinner, as it far exceeded the county meal allowance. We enjoyed fresh oysters as an appetizer and never spoke another word about the project that evening, so we covered our own expenses.

NOTES

1. Benjamin Franklin, "Poor Richard's Almanac," *The Astronomical Calculations.* Annual Illustrated ed. (New York, NY: John Doggett, Jr., 1849), 27.
2. Ibid., 48.
3. Harrison, *Introducing the Accelerating Implementation Methodology (AIM) A Practical Guide to Change Project Management*, 105–111.

4. Ibid., 121.
5. Ibid., 97–103.
6. Ibid., 20–23.
7. Ibid., 115–122.
8. Ibid.
9. McCarthy, Eastman, and Garets, *Effective Strategies for CHΔNGE*™. Chap. 7, Google Books.

8

Philosophy

Renee and I sat in a DHS conference room, arriving early for our meeting. Previously, DHS ensured that members of the Scrum Team received Agile training. Renee planned to review Agile with the Project Team to broaden their understanding of it, including project implications. Renee also asked that I take part to offer input on how Agile affects project and change management. The meeting included Tina Green, KDMC CIO and PM; Marissa Mulby, certified AIM consultant and CM; Layla Washington, KDMC chief change agent, Nolan Hursey, DHS senior programmer analyst and SM; Shirley Walker, KDMC staff nurse and WAM, Walter Ming, KDMC nurse informaticist and CSU; and Billy Davis, DHS senior business analyst and CPO.

AGILE MINDSET

After introductions, Renee explained, "The reason for everyone attending this meeting may not make sense to all of you. The board mandated change, demanding DHS no longer continue to fail like it did before. Now it's time to get into the details, working through momentous change, including how to adapt as the Recovery Project proceeds. Agile is a mindset designed specifically to embrace this change and associated ambiguity."

Shirley had a plain face that looked a little worse for the wear, but that was part of her charm. With warm, deep brown eyes and a rock-steady look, she asked calmly, "I am not an IT person, so I still don't understand why I'm here. If it's not too much trouble, could you offer me more details?"

DOI: 10.4324/9781003003809-8

Both Walter and Billy joined Shirley, actively nodding in agreement to Shirley's question.

Renee responded, "Why, of course. I'm here to share a philosophy originally meant for software development that now drives all kinds of endeavors with input from diverse experts like you three. Agile offers great ways of collaborating to achieve a common goal. It includes a set of values and principles on how to work together.

"As we go ahead today, I'll refer to Agile as an underlying philosophy affecting the entire project, not IT only, so don't you worry. I'll also discuss Scrum; the Agile approach DHS will use during the Recovery Project. Scrum requires a team of experts to build a product. Scrum Team members collaborate and create the product within a specified timeframe to achieve the greatest customer value. The team members include software and systems engineers, a PO, and a SM. Collectively, they are often cross-functional. They may represent different organizational perspectives. They come from various areas depending on the product the team expects to create. Their role is to complete the product according to priorities set by the PO."

Renee then summarized how the Scrum Team functions. "The Scrum Team completes parts of the product through a repeated series of specific timed sessions or Sprints. A Sprint is a unit of work, like two weeks, where the team delivers a functioning product increment in a short period.[1] At the start, there is a planning meeting where the PO prepares a Product Backlog with the team.[2] This is a prioritized work list the team executes in individual iterations. During the two weeks, there's a 15-minute standup session at the beginning of every day. At this Scrum session, everyone takes a turn by standing and speaking about their progress on the product: important tasks just completed, in progress, and about to start.[3] At the end of two weeks, there's a Sprint review lasting up to two hours. Here, the customer offers feedback on the working product increment completed during that Sprint.[4] Afterward, there's a Sprint retrospective meeting, lasting no more than one hour. This is an opportunity for the Scrum Team to define lessons learned during the earlier Sprint, including what they want to start, stop, and continue doing during the next Sprint.[5] With this information, the team fine-tunes their schedule to complete remaining work.[6]

"The PO drives the results created by the team. The PO understands how the product fits within DHS's strategic plan, what customers need, and how to validate that with them. This includes the PO actively collaborating with the customer to keep them fully informed about product features and priorities. This also requires updating the prioritized list of product features maintained in a Product Backlog.[7]

"The SM is a Scrum expert and facilitator who collaborates with the team to overcome impediments affecting product creation.[8] One of the SM's primary roles is to train the team to work collaboratively on each task instead of breaking work down by everyone's expertise. This includes fostering and supporting an understanding that each team member must listen. If team members just talk, they're not learning. And this job is all about learning—learning what the customer needs. This means everybody has an obligation to hear and consider each other without judgment in a safe environment. This is a critical type of interaction that requires understanding Scrum and specific facilitator techniques to sustain it."

Now that Renee had finished her introduction, I interjected, "The concepts of Scrum Team collaboration are remarkably like the viewpoint taking and involvement requirements found in AIM and used to engage Targets and other stakeholders in change and project management. It's not just about gathering facts; it's about how people feel, too."

Tina, an austere woman with short-cropped grey hair and a square smooth face, asked, "Where's the project manager?"

I clarified, "Standalone, Agile is more about product than project management. When combined, Agile and project management work well together. As such, a complex endeavor like the Recovery Project requires a PM, who coordinates all the teams in the project governance structure. Examples include working with the SM and Scrum Team on product delivery and PO for project schedule preparation and adherence. Input to the PM also comes from the CMT and PMT members, WAM, CPO, and CSU. The PM also coordinates external stakeholders, for example, ISD procurement and network services, third-party contractors, and the COTS vendor. This requires project management skills like integration, scope, schedule, cost, communication, risk management, and so on.

"In contrast, the SM replaces the traditional role of an IT development manager responsible for delivering a product. For example, the SM facilitates methodological compliance and removes impediments as the Scrum Team completes tasks during each product development iteration. The PO manages trade-offs between scope and schedule associated with product requirements management, and the whole Scrum Team manages quality."[9]

AGILE VALUES AND PRINCIPLES

Renee distributed a document, including Agile Values and Principles, to the meeting participants. It listed the four values and 12 principles created by the Agile founders. Renee's document organizes the 12 principles by the four sequential Agile values to define how they relate to each other. While it portrayed a precise organization of principles by values, Renee commented that they overlap.

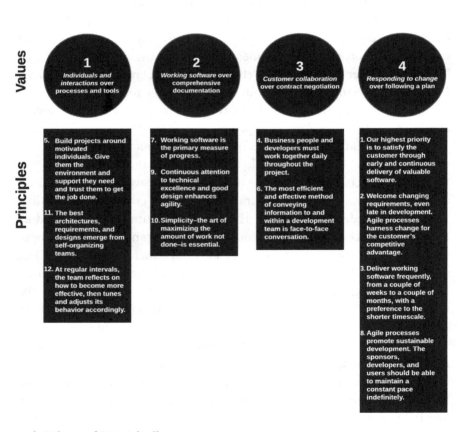

Agile Values and Principles.[10]

Renee said, "The values are concepts of Agile philosophy, points of departure for organizations just like DHS. They juxtapose where DHS is and where Agile expects the department to go. The principles add detail to the values as steps used to execute Agile."

"Before we begin discussing Agile," suggested Nolan, "Why use it on a COTS procurement project?"

"There is a fundamental reason," responded Renee. "Concentrating on the value customers seek when acquiring, configuring, and implementing a COTS solution requires the same rigor applied to software development.

"Software development includes building entirely new programs or customizing existing ones. In either case, this refers to writing software code to achieve the value customers seek.

"Configuring uses available tools in the COTS solution to tailor the existing standard software for the customer. This involves changing a setting, like adapting an email program to put my boss's messages in an Important folder automatically. While not programming, as in software development, we still must define customer requirements, *configure* and unit test software that delivers customer value, complete integration testing of all system components together, and implement it successfully."

"I get that," countered Nolan. "Why introduce Agile, though? Waterfall includes the same rigors, whether applied to developing or configuring software."

"It's about change," emphasized Renee. "DHS has to stop continually delivering failed IT projects. Agile offers a successful alternative to waterfall."

"I don't agree. That's an oversimplification," objected Nolan. "We could drink a pot of coffee or a bottle of wine arguing this. I'm not going to spend our time now learning about Agile just because you think it's better. DHS has too much to do. While the rigors of software development certainly apply to COTS solutions, you must convince me we need to use Agile. I'm not okay with just following whatever you say."

"I never suggested anything like that," parried Renee. "I have no intention of assuming you will accept Agile just because I say so. By the end of our discussion, you will accept Agile as a far better alternative. In fact, I'll buy the wine if I'm wrong."

Nolan just shrugged and asserted, "Suit yourself."

"I don't want you to comply," offered Renee. "Instead, I ask that all of you explore Agile as a new way of thinking, a mindset with different values and principles. The more you do that, the greater your success when applying Agile to your work."

Value 1—Individuals and Interactions over Processes and Tools

Renee jumped forward, deliberately not allowing a response from Nolan. "Let's begin with exploring how we communicate. Agile Value 1 is about embracing how people solve problems instead of strict reliance on methods and techniques. People interacting find answers to problems. This means we concentrate on people communicating first, followed by the methods and techniques.[11]

Principle 5

"Value 1 is a theory Agile refines in Principle 5. This principle says: *Build projects around motivated individuals. Give them the environment and support they need, trusting them to get the job done.* This means we encourage the organization to trust customer input about system needs and the IT staff responsible for building a corresponding solution. We leave them both alone to collaborate and complete their work."[12]

"This is the reason we need a dedicated software configuration team, isolated from the rest of the organization, in a separate project office," noted Nolan.

"Correct, at least from a software configuration standpoint," Renee said curtly.

Renee added, "This value and principle apply to all project teams, including the Scrum Team, PMT, WAM, and CMT. We need to dedicate these participants to the project and emphasize the importance of trusting them to get their assigned job done. Trust is a key driver for their successful interactions.

"We also use Kanban, a complementary method that considers customer demand, displays workflow on a board, and limits work in progress to what's most important to the customer, particularly continuous improvement. So instead of just doing Agile work with task tracking tools, we use Kanban."[13]

Renee got up from her seat and went to the whiteboard. She started drawing a Kanban or Scrum Board, noting, "The board is a swimlane diagram. This is a kind of flowchart that relies on the metaphor of lanes in a pool. The labels for each lane or column are Backlog, To Do, In Progress, and Done. On the far left is the backlog of customer features or stories, workflows, or other assignments arranged in prioritized order, starting with the most valuable. Tasks for this work move from left to right on individual Post-It Notes in each lane, tracking the progress on the prioritized work. Focusing on the top row of the Scrum Board directs attention to the highest-priority tasks, the ones with the most customer value. Once completed, the team moves to the next top value work listed in the far-left column. This is about value-driven activity, not just a tool- or method-based technique."[14]

Tina noted, "I like the twist from tools and methods to emphasizing value. You make a good point. What do you think, Nolan?"

Nolan just shrugged and didn't respond.

"I haven't really started yet," Renee interrupted, "As I share each principle and value, I'll offer other ways Agile promotes project team interaction to support customer value."

Nolan looked up at the figure on the whiteboard. He then looked up at Renee and just bristled with, "This is hardly enough to enchant me with Agile."

He appeared angry about something, with no intention of doing anything except disputing whatever Renee said.

Scrum Board.

"It wouldn't work for me either at this point," Renee proclaimed. She paused for a moment, not knowing the source of his anger. I thought Nolan was annoying.

Principle 11

Renee proceeded with, "Principle 11 states: *The best architectures, requirements, and designs emerge from self-organizing teams.* This means the best work comes from a team left alone to complete their work. Self-organizing team members understand their roles and responsibilities clearly and do what's expected of them with sufficient autonomy to perform at the best of their ability. This includes collaborating teammates, each with different ability, to do the work. Team diversity gives them strength, while their unity is their power.[15] This extends Value 1 and Principle 5, moving from the importance of individuals to teams."

"I know about self-organizing teams," quipped Nolan, derisively.

Everyone felt the tension. Renee stopped and Nolan just looked at her menacingly without saying anymore. Cigarettes saved them.

Without fear of recrimination, Renee said, "Let's take a break. I need a cigarette. Will anyone join me?"

Later, Renee told me that is what happened:

No one except Nolan responded. He grabbed his Camel straights from his breast pocket. He brusquely led the way to the designated smoking area, separated from a disapproving world, in front of the building. Good old cigarettes. Breaking barriers and putting us on the same side.

As they lit their cigarettes. Renee started with, "There's tension in our communication. I can help you with or without it."

Nolan took a deep pull on his cigarette and exhaled. "Renee, don't waste my time with the virtues of Agile when it's never going to matter."

"It's your choice on how this goes, Nolan. It's a whole lot easier without the tension. Clients interact and know each other as coworkers and even friends. They're comfortable outwaiting the consultant and continuing as if we never existed. I'm always the outsider, explaining proven practices, asking necessary questions, without forming a relationship with anyone. There's one thing that unites all consultants: our inherent loneliness. I often can't afford to get to know client staff, especially while they remain wary of me. Once I finish helping you, I leave, never seen again. In fact, in your case, you'll be rid of me."

Renee took a deep breath, adding. "Zelda virtually handed the Recovery Project to you, calling you the best on her staff. I thought you embraced this assignment."

"Look, I completely support this project," responded Nolan. "It's just that DHS and the board have plans that I'll follow without Agile."

"What are you talking about?" Renee asked.

"IT Advisory Solutions (ITAS) has a board contract with a report due shortly. Their charge is to explain how best to combine all county health services under DHS control. That includes the Sheriff's Jail Health, who has the only county EHR project currently. Jail Health selected a vendor solution from Cerpix, which the Sheriff is implementing.

"ITAS is all about consolidating and standardizing health care services county-wide. The follow-on work for them is too huge for any other recommendation. There's no reason for us to talk. DHS will implement the vendor software selected by Jail Health in our six hospitals and 24 ambulatory clinics without Agile."

Nolan stubbed his cigarette in the filthy sand ashtray and promptly lit another.

"Oscar already shared with me much of what the Recovery Project involves, Nolan. None of it matters. Health service consolidation or not, we must define what the hospitals and ambulatory centers need. We must do this in the most successful way available to us. That's why we're talking about Agile. We cannot take all the clinical practices and procedures from the jail and just implement supporting software in each hospital and outpatient clinic."

Renee added, "While this may be a worry for you, consolidation makes our work easier. Assume DHS is responsible for all county health care. As you said, standardizing is important. This means the county uses the EHR vendor already selected by Jail Health. While the Recovery Project will review that EHR to decide its suitability, DHS will select it. It's not politically workable to do otherwise, even if we find it unsuitable. I don't support this approach, but that's how the county operates, like it or not. In any case, we will save months of project time and effort because we can eliminate the entire public procurement process needed to select an EHR if we end up with Cerpix due to health care consolidation."

"I can't afford to let anything go wrong," said Nolan, while sticking his second Camel in the ashtray.

"Nolan, I hate to repeat this, but the current way fails, so you can't afford to continue doing it. I didn't pull Agile out of a hat. It works. Can you honestly tell me you know everything, you don't need help, no one is sorry for the past IT mistakes, and nothing was ever wrong about how DHS went about these failed projects? Are you not willing to try something new, especially given DHS's history and an available successful alternative?"

"Of course not!" he said, now putting his Camel cigarettes in his shirt pocket.

"Okay, then," Renee said, moving toward the building entrance.

Renee and Nolan rode up in the excruciatingly slow elevator alone and in silence.

Renee changed the subject as they continued up in the elevator, "What's your Ph.D. dissertation about?"

"The Third Reich."

"Whoa!" Renee exclaimed as the elevator doors opened. "I thought your degree was from the University of Chicago's Divinity School."

Nolan and Renee paused in the hall by the meeting room as Nolan explained, "It is. When I went there, we studied German philosophers from the 1930s and '40s. I found this unsettling, given that's when the Third Reich started and ran its barbaric course. I began researching the lives of these philosophers and how they co-existed or died alongside the Third Reich. Many died because of Hitler. Some went underground. Others supported him. Suffice it to say, I found it troubling. I went on to focus on the Third Reich for my dissertation."

"Where'd you go afterward?"

"While I was born in the UP, most of my family is from Los Angeles. My folks moved back there, and that's why I returned after finishing my degree.

"I'm an ordained minister as well, and I was highly active in civil rights before the Rodney King riots. I ended up working for the Los Angeles Police Department (LAPD) shortly after that time. That's where I really started in IT. My academic career included a statistics concentration and computer modeling. This helped me to supply insights about policing and reducing how they applied force. Years later, I met my wife, who also worked for LAPD. I joined DHS IT to avoid any potential issues with us both working for the same employer."

"We've both had first-hand experience with change induced by IT," Renee offered. So why the pushback?"

"To be honest, Renee, I'm not sure. It's all the political mayhem, the failed GMIS project, the Recovery Project demands, county health care consolidation. I don't know. I'm sorry."

"I didn't help by just swooping in on my broom and telling you what to do," Renee offered.

"I appreciate your apology, but it's not necessary," shared Nolan. "My wife is from Spain, and I jokingly call her *la bruja*, or witch in Spanish. We've got work to do. Let's get back at it."

Renee smiled as they returned to the meeting and resumed as if she and Nolan no longer had a problem.

Renee began again with, "A self-organizing team doesn't wait for their manager to tell them how to build the customer product successfully. Without intruding supervision, all team members help each other where and when possible, including teaching each other new skills."

Nolan responded, "I see this is contrary to how we split our organization into functional areas. DHS separates its business people, software developers, QA, and so on. Each silo has its own supervisors controlling and directing work. Agile appears to empower team members to work together across disciplines without intrusion from supervisors. It sounds productive, but how do you get the right mix of generalists and specialists together on a team? How do you encourage self-organizing team interaction?"

"There are a few ways," said Renee. "A self-organizing team includes a group of different experts. These experts collaborate for a common purpose, creating a product within a specified timeframe to achieve greatest customer value. In keeping with Agile, the project recently defined a governance structure, including teams with a variety of experts. Most of you are the facilitator and knowledge expert, training your team members to work together.[16] As facilitators, it is your job to engage the diverse DHS viewpoints and expertise within your self-organizing teams. Further, these teams embrace DHS's purpose-driven visions with customer value at its core.

"Autonomously, each self-organizing team selects the best way to do their work instead of assigning work based on an individual's siloed specialty or a manager's direction. This means no single team member has all the answers. The dynamics of a self-organizing team requires appreciating diversity. Listening to different ideas supplies opportunities for finding common ground. Encouraging common ground among diversity finds new and beneficial ways of thinking and improving how to get work done better.

"To do this, the team must engage in communication about diverse ideas, in a safe environment, where the membership listens without judgment. This helps everyone reach a better understanding of themselves and each other, which enhances the team's ability to solve problems together.

"Conversely, each team member could join with their own specialty and management practices. They could complete their part of the work and hand it off to the next team member, each working within their silo inside the team. If you look carefully at these handoffs, you'll see piles of partially completed work. These are bottlenecks that create backlogs of work waiting for each team member in the process to complete their part. Each silo member works at their own pace, managing only so much capacity before work in progress begins to pile up. Bottlenecks create costly hold ups when each process depends on the next and when countless constraints cause variation in each processes production rate."[17]

"I see how this collaboration style works to remove silos and handoffs, but there's a tradeoff," noted Nolan. "While eliminating silos, there's the cost of training everyone so they can work together."

"This tradeoff has a lower cost when compared to continuing with silos," Renee countered. "Yes, there's time dedicated to team member cross-training and striving to be good enough at contributing to customer value. Every team member is not likely to become an expert in each skill needed from them. However, self-organized teams are far more efficient than their siloed alternative because required training is a one-time cost, diminished after initial team development. The siloed approach has ongoing costs."

Nolan nodded, adding, "This certainly reaffirms the importance of the Sponsor's role in preventing supervisors from prematurely taking their staff from one of our teams. The moment that happens, team productivity drops to accommodate incurring the cost of training replacements."

Renee responded with, "The SM has a challenging role to ensure that doesn't happen."

I could see Layla felt the positive vibe in the room as she added, "Like Tina, initially I wasn't sure why I was here. I get it now. Each self-organizing team member must learn and adopt the viewpoint of each of their teammates. This is a fundamental AIM concept."

Principle 12

"You've got it!" Renee said, moving to the next topic. "Principle 12 motivates team continuous improvement, another critical attribute of Value 1. Principle 12 states: *At regular intervals, the team reflects on how to become more effective, then tunes and adjusts its behavior accordingly.* Agile has an inherent quality focus at every step to refine the product and customer value. At the end of each Sprint, the team meets face-to-face on how to enhance its effectiveness. The team executes these improvements at once in the next Sprint."[18]

Value 2—Working Software over Comprehensive Documentation

"Value 2 says there's no better way to communicate about the software than working examples of it," continued Renee. "That's far better than a PowerPoint status report, documenting project progress."

Nolan smirked and interrupted Renee with, "Value 1 puts a solid team structure in place, and now Value 2 jumps to software delivery. How did we get there? Where's the plan?"

"Remember, you need to adopt an Agile mindset and stick with the values as theories that drive everything else," said Renee. "Evidence on how to accomplish those values begins to appear in the principles I'm describing now. The clarity increases as we more fully define Agile. Consider what I've already said about Scrum and Kanban. Think about how they reveal practical details about delivering working software. Keep what I just said in mind as I answer your planning question later in this meeting.

Principle 7

"Principle 7 delivers Value 2, *working software as the primary measure of progress*. It includes significant planning, but with flexibility that encourages change. For example, Scrum defines a User Story as a description of a feature from the PO's perspective.[19] The team selects the highest-priority stories and includes them in continuous two-week Sprints. Each Sprint concludes with working software shared with the customer for improvement.

"We combine producing working software with collaborative teamwork to maintain continuous product improvements. Waterfall virtually waits to the project end to deliver working software. In the interim, evidence of headway is not much more than a notation of completed tasks on a documented plan and status report."

"I'll accept that as limited planning only, for now," argued Nolan. "I'm still not convinced, but I'll wait until you get through the remaining principles. However, what you just said raises another question. How can a team deliver high-value software every two weeks?"

"We use an iterative incremental approach," Renee retorted. "This approach uses a software development lifecycle that repeats or iterates successively, building small pieces or increments in a sequence. Each iteration is an understanding of the final product based on the currently available set of highest-priority features identified by the PO. We iterate, building on prior increments, with new additions until we completely realize the value the PO looks for on behalf of their customer.[20]

"The team gains a better understanding of the product during each iteration. Likewise, the PO increases their knowledge about the product. You can imagine the powerful discussions the team and PO have during development and the Sprint review meetings. They welcome change, increasing product value in the next iteration. You can also see how conducting a retrospective on work completed by the Scrum Team increases their effectiveness and impact on the project."

"Terrific." Nolan smirked. "That still doesn't answer my question about a plan."

Ignoring Nolan for the moment, Renee pointed out, "There's a misunderstanding about Agile. Principle 7 says *working software* is the chief success measure of progress. While the product might be EHR lab ordering, Principle 7 only means develop and test working software, not a fully functioning solution. The value is about showing this working software to get feedback about what to improve and include in the next increment.

"In contrast, waterfall may build the entire lab ordering system, starting with one team building the database, another team building the user interface, and linking the two together. Individual teams may work on each part concurrently, with associated handoffs and backlogs.

"Agile dedicates the entire team to building the top-value priority from the start, for example, a physician selecting a lab order. The team delivers a functioning tool to select a lab order from a database in Sprint one. The team receives input during development and feedback at the Scrum review meeting. In Sprint two, the team delivers a link between the lab order and the patient and gets more feedback. The team continues with an interface to the lab system in the next increment, which is a basic lab order system in Sprint three. These Sprints or iterations continue until the team captures and delivers all the value sought by the PO."

Nolan, appeased for the moment, declared, "This frees me of a basic worry. It takes too long for my team to develop a customer solution. We freeze requirements so we can begin and complete the build. Customers see the software for the first time during testing and request previously undocumented requirements. We have a tough time accommodating them because we cannot keep on schedule and budget without scope change, particularly this late in the project. Post-live, we have a large backlog of enhancements. This is a testimony to Agile's customer involvement in an iterative and incremental approach that embraces change."

Marissa chimed in, "This continues to emphasize Agile, like AIM, underscores a crucial change tenet, Target involvement."

Renee was using a bit of the Agile iterative incremental approach with her meeting participants. It was building involvement, even including Nolan.

Then Nolan asked, "Where does integration testing fit in?"

Renee replied, "The Scrum Team tests each feature, interfaces, and conversions individually and in combination, as necessary to complete Sprints. Eventually, integration testing involves users proving all EHR features, conversions, and interfaces work together as a coordinated whole. Completing this test is one of the final milestones confirming go-live can occur. It happens after the Scrum Team completes configuring the EHR, building interfaces, and developing conversions that integrate with workflow improvements."

Principle 9

"I have more to say about planning," reasoned Renee as she glanced at Nolan. "We also have a good amount of work ahead of us. Do you want to continue?"

Everyone said yes, except Nolan. He said, "I guess so."

Renee relied on peer pressure to help Nolan comply.

Renee did not hesitate, she plowed ahead with, "Principle 9: *Continuous attention to technical excellence and superior design enhances agility.*

"As I've said, Agile thrives in an environment where there's change. To do this, Value 2, expressed through Principle 9, means it's important to routinely pay attention to high technical quality, making sure the software development or configuration processes continuously improve. Superior design and technical excellence are about preventing errors and getting work done right the first time. It's simply good practice that positions the Scrum Team to move easily and respond successfully to customer change.

"Any questions or comments?" Renee asked, hoping to avoid Nolan's comments.

Tina said, "Agile complements the project management quality knowledge area."

"You're right," Renee said.

Principle 10

"The phrasing in Principle 10 is a bit unusual," Renee explained. "It says, *Simplicity—the art of maximizing the amount of work not done—is essential.* It reinforces Value 2, saying: develop software that includes only what the customer needs, leaving everything else behind. Again, this makes sense in a broader context applied to all project teams."

"Any questions?"

Surprisingly, there were none.

Value 3—Customer Collaboration over Contract Negotiation

"Value 3 promotes regular communication, replacing an adversarial customer and IT relationship with a collaborative one," Renee said.

"I have an example," interrupted Billy, a chiseled-faced former career Navy sergeant. "Years ago, when I started as a business analyst, I prepared requirements by interviewing customers. I'd assemble these requirements in a single document, distributing them at a customer meeting for review and sign-off. They needed significant revisions before sign-off. In fact, I rarely received approval outright without considerable reluctance. I then handed these requirements to developers, who built a solution customers rarely wanted. IT was the adversary, demanding user compliance.

"Years later, I prepared requirements in self-organizing teams. I never needed customer sign-off. The team created requirements with customer collaboration from the start, as I facilitated the process.

"It was always confounding to a supervisor when they asked a member of the customer team, who was happy with the results, for the sign-off document. The supervisor didn't get the concepts of self-organizing teams or customer involvement."

Principle 4

Renee welcomed Billy's understanding of Value 3, explaining Principle 4 took this even further.

"Principle 4 says, *Business people and developers must work together daily throughout the project*, which reinforces team collaboration. The PO's role as the customer representative on the Scrum Team offers an example of how this relationship works. IT representatives on the Scrum Team work with the PO collaboratively; evaluate product features; and develop, test, and demonstrate them for incremental improvement in each Sprint. There is no reason for an adversarial relationship. This principle also illustrates how other project teams can reinforces collaboration.

"Contrast this with waterfall. The business analyst prepares requirements, and there's a handoff to users for approval, just like you said, Billy. The business analyst does another handoff to developers, and so on. There's little opportunity for involvement and collaboration of all participants, which often breeds an adversarial relationship."

Nolan indicated this made sense.

Principle 6

Renee charged ahead with, "Principle 6 stresses, *the most efficient and effective method of conveying information to and within a development team is face-to-face conversation.* This supports Value 3.

"This is controversial given teams with remote workers are necessary. I know face-to-face does not exclude virtual meeting, but it's difficult to communicate when it's not in person. A critical reason remote communication is less effective than in person is that it limits physical cues, like gestures, reducing our levels of trust among team members.[21] We cannot take part in hallway and cafeteria conversations, meet peers in the elevator, and interact impromptu, which builds relationships and trust organically.

"Virtual meetings don't work if we just put them on top of our old in-person ways of doing things. We need to rework the process so everyone interacts better together in this new medium. For example, a day of virtual meetings requires looking directly at a person's face. This can be incredibly stressful. They're no frequent coffee breaks to re-energize. However, there are innovations available. For example, there are now, more than ever, virtual tools to protect employee mental health and well-being, promoting self-care in times of remote work isolation. There are headsets designed to send sound directly to the wearer's inner ear, leaving the ear uncovered and comfortable. Tools for Scrum now support online sticky notes; shared digital whiteboards; and live co-editing of spreadsheets, presentations, and text documents. Tools also promote success by combining video, voice, and chat to help collaboration easily for all team members, flattening hierarchical difference. Finally, innovative tools now support virtual serendipitous encounters to organically build trust by letting you know which of your teammates is available to start instant video chats with a single click."

"Let's assume we use both in-person and virtual communication, a mix of both worlds. Why is this effective at getting work done?" asked Nolan.

Renee said, "Examine the challenges Billy had gaining acceptance of requirements prepared from separate interviews. Even though he worked to create requirements with precision beyond any interpretation by software developers, customers remained reluctant to accept his work. It was not solely because he used interviews instead of a team. It's also because IT couldn't deliver the desired final product from those requirements unless there was constant customer involvement. Face-to-face combined with virtual communication offers opportunities for increased customer involvement when compared to just one or the other methods of interaction.

"Scrum also relies on User Stories. A User Story is a note for a Scrum Team conversation with the PO.[22] During a meeting, where it's easy to achieve full attendance because it includes face-to-face and virtual participants, the team discusses how to best deliver customer value from those stories. There's no illusion that the Scrum Team plans to force customer acceptance of the requirements."

"You still must identify customer needs," prompted Nolan. "How does a User Story do that?"

Renee got out of her chair, went to the whiteboard, and wrote a User Story structure:

As a <type of user>—Who is the user?
I want <some feature>—What does the user want to achieve?
so that <some reason>—Why is this valuable to the user?[23]

Renee returned to her chair and explained, "This structure helps the Scrum Team developers and the PO ask the right questions. This starts a dialog and builds understanding on how to achieve customer value."

Nolan considered what Renee had just described and nodded.

"Oh, and once again," ventured Marissa, "this is a good example of Agile and AIM working together. It emphasizes more communication and involvement. Agile Value 1 extends trust to Principle 6 as well to AIM."

Renee leaned forward and gave Nolan and Marissa each a high five.

Value 4—Responding to Change over Following a Plan

"Value 4 embraces evolving customer needs instead of following a prescribed to do list. All of the associated principles welcome change," Renee reported.

Principle 1

To begin with, Renee said, "Principle 1 proclaims: *Our highest priority is to satisfy the customer through early and continuous delivery of valuable software.* To do this, the SM, PO, and rest of the Scrum Team refine the backlog of User Stories. The PO prioritizes the backlog for Sprints, based on customer input, allowing early and continuous delivery of software with the most value."[24]

Nolan suggested, "One of the toughest problems for IT is getting a customer to prioritize requirements. They always rank everything as top priority, until we assign cost. Unfortunately, we often don't know the cost until a vendor gives us a price or we plan to write the code. These methods are too late. How does Agile solve this problem?"

Renee replied, "The simple answer is, the PO prioritizes the Product Backlog according to customer value. The PO reviews each feature and gets clarifying feedback from customers. There's a more detailed process that customers use, which we will review later.

"Also, Agile imposes constraints to motivate customer identification of the highest-priority features. For example, Agile, particularly Principle 10, challenges the axiom that more is better. We do this by applying the 80/20 rule or Pareto principle. Research shows users only rely on about 20% of a software product's features.[25] Agile teams start by homing in on what the customer values most about their product, the highest-priority features.

"The team also has another constraint; it must deliver working software in two-week Sprints. There's little time for low-priority features. The team keeps releasing new Sprints including next-level priorities until the customer has the fully functioning software they need. This often results in a product far less grand than the customer originally envisioned."

Nolan agreed, "According to waterfall, we presume the requirements are precise and reflect customer priorities with few opportunities for change. We start building and begin reporting milestones. We complete the whole product, the customer sees it for the first time, and they express dissatisfaction, at a minimum, if we're lucky."

At this point, Renee told the meeting participants that *Hook* was one of her favorite films. The movie is about Peter Pan, who forgot who he was, and his return to glory. The Lost Boys start to teach him all about his magic. During a meal, there's a food fight where Peter's magic returns. The Lost Boys are in awe, saying, *You're doing it, Peter.*

Nolan slammed his chair back from the conference table, and it hit the wall behind him. "I love that movie!"

"Well, Nolan, or should I say *Peter, you're doing it.*"

During the following cigarette break, Renee and Nolan shared favorite scenes from *Hook.*

Principle 2

Back at the meeting, Renee clarified with, "Principle 2 says, *Welcome changing requirements, even late in development. Agile processes harness change for the customer's competitive advantage.* This means each time the Scrum Team finishes a Sprint, they learn what to change. The benefit of those changes, whether it's to include or exclude features or maximize value, finds its way into the next Sprint. This is a dynamic process, impossible to identify in an initial plan."

Nolan remarked skeptically, "Okay, Agile embraces change. I have no issue with that, especially how this maximizes customer value. What concerns me still is the notion of a plan. A project, by definition, has a start and end date. We cannot do without that information. When are you going to explain how Agile responds to this fundamental requirement?"

Principle 3

I could see Renee was glad they could get back to this question now because the next Agile principle addressed planning. While Nolan had practical concerns, he still failed see the power of delivering working software as a measure of progress instead of a status report about a plan or schedule.

Renee stated, "Principle 3 states, *Deliver working software frequently, from a couple of weeks to a couple of months, with a preference for the shorter timescale.* It's about iteratively producing working software increments. Delivering software predictably, in this manner, measures progress."[26]

"Progress against what? We don't have a plan, so we can't know how much work we finished or what remains simply because we completed another Sprint," argued Nolan.

Renee reassured him. "It's progress against the product. Customers see actual progress by comparing the earlier product version to the current one. This has far greater value than an update to a schedule and a status report.

"Configuring the EHR is a primary schedule driver, within a large and complex project that is far more than a team producing software. The Recovery Project governance structure illustrates that there's a substantial number of moving parts, requiring a PM, schedule, and updates to keep everything coordinated."

Renee rose again and went to the whiteboard, talking while drawing a Burndown Chart, a graphical representation of work remaining versus time.

She clarified that to start, there's a Product Backlog or a prioritized list of what the customer wants in the software. Because change is desirable, the Scrum process encourages collaborative contribution to this backlog.

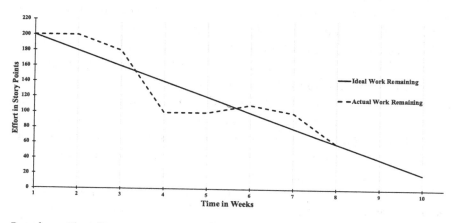

Burndown Chart.[27]

Contributions, each individually expressed as a product feature, include user needs, technical requirements, configuring, testing, defects, corrections, and so on.

The PO reviews each feature and gets clarifying feedback from customers to prioritize this backlog. This includes defining each feature as standalone to avoid dependencies where possible. The PO organizes the backlog in an ordered list, with top-priority items the Scrum Team completes in the near term. Features at the bottom may never make it into the final product because they have limited customer value. Finally, as the Scrum Team completes their work, they receive ongoing feedback about the product, and the PO refines the backlog priorities to increase customer value.

Once the Scrum Team has a prioritized Product Backlog, it becomes the scope of work to complete for their customer. As work begins, the backlog becomes the amount of work or effort remaining after the team completes each Sprint. At the beginning of the project, the Scrum Team plots the height of the backlog on the vertical access of the Burndown Chart. Drawing a line from the top of this axis, Renee decreased it by one Sprint, in this instance, every two weeks, to the point where no work remained on the horizontal axis of time. This is the ideal work remaining line, predicting the date the Scrum Team plans to complete their work. We derive the duration of this plan based on the velocity of the team completing User Stories over time.[28]

The Scrum Team plots an actual work remaining line on the Burndown Chart at the end of each Sprint. This displays actual against planned work. With consistent velocity achieved as the team matures, they will complete or *burn down* the backlog according to the planned schedule.[29] A Burndown Chart illustrates work left to do versus time. While Scrum uses it to measure development or configuration progress, Burndown Charts apply to measuring progress involving other work items over time, like completing a backlog of workflow improvements.

In addition, plans are imprecise and imperfect, especially at project start. We don't know the team members, technologies, user requirements, or customer details yet. As a project progresses, we gain a considerable amount of knowledge about each of these. Scrum assumes this is the case. It categorically requires it for success, introducing planning as the first step of each new Sprint. Taking account of newly acquired knowledge may or may not require plan revision. However, it does sharpen team focus on doing the most they can to build the best customer product. This eliminates wasting time building and following the unachievable, a perfectly prepared schedule or plan.

Waterfall requires long-term planning, relying on predictions without actual work completion, to prepare a project plan. Unfortunately, we underestimate time, costs, and risks of future actions, while we overestimate the benefits of those same actions.[30] Developing software is knowledge work. It's messy, like so many human endeavors. It simply doesn't lend itself to correct plan predictions. It makes much more sense to rely on actual incrementally improved working software, every two weeks, as we progress according to a planned completion date.

"That's great, but how does the team do that?" objected Nolan.

Renee assured him that there are many estimating methods; the most popular is Planning Poker. I know this sound crazy, but Scrum gamifies the estimating technique using a special set of cards designed for this purpose. The Scrum Team sits together at a table with the SM and PO facilitating, while all other members estimate. Included in the game is a timer, a special card deck for each team member, and a list of User Stories describing a software product the team expects to develop or configure.[31]

Every card in the deck has a number from the Fibonacci sequence, a series where each number is the sum of the two preceding numbers. Scrum uses Fibonacci numbers mostly because they're far apart and imprecise enough to show differences and uncertainty naturally found in estimating.[32]

During the game, each team member assigns Story Points to each User Story to estimate the level of effort needed to complete that feature. A Story Point is a relative unit of measurement used to estimate total effort to completely implement a requirement in a Product Backlog. Effort considers all work, complexity, risk, and uncertainty involved to finish implementing the requirement.[33]

The *absolute* point value assigned to each Story Point is not meaningful. The importance lies in the assigned *relative* value. This means a Story Point assigned a four requires twice the effort of a Story Point given a two.

The team never assigns Story Points based on time. Time is an absolute measure, so it destroys the importance of relative value and estimation consistency. Everyone is also notoriously bad at accurately estimating time. Finally, translating Story Points into time is not even necessary. What is important is how many Story Points a Scrum Team typically completes in a Sprint, for example, two weeks. This defines the team's velocity.

Once the team knows its velocity, it can predict the total schedule needed to complete the Product Backlog from actual experience.[34]

Planning Poker starts with the SM facilitating the team. Typically, the PO summarizes a requirement. The estimating Scrum Team members ask the PO questions, followed by the SM summarizing and concluding the discussion. Each Team member then assigns their estimate of Story Points, placing their card face down in front of them. This avoids affecting the estimates of all other teammates. Everyone announces their estimate, simultaneously turning their card over. Team members with the highest and lowest numbers then justify their estimates. The game resumes until the team arrives at consensus, total agreement on a Story Point estimate. At any time during the game, the SM or PO may use the timer to end the discussion and resume another estimating round.[35]

Nolan smiled and said, "That's impressive. I really thought this card game would be a silly waste of time."

"Oh, and one more thing, Nolan. To feed your interest in Agile, there's lots more for you and me to discuss. I would enjoy doing that with you."

Nolan nodded, "That would be great. I look forward to it. Thank you."

Principle 8

Renee concluded, Principle 8 indicates, *Agile processes promote sustainable development. The sponsors, developers, and users should be able to maintain a constant pace indefinitely.* This principle reinforces what we just talked about but adds sustainability. In each example we've used, the self-organizing team repeatedly delivers working software every two weeks. They do this successfully based on proven estimating techniques and strict time constraints. By committing to only what they can build, within strict time and feature constraints, the team creates an environment that maintains a sustainable pace.[36]

The Scrum Team works under the constant constraints of a time box, a *container* with a fixed start and end. This focuses the team. For example, all meetings have strict start and end times, and each Sprint completes with working software within two weeks.

Deviations occur when the team first begins working together. Other variations occur throughout product development. The team uses planning and retrospective meetings to find adjustment so they stay within the time box. They aim to cut deviations that occurred in the prior Sprint by implementing corrections in the next. Again, predictability and continuous improvement are key.

Kabir spoke, with a question, "All of this narrowly applies to the software engineering domain of requirements, design, development, and testing. How does Agile apply to the systems engineering domain like, infrastructure, networks, security, and other integral categories necessary for customer product delivery?"

Renee explained, "Scrum is about a single team developing, delivering, and sustaining a product. To avoid handoffs and bottlenecks, the Scrum Team includes software and system engineers. Alternatively, DHS could train software engineers to use Agile in a separate Scrum Team. There could even be more Scrum Teams working simultaneously. These options involve complexity that are difficult for an organization like DHS to tackle in its first Scrum experience but worth considering in future projects."

Nolan peered over his glasses at Renee. "You said you would convince me. You did. At the beginning of this meeting, I mentioned we might need to debate our opposing positions over a pot of coffee or a bottle of wine. I owe you that wine."

"I'll toast to all of you for doing what we did today, but only one glass. I'm beat. Sharing a bottle would do me in," Renee replied wearily.

NOTES

1. "Scrum (Software Development)."
2. Stellman and Greene, *Learning Agile: Understanding Scrum, XP, Lean, and Kanban*, Chap. 4, Kindle. Republished with permission of O'Reilly Media, Inc., from Learning Agile: Understanding Scrum, XP, Lean, and Kanban, Andrew Stellman and Jennifer Greene, 2013; permission conveyed through Copyright Clearance Center, Inc.
3. Ibid., Chap. 2, Kindle.
4. Ibid., Chap. 4, Kindle.
5. Ibid., Chap. 2, Kindle.
6. Ibid., Chap. 4, Kindle.
7. Ibid., Chap. 1–3, Kindle
8. Ibid.
9. Ibid.
10. Kent Beck et al., "Manifesto for Agile Software Development," *Agile Alliance*, 2019, https://agilemanifesto.org/; Beck et al., "12 Principles Behind the Agile Manifesto."
11. Stellman and Greene, *Learning Agile: Understanding Scrum, XP, Lean, and Kanban*, Chap. 2–3, Kindle. Republished with permission of O'Reilly Media, Inc.,

from Learning Agile: Understanding Scrum, XP, Lean, and Kanban, Andrew Stellman and Jennifer Greene, 2013; permission conveyed through Copyright Clearance Center, Inc.

12. Ibid.
13. Ibid.
14. Ibid.
15. Ibid.
16. Ibid.
17. Eliyahu M. Goldratt, *The Goal: A Process of Ongoing Improvement*, 30th ed. (Great Barrington, MA: North River Press, 2014), Chap. 18, Kindle.
18. Stellman and Greene, *Learning Agile: Understanding Scrum, XP, Lean, and Kanban*, Chap. 4, Kindle. Republished with permission of O'Reilly Media, Inc., from Learning Agile: Understanding Scrum, XP, Lean, and Kanban, Andrew Stellman and Jennifer Greene, 2013; permission conveyed through Copyright Clearance Center, Inc.
19. Ibid., Chap. 4, Kindle.
20. Ibid.
21. Vanessa K. Bohns, "A Face-to-Face Request Is 34 Times More Successful Than an Email," *Harvard Business Review*, no. April (2017): 1–4, https://hbr.org/2017/04/a-face-to-face-request-is-34-times-more-successful-than-an-email.
22. Stellman and Greene, *Learning Agile: Understanding Scrum, XP, Lean, and Kanban*, Chap 2–3, Kindle. Republished with permission of O'Reilly Media, Inc., from Learning Agile: Understanding Scrum, XP, Lean, and Kanban, Andrew Stellman and Jennifer Greene, 2013; permission conveyed through Copyright Clearance Center, Inc.
23. Ibid.
24. Ibid.
25. Jim Johnson, "ROI, It's Your Job," in *Third International Conference on Extreme Programming* (Alghero, Italy: Standish Group, 2002).
26. "Burn Down Chart," Wikipedia, 2021, https://en.wikipedia.org/wiki/Burn_down_chart.
27. Ibid.
28. Ibid.
29. Ibid.
30. Amos Tversky and Daniel Kahneman, "Judgment Under Uncertainty: Heuristics and Biases," *Science* 185, no. 4157 (1974), 1129.
31. "Planning Poker—Wikipedia," accessed July 9, 2021, https://en.wikipedia.org/wiki/Planning_poker.
32. "Fibonacci Number," Wikipedia, 2021, https://en.wikipedia.org/wiki/Fibonacci_number.
33. Stellman and Greene, *Learning Agile: Understanding Scrum, XP, Lean, and Kanban*, Chap. 2–3, Kindle. Republished with permission of O'Reilly Media, Inc., from Learning Agile: Understanding Scrum, XP, Lean, and Kanban, Andrew Stellman and Jennifer Greene, 2013; permission conveyed through Copyright Clearance Center, Inc.
34. Ibid.
35. "Planning Poker—Wikipedia."

36. Stellman and Greene, *Learning Agile: Understanding Scrum, XP, Lean, and Kanban,* Chap. 2–3, Kindle. Republished with permission of O'Reilly Media, Inc., from Learning Agile: Understanding Scrum, XP, Lean, and Kanban, Andrew Stellman and Jennifer Greene, 2013; permission conveyed through Copyright Clearance Center, Inc.

9

Procurement

On Friday morning, Jacqueline left Seattle and joined me for a weekend in Los Angeles of much-needed relaxation. Finally recovered completely from my illness, I could now support her and celebrate our wedding anniversary.

Monday morning struck hard with Jacqueline's departure and my requisite county CIO meeting. The shocking commotion outside the CIO's office contrasted with the normally stark corridors of the County Hall of Administration. I neared the scene and saw a DA investigator carrying a computer out of the CIO's office.

I joined one of the assistant CIOs, Harry Bernosky, who was among the crowd.

Harry told me, "DA investigators with the Public Integrity Division served search warrants at 13 locations, including the CIO's office and home, and a list of contractors. They're seeking evidence included in proposals, contracts, correspondence, and computer files. They suspect contractors abused their relationship with the county. Contractors allegedly solicited and paid Willoughby for insider information. These contractors supposedly made millions on county IT projects, given they had an unfair advantage over their competitors."

Not betraying what I thought of Clarence, I asked, "Where is he now?"

Harry explained, "Clarence is on administrative leave."

Willoughby's aura of intimidation, at least temporarily gone from the project, kindled worries of whether the county's acting CEO had played a role in the CIO's downfall.

Homer Jons, the deputy CIO, was nearby. I thanked Harry and went to Homer. As deputy CIO, Homer always took part in our meetings with Willoughby. I sought him out just in case he wanted to meet with me

DOI: 10.4324/9781003003809-9

separately. Homer, a Stanford Law School graduate, enjoyed his county position because he could avoid doing anything, like making decisions. He dodged stepping into his new acting CIO role by canceling our meeting. That gave me time for coffee with Renee before we met with KDMC to complete the EHR procurement.

KDMC, situated in South Central LA, opened in 1971 as a county response to the Watts Riots.

After the 1992 acquittal of four LAPD officers for beating Rodney King, another South Central riot occurred. While KDMC supplied requisite health care and jobs to the community, it could not stem the sheer enormity and extent of racism.

Located at the interchange of some of the world's most crowded highways and in one of LA county's highest-crime areas, KDMC's ED is one of the busiest. The neighborhood violence is so great that the U.S. military once relied on KDMC to train their trauma teams on how to handle gunshot wounds and other life-threatening injuries.[1]

Now, as we walked from Renee's rental car to the facility's main entrance, I said my usual hello to the man living in the nearby dumpster.

PRODUCT PLANNING

While the county sheriff previously selected Cerpix's COTS solution, DHS still needed to make an informed decision before selecting Cerpix or procuring an alternative for the Recovery Project. County procurement previously approved acquisition of Cerpix's EHR by Jail Health. Based on this, the Recovery Project could evaluate Cerpix's EHR first without considering any other options or violating procurement rules. If Cerpix met Recovery Project needs, the parties could amend the Jail Health agreement and go ahead without competitive procurement.

Renee and I had previously met with Oscar and agreed the Recovery Project, like all others, had resource constraints including time, cost, and personnel. This required prioritizing product features, or User Stories, by customer value before evaluating a vendor's proposed solution. This also contributes to setting the product and project boundaries, or scope, on what was most important to include and exclude within reasonable constraints. Using this approach, DHS's customer could evaluate and select a vendor's product that met the highest-priority features at the lowest cost.

Jail Health supplied its ambulatory Product Backlog of User Stories, and NYHH, who was also a Cerpix customer, supplied theirs for inpatient. To make the Product Backlogs manageable, both Jail Health and NYHH previously organized their User Stories into EHR modules, including clinical information, results management, computerized provider order entry, and clinical decision support (CDS). Delivered as separate ambulatory and inpatient Product Backlogs, DHS now had Jail Health and NYHH's prioritized User Stories by module, including all components required to configure the EHR software and technology. DHS had only to revise and customize these backlogs, tailoring and prioritizing them to meet their own needs. DHS could then compare these updated backlogs to Cerpix's EHR. Assuming DHS found Cerpix's EHR suitable, these backlogs also supported preparing a high-level project schedule for the Scrum Team.

At an earlier meeting with Oscar, I had explained how the Kano model worked to prioritize product features based on customer value. The model's first category includes *basic* or *minimum mandatory* features. Customers are neutral about these features, assuming they are ready fully for customer use. However, customers reject the product altogether if these features are not available completely. For example, a customer selects a software subscription with an *unsubscribe* option only. Assuming the vendor meets all minimum mandatory features, the PO can quickly focus the Scrum Team's limited resources on other priority items to select or reject a product.

The second category includes *one-dimensional* or *highly desirable* features. These features are not mandatory but satisfy the customer when available and dissatisfy when not. Such features are linear: more increase value.[2] For example, a call center software solution lets a customer reserve their place in line during a telephone support call, requesting a call back instead of waiting on hold. The PO includes these features next, without bloating the product, to increase customer value.

The third category is *attractive*, or *value-added*, features. In this instance, these fully supplied features satisfy the customer, while their absence does not cause dissatisfaction. However, the more a customer invests in these premium features, the more they gain. Value-added features are often previously unforeseen and are a product differentiator.[3] For example, a customer can access a free app subscription and receive basic functions. The customer can also opt for one of many tiered pricing plans. As the customer pays more for each tier, they receive more innovative features.

Using a Kano questionnaire, like the one Renee shared with Oscar, POs survey their customers and measure the EHR product features according to the model. Survey respondents rank the presence of the product feature according to two affirmative questions and then their absence based on two negative ones.

Such a survey, custom built or available online, may have illogical answers.[4] For example, a customer may show they both expect to have and not have the same product feature. After removing illogical answers, the analysis proceeds, aggregating customer responses that prioritize the value of product features.

DHS wanted to select one EHR serving both ambulatory and inpatient care. DHS also wanted to ensure the EHR selection was department-wide and not by the Recovery Project hospitals only. At Oscar's direction and with Renee's support, each of the six county hospitals and ambulatory care centers named CPOs. These facility CPOs managed their respective PO teams. The individual POs on each team, supplied with the Product Backlogs from Jail Health and NYHH, then met with their customers. Customers reviewed and updated EHR features to reflect their needs. When

Kano Questionnaire[5]

Questions and Evaluation Criteria	I Like It	I Expect It	I Am Neutral	I Can Tolerate It	I Dislike It
Functional					
How do you feel if the product has . . . ?					
How do you feel if there is more of . . . ?					
Dysfunctional					
How do you feel if the product does *not* have . . . ?					
How do you feel if there is *less* of . . . ?					

complete, each CPO had their hospital's first EHR ambulatory and inpatient care backlog, including features for system and software engineering.

Agents took part in later customer or Target meetings. During these sessions, Agents explained DHS will send an electronic survey to each Target to update all feature priorities across the six hospitals and ambulatory centers according to the Kano model. The survey results combine all prioritized features and serve as the basis for evaluating whether DHS should select Cerpix's EHR.

Renee built and administered the survey for both ambulatory and inpatient services. After receiving and analyzing the results, the CPOs now had a customer-defined DHS Product Backlog to compare priorities to the demonstrated EHR.

Cerpix demonstrated their EHR to seven participants, including the six hospitals and one ambulatory services CPO. Also in attendance were the hospital project managers, Nolan, Oscar, Renee, me, and Cerpix representatives. Agents and Targets or customers, encouraged to attend, saw the evaluation as participating audience members.

Before formal demonstrations, Nolan prepared and distributed an evaluation guide for the CPOs, with Renee's support.

Nolan addressed the CPOs, saying, "These demonstrations include an agenda, interview questions for Cerpix participants, a scoring method, and an issue documentation process."

Nolan then addressed Cerpix, "We expect you to demonstrate how your EHR supports selected prioritized features in the Product Backlog. As you perform each demonstration, CPOs may ask clarifying questions. When you complete showing us a feature, I will ask you to leave the room so the CPOs can discuss and evaluate what they just saw. Evaluation concludes with a single consensus score awarded for this most recently showed feature. I will then ask you to return. I will invite customers from the audience to sit at individual computers, where they will explore the recently demonstrated EHR features with your guidance."

Nolan, speaking to all in attendance, concluded, "The CPO evaluation will start with minimum mandatories. If Cerpix cannot show us any of these minimum mandatory features, allowing for configuration updates only, DHS will reject their EHR and cancel this demonstration. Assuming Cerpix meets minimum mandatories, demonstrations will continue with highly desirable and then value-added features. At the conclusion of each demonstration day, I will total Cerpix's scores by Kano priority. When the CPOs complete all demonstrations, I will update the evaluation results and announce the outcome."

The evaluation process worked as planned. It showed significant Cerpix support for the DHS Product Backlog and features requiring configuration. It also revealed where 1115 waiver requirements needed EHR application software modification.

Not surprisingly, Cerpix met all minimum mandatories. They also met 93% of inpatient and ambulatory highly desirable and 87% of value-added needs. Cerpix surpassed expectations. DHS and Cerpix agreed to begin work at once under a short-term amendment to the existing contract. Concurrently, DHS and Cerpix planned to prepare an agreement to serve all DHS inpatient and ambulatory functions even though the Recovery Project focused on the inpatient EHR only.

There was a problem. During the failed project, county counsel did not negotiate the GMIS contract using an attorney with large-scale IT procurement expertise. As a result, the CAP recommended, and the board ordered, county counsel deliver this expertise when such an agreement exceeded $3 million. County counsel remained without sufficient IT contract expertise, so they needed to procure services from a qualified attorney. This entailed a procurement, which could delay negotiations with Cerpix.

TRAINING

Before ending the meeting, Nolan announced, "We will begin Cerpix EHR training now because it is the best place to start. Training is one of the most important ways to improve EHR system adoption for better patient care."

Nolan added that Cerpix would provision the hardware platform in the cloud. This let work begin quickly on readying and testing the infrastructure required to configure their EHR and subsequent user training and practice.

Nolan also explained DHS would start the project with Cerpix training Scrum Team members, Workflow Analysts, Superusers, POs, and a knowledgeable cadre of KDMC clinical leaders and frontline Targets.

After receiving training, these individuals would begin configuring the EHR with KDMC users.

While training is one of the highest EHR costs, it delivers a valuable payback. Cerpix certified Scrum Team members, Workflow Analysts, Superusers, and POs will gain new expertise and responsibilities embedded in their job description. As DHS employees, they start the project and continue long after cutover, delivering improvements. In contrast, hiring Cerpix product specialists is more costly since they leave with their expertise about both the EHR and KDMC after cutover. Even when accounting for the loss of Workflow Analysts, Superusers, and POs from performing their regular jobs, employing them early in the project hastens a smooth transition to the EHR. Hospitals that implement an EHR, and who then invest in training, spend far more money undoing what they implemented while failing to gain product benefits.

Nolan announced, "All Cerpix EHR training will begin next week. Are there any questions?"

One of the POs turned and thanked Cerpix. Someone started to clap, and the rest of the attendees joined in the applause.

NOTES

1. "Martin Luther King Jr. Outpatient Center," Wikipedia, 2020, https://en.wikipedia.org/wiki/Martin_Luther_King_Jr._Outpatient_Center
2. "Kano Model," Wikipedia, 2021, https://en.wikipedia.org/wiki/Kano_model
3. Ibid.
4. Ibid.
5. Ibid.

10

Plan

I thought Nolan might be unqualified as Recovery Project SM, given his manner in the first meetings with Renee and me, although he excelled during the procurement as a facilitator.

Renee worked with him extensively, believing he was exactly right for the challenge. Nolan and Renee spent hours together planning the EHR software configuration for the project.

The week following the Scrum Team completed their Cerpix EHR training, they met in their project office with Renee and me.

Renee and I observed as Nolan began his inaugural Scrum Team meeting with, "Let's each share what we found most satisfactory when completing a project."

After a brief silence, the software developer, Cliff Jones, whom everyone called Jonesy said, "My team implemented the call center system. I used to sit in the supervisor's office and observe call takers using the system. I felt such pride. I could point at that system in use and say, 'I did that'."

As team members went around the table, they all supplied different versions of the same experience.

Nolan smiled, offering, "Let's keep that power of delivering customer value in the forefront throughout this project. To support that focus, I posted the DHS vision and Recovery Project SMART objectives on the wall behind me.

"Also, once we agree, I'll list our Definition of Done on the wall to my right. Just to be clear, this defines what our Scrum Team must do successfully for all work items in the Product Backlog. For example, configure software, document configuration, review configuration, and pass tests.[1]

"Last, I assume George Fleming, our first PO, will prepare Conditions of Satisfaction for each User Story. To be clear, Conditions of Satisfaction are what our Scrum Team must do to a specific User Story before the PO considers it complete. The PO uses one of these pads of 3-by-5 sticky notes and a marker for each User Story. George will write the name of a selected User Story on the front, record the Conditions of Satisfaction on the back, and post it on the Scrum Board to my left."[2]

SCRUM ASSUMPTIONS

Nolan continued, "Defining Scrum assumptions is our next step. Assumptions supply information for a variety of estimates; for example, they support our Scrum Team's product configuration time included in the project schedule. We prepare our part of the schedule by starting with assumptions. Of course, once we make estimates based on these assumptions, everyone other than us will ignore or forget our approximations and believe our configuration schedule is an absolute guarantee."

Scrum Team members chuckled in agreement, as Nolan stressed, "We must take steps to reinforce that while our assumptions take uncertainty into account, they are subject to change. For example, we'll always supply estimates as a range."

Sprint Length

Nolan announced, "Let's start with team agreement on iteration length. Sprints are between two and four weeks. Virtually all of us are new to employing Scrum. Few of us have prior experience with system projects driven by principles like inviting ongoing product change and repeated delivery of working software in short intervals. These principles, coupled with risk and uncertainty, require early and frequent feedback to help us understand and address the significant learning curve that lies ahead. What iteration length do you propose?"

Understanding what Nolan just said, the team quickly chose two weeks. They knew keeping to two-week iterations forced work into a short interval. For example, each interval had to include ongoing refinement of the Product Backlog according to customer priorities, time for development, and thorough testing to attain high-quality Sprint results. On the other hand, the brief period communicated early corrective feedback and helped to set up a consistent team rhythm promptly, key to sustained Agile development and better planning.

Ideal Days

"That was easy," noted Nolan, who then said, "With an agreed Sprint length, let's consider factors included in task estimating assumptions.

"To date we've used Story Points, a relative measure of effort, not time. With Sprint planning we shift to tasks instead of Story Points. This requires assumptions about time estimates, so we use ideal days.

"An ideal day is the number of hours of effort the team needs to complete work without any interruptions. Interruptions vary, like the time to prepare and respond to emails, take part in telephone calls, socialize with co-workers, get coffee, and perform that endless list of administrivia we all do. If we take interruptions out of our day and agree on the amount of time for pure work only, we have the basis for estimating clarity. If we assume an ideal day is six hours and interruptions are two, total duration is an eight hour day. From a Scrum standpoint, we also assume it takes the duration of one eight-hour day to complete each task. This approach reinforces self-organizing team confidence to control their daily work.

"Any questions?"

Everyone nodded or stayed silent.

Accountability

Nolan suggested, "It's also our responsibility to define Scrum tasks and attribute that work to the team, not individual members. Attribution to an individual may defy teamwork, so we estimate tasks based on what it takes to complete them, without necessarily considering a specific team member assignment. For example, it may seem justifiable to assign database design work to Yolanda Mayfield, our team's database analyst, during planning. However, when it's time to do the work, she may not be available, while another team member is."

Yolanda interrupted, "Don't we want to assign tasks to those on the team with the most expertise? How else are we going to ensure we get work done as well as possible for the customer?"

Nolan explained, "That's not necessary. Our goal is to produce good-enough results, not perfection. Perfection isn't essential. The team needs to put time and effort into what adds value only. Anything else wastes time and prevents moving on to the next task listed on the Scrum Board, including the daunting list of all work the team must complete within each two-week Sprint.

"Remember waiting for the team member with expertise to complete a task causes bottlenecks and handoffs. So, we assign tasks based on team member availability. While there's a learning curve for each of us as we improve our understanding of a new skill, overall team velocity does get better."

Yolanda chimed in again, "Okay, but what does this have to do with accountability?"

Nolan put in, "Sorry for not making that clear. The team does not find, organize, and assign each task to individual members based on their expertise, holding them responsible for getting each piece of work done. Accountability means everything about all work applies to the entire team, who creates customer value by the end of every Sprint."

Dependencies

Nolan continued with, "Working on User Stories identifies dependent functional and technological tasks, often completed by third parties, which the Scrum Team must address to complete Sprints."

Loretta hesitated and asked, "How do we plan for third-party dependencies and avoid changing our product configuration schedule?"

Nolan asserted, "Our Scrum Team cannot resolve all dependencies that must occur to complete each Sprint without any schedule adjustments. While we expect change, and we need to accommodate it, we must minimize associated schedule risk and uncertainty while accommodating third party dependencies.

"The Scrum Team reduces dependency schedule risk and uncertainty by grooming or refining the Product Backlog every week. The PM and I, as SM, work together on the project schedule and risk management, using milestones alerting third-party dependencies that their work must start, reach halfway, or finish soon. Also, I take part in frequent status reporting on work involving these dependencies during weekly project meetings. I share this with our team while grooming the Product Backlog. While this doesn't guarantee the resource will complete their dependent work on time for the Scrum Team, it offers a practical risk management technique that minimizes schedule adjustments."

Loretta smiled kindly and thanked him.

Spike

Nolan grinned and then said, "As you know, our Scrum Team *always* understands how to define each task. Joking aside, when there is an unclear situation, we add a placeholder. We use this placeholder to perform a spike or a short task to explore how to do this technical or functional work. The team discusses the outcome and then decides how to estimate the task to complete that work. Replacing the placeholder with this new task may require adjusting the involved Sprint."[3]

George added, "That's a perfect example of doing product work to refine assumptions and associated estimates instead of predicting from prior experience or guesstimating."

Velocity

Nolan then said, "Now that we have our Sprint length and we know how to prepare Story Points, we can define team velocity, or how much work we can complete in a single Sprint. We figure this out by calculating the sum of all assigned Story Points completed within a Sprint."[4]

Nolan explained preparing assumptions for a stable velocity was difficult for the team right now since this was the first project together and there was no meaningful data available for estimating. He suggested running three Sprints to create this data. He would then use this evidence to estimate team velocity for future work and revise it as new data suggests. Each Sprint covers everything needed to deliver a working increment of the full product, for example: features, technical architecture, user experience, interfaces, conversions, and testing needed to deliver customer value. Once the team reaches stable velocity, Nolan will have the data needed to prepare this part of the project schedule.

Nolan continued with, "To prepare a stable velocity, I'll compute a moving average that calculates the team's trend as we improve our Scrum skills and adjust to working together. I'll calculate the average velocity from our initial three Sprints. The next calculation of the average drops the oldest

Sprint velocity and adds the newest or fourth Sprint velocity, and so on. Over time, the trend stabilizes and offers a suitable basis to any adjustments to initial planning and scheduling."

Nolan knew he had reviewed a significant amount of complex information, so he suggested the team take a break before starting.

After everyone returned, George moved to engage the team with a description of the top-priority User Story in the Product Backlog. Everyone sat quietly, as if they had forgotten all their training.

Quickly, George offered, "Let's go around the table, with each of you offering clarifying questions and comments."

Briefly, people asked questions and discussion ensued, but then everyone stopped again and looked at George for guidance.

Jonesy remarked, "This is our first real go at a Sprint aside from Agile training. Before that, I estimated size in terms of time and cost. That's not the correct way to figure out the work needed to find Story Points. I don't think any of us really know how to do this. We need help."

Nolan suggested, "Story points are what the team decides. There is no one else who defines the standard for you. For example, In 'N Out Burger labels small, medium, large, and extra-large drinks as a way of sizing them relative to each other. We don't have to know the actual number of ounces, but we all understand their relative differences. When applied to Agile, each Story Point involves varying categories of effort only. Effort is the amount of work, risk, uncertainty, and complexity needed to achieve our Definition of Done. That's what we mean by Story Points.[5]

"As you remember from your training, we use the Fibonacci sequence for estimating. The Fibonacci sequence is a system for relative estimating of Story Points associated with a task. A larger, more complex task receives a higher Fibonacci number or Story Points. Relatively speaking, a smaller, less complex task receives fewer points. So, let's assume we agree as a team to use the Fibonacci sequence of 1, 2, 3, 5, 8, 13, 21, 34, 55, and 89. Now, suppose we select a User Story and assign it 13 Story Points and name it mid-size. We continue by assigning Story Points to other User Stories relative to this first one. Once we've done that, we have a team reference point for a mid-size User Story. Of course, we'll only use it for a while, until we get better at completing tasks because of our greater understanding of Scrum, each other, the product, and the project. Once we reach that position, we'll update this team reference point and hopefully have few reasons to change it or the schedule we created from it."[6]

George moved to engage the team in defining Story Points for what he thought was the first mid-size User Story. There was indecisiveness.

George suggested, "Let's play Planning Poker."

Nolan winked at George, who distributed Planning Poker decks to each team member. Fun and serious, they began negotiating assignment of Story Points to what became a mid-size feature. This continued successfully for other features as well. By the end of playing Planning Poker, George posted 3-by-5 sticky notes under *Backlog*, the far-left column of the Scrum Board. Each had the User Story name and the number of Story Points on the front and the Conditions of Satisfaction on the back.

Afterward, Jonesy suggested, "We agreed a Sprint is two weeks, so let's start by estimating how many hours we have available."

The rest of the team nodded or voiced consent.

Jonesy calculated, "There are five permanent members and 6 hours of work in an ideal day, so we have 30 hours per day of work. One two-week Sprint or 10 work-days times 30 work hours per day equals 300 hours."

Yolanda got up from the table and grabbed a pad of 3-by-5 sticky notes. She walked to the Scrum Board and pointed to the *To Do* column to the right of the highest-priority User Story in the *Backlog* column.

Yolanda turned to the onlooking team and announced, "Let's add tasks to the top-priority User Stories in the Product Backlog that include estimated Story Points."

The team completed a discussion of the first task, and Yolanda documented it on the sticky note and posted it on the Scrum Board. Zara Kumar, the tester on the team, went through the same process and posted the next task on the Scrum Board. The team continued to assign tasks to all User Stories with Story Points. They had more than enough User Stories to complete in three Sprints.

The meeting ended with everyone agreeing to start the following day on the six-week period to define the Scrum Team's velocity.

At the beginning of the first Sprint, the team assumed they could complete the tasks in four User Stories totaling 36 Story Points. At the end of this Sprint, they completed three User Stories, resulting in a velocity of 24 Story Points. As the team progressed through the remaining two Sprints, the gap narrowed between what they thought they could do and what they did. By the end of all three Sprints, the Scrum Team proved an average velocity of 32 Story Points.

OTHER ASSUMPTIONS

After the Scrum Team defined their velocity, Renee asked Oscar to join the next meeting, including me to define other DHS assumptions needed to finish the project schedule. Nolan explained that while the team defined schedule assumptions for configuration and development, the project had other significant requirements and associated schedule estimates. For example, construction and the network upgrade requirements don't have User Stories, Story Points, and velocity. While these requirements may or may not involve the Scrum Team directly, the project must define assumptions to estimate and complete the other parts of the project schedule.

Workflows

"One of the first examples is workflow," Nolan suggested. "The reason is that we cannot configure the EHR or improve workflow independently."

"Can you explain this configuration and workflow relationship further?" said Yolanda.

"Sure," responded Nolan. "While not all workflow improvements entail configuring the EHR, many do. Implementing an EHR disrupts current workflow. The WAT improves workflow, and the Scrum Team configures the EHR collaboratively. Each focuses on improving service quality. These teams do not add the EHR software and accommodate workflow to simply support current operations. They need to integrate and serve a future state. EHR configuration and workflow changes inform each other, finding opportunities to cut waste, improve communication, increase accountability, enhance safety, and enrich the quality of a patient's experience. This is Level 3 organizational maturity, where the WAT and Scrum Team collaborate, tailoring and improving processes and the EHR proactively rather than reacting to integration problems after cutover.

"There's more," explained Nolan, "but that's a start for now. Does that make sense?"

Yolanda said, "It does."

Nolan continued by noting, to be effective, the WAT makeup requires multidisciplinary representation because so many workflows span multiple functions and departments.[7] Communicating across multiple disciplines and departments about how best to update a workflow and configure the

EHR fosters involvement and respect among the participants. Collectively, workflow improvements and associated configuration changes introduce Targets to the EHR implementation and how KDMC will deliver health care in the future.

A Workflow Analyst, from the WAT, helps a subset of Targets included in each department or operational area, who routinely execute processes as part of their work responsibilities. They begin by examining processes associated with the top-priority User Story in the Product Backlog.

The PO works on the Scrum Team to ensure the EHR configuration meets Target needs. These Targets work with this PO to ensure workflow improvements and EHR configurations integrate. To reinforce this, the Workflow Analyst helps Target definition of an objective for each work-flow, tied to the DHS purpose-driven vision, like compliance with specific proven practice care guidelines as measured by lower patient readmission rates. The PO shares this objective with the Scrum Team. Conforming with the Agile philosophy, the Scrum Team uses this objective to define the goal for each EHR Sprint configured and integrated with the workflow.

With the objective in mind, the Workflow Analyst facilitates Targets, as SMEs, in mapping or preparing a workflow description. Targets confer with their supervisor or manager of the operational area and ensure the workflow follows mandated internal and industry standards. Finally, the team collects and catalogs all paper forms associated with each workflow task, documenting all systems interacting with these processes and find-ing the type and volume of staff involved.[8]

Following this, the Workflow Analyst prepares a diagram of existing pro-cesses. The team uses sticky notes on a whiteboard or 3-by-5 cards posted on a corkboard for each task and decision. These temporary postings allow easy reorganization for corrections. Now the analysis begins, changing tasks and decisions by updating their sequences, removing them, limiting variations, minimizing repetition, cutting delays and handoffs, revising them, preparing new ones, and adding innovative EHR proven practices.[9]

The result is typically a one-page diagram of the future state that the Workflow Analyst verifies with repeated SME walkthroughs. At this point, the analyst documents the future state in Microsoft Visio or a simi-lar tool. After posting the diagram on a wall for review, the analyst finishes it with supplied updates.[10]

Once completed, the results included in the final future state work-flow diagram prove particularly helpful. This and all other future state workflows combined with the configured EHR reveal changes to Target roles and responsibilities. These changes define how to achieve SMART objectives tied to DHS's vision. They define new skills requiring job training, revisions to onboarding for new hires, and updates to position descriptions. The Agent involved in the effected operational area works with associated Targets and the HR representative on the CMT to make this happen. The result is that it promotes Target reinforcement, better coordination among departments; changes standards, policies, protocols, and compliance requirements; ends chart pulls, paper forms, and note routing; improves the patient experience; and defines technology access requirements. In one example, if a workflow produces a printed document, IT now knows where to install a nearby printer. By the end of analyzing every workflow combined with associated EHR configuration, KDMC has a catalog of all manual and automated systems the EHR replaces or interfaces with before cutover.[11]

Finally, since KDMC's environment is dynamic, workflow, the associated EHR configuration, and training continue to change after cutover. This means the DELTA Team conducts EHR quality improvement audits and resulting updates as an ongoing process during and after the project.

Jonesy, with his red cap of hair and mountain-man beard, asked, "How many workflows are there?"

I said, "An EHR implementation can involve up to 100 workflows. Each workflow often requires Target commitment to achieving at least one objective."

Jonesy then inquired, "I understand what you just said, but how does *our* Scrum Team interact with specifically named individuals involved in workflow analysis?"

Nolan clarified, "Both Tomo Yasuda, a Superuser with Cerpix EHR training, and Loretta Peabody, a Workflow Analyst, are temporary members of our Scrum Team with KDMC experience. When the Scrum Team plans a Sprint, the PO invites Tomo, Loretta, and SMEs to share their workflow analysis with the User Stories involved in EHR configuration changes. They attend Scrum Team meetings and work directly with the PO. The PO, Workflow Analyst, and Superuser leave the Scrum Team when we move to the next Sprint. Their replacement depends on what prioritized part of the EHR the Scrum Team configures next."

"Any questions before I share another example?" Nolan inquired.

"Well, yes, but I'll wait until you finish with the examples," noted Jonesy.

There was a knock on the door and Amanda, Oscar's assistant, stepped into conference room and handed Oscar a note. He excused himself apologetically, and he and Amanda left the meeting.

Chart Abstracts

Nolan then said, "It is our job to work with Superusers, Workflow Analysts, and Cerpix to plan and migrate selected chart data electronically for testing, training, and cutover. So, it's important for our Scrum Team to know about this next topic, the chart abstracting process."

Nolan pressed on with how EHR technology and workflow changes would inevitably disrupt KDMC, causing decreased productivity during cutover and for the near-term future, if we were lucky. A principle way to minimize this is to prepare now for populating electronic patient charts with clinical data from the paper ones. Actual data migration cannot occur fully until shortly before cutover because we cannot forecast *all* patients scheduled for admission to KDMC. Nonetheless, this is a significant undertaking that requires input from HTAC to enable preparing, testing, and executing a successful strategy.[12]

Considerations for this strategy include what data to migrate; how data migration varies by patient type, schedule, and condition; how to resolve data quality issues; where and how KDMC currently stores the data; what data triggers other processes; how to migrate data to the EHR and when to migrate it; and how the EHR handles the data differently, including how to train Targets about these changes.[13]

HTAC is the forum for defining and executing an abstracting strategy. This includes the Physician Subcommittee and others, like HIM, Health Informatics, quality improvement, and revenue management, whose input is critical to a well-thought-out strategy. Overall, the objective is to have the most pertinent information loaded and ready in the EHR at the POC, upholding patient safety while retiring paper charts.

There's a large amount of information to move on time. The project begins with basic data extraction, populating the electronic chart for current patients and others seen in the past 12 to 18 months. This includes, for example: allergies; recent medications and lab results; diagnostic, medical, surgical, and family histories; near-term nursing and physician notes; and disease management indicators.[14]

This is challenging by itself. Compounding it is KDMC's reliance on external data sources outside our control. For example, paper-based consultation reports, arriving from external sources, require scanning documents into the EHR. Consequently, data migration must combine manual, electronic, and scanning options.[15]

To help ensure safe and correct information, chart abstracting relies on nurses and providers to migrate data from paper charts to the EHR. This adds to their already hectic schedules, which requires reducing their patient load and paying for their time. HIM staff ready the charts ahead of schedule, and nurses and physicians update records with pertinent information defined by clinical standards. This conversion processes also starts to train nurses and physicians on how to use the EHR before go-live.[16]

While providers want more data than what the project can supply, they will receive what's pertinent to current patient circumstances. Unfortunately, there are exceptions. For example, many patients from KDMC's disenfranchised community suffer multiple chronic co-morbidities. HTAC will find that there is an imperfect balance between the data needed and the cost of migrating it.[17]

Jonesy confirmed, "I assume additional Superusers and Workflow Analysts will assist George and other POs as we work on this migration."

Clinical Documentation

Nolan responded that Jonesy was correct. Nolan then noted this also applied to clinical documentation, the last example involving other requirements.

Nolan said, "The Scrum Team will support electronic migration of clinical documentation to the EHR. Knowing this now helps us prepare for clinical documentation migration to the EHR before testing, training, and go-live."

Nolan continued with how clinical documentation is the record of provider medical treatments and tests delivered to specific patients. Internal hospital providers, care teams, HIM, billing, and quality improvement use clinical documentation. External entities like insurers, public health, and researchers also use this documentation. In KDMC's current paper-based environment, clinical documentation is difficult to access and distribute and contains large amounts of non-uniform free text. An EHR helps reduce all these deficiencies while increasing standardization.[18]

Of considerable significance, an EHR supplies information from clinical documentation for CDS. CDS delivers, often at the POC, the best available body of knowledge to support clinician expertise when making health care decisions. This is a good example of how an EHR will standardize care across KDMC.

Clinical documentation also supports population health that relies on data patterns and trends. For example, data trends on KDMC's diabetic patient population may show when to schedule provider follow-up as part of a treatment plan in certain circumstances.

An EHR requires limited free text to improve uniformity, completeness, credibility, and compliance to support CDS and population data needs. EHRs rely on standard nomenclature, including structured data and vocabulary, to help ensure a collective understanding of clinical documentation content and its patient care impact.[19]

Changing practices from free text to an electronic environment, with standard nomenclature, is painstaking and time consuming. Like chart abstracting, the HTAC must define, test, and execute a successful strategy to ready providers as data migration occurs shortly before go-live.[20]

Again, there are many ways to approach this, and the best way is to combine some of them. For example, structured vocabulary, like Systematic Nomenclature of Medicine Clinical Terms (SNOMED-CT) or (SNOMED), understands key words and their synonyms but does not understand important free text nuances. So, free text is still necessary but with a limited purpose now.

Also, like abstracting, there are tradeoffs that HTAC must balance between the value of CDS and population health needs and the flexibility of information capture. For example, there are widely different data migration techniques, with pros and cons. Overall, a practical solution is using electronic migration of basic patient demographics from medical records, followed by nurse and provider manual data entry, given their professional standing working with a trusted source.[21]

While most migration from paper clinical documentation to the EHR occurs just before and at once after cutover, the care environment and technology are dynamic, continuously evolving. This results in configuration, template, and training changes, often related to evidence-based medicine. Unfortunately, there are instances where providers believe they need a special template for their unique technique, despite evidence-based medicine to the contrary. For example, when applied to certain cancer chemotherapy protocols, evidence-based medicine includes patient safety improvements. A provider not familiar with the latest safety protocols may insist on adhering to their own approach based on years of practice even though recent research proves otherwise. This requires frequent quality improvement audits and Reinforcing Sponsor intervention to ensure compliance.

Involvement in the strategy and its execution, when including clinical documentation, requires listening to provider input from their FOR and refining solutions to meet their needs while complying with evidence-based medicine. This means EHR and workflow process improvement requires Reinforcing Sponsors meeting often with Targets to strengthen using the EHR safely.

Loretta asked, "I appreciate that this is important, but I still don't understand what these other requirements have to do with Scrum Team and our assumptions."

Nolan offered, "I'm sorry for failing to make that clear. The last three examples include Scrum Team participation. Each example affects our assumptions about what our team does, how long it takes, and the impact on the project schedule. For example, migrating from paper to the EHR involves automated conversion that requires development by the Scrum Team."

Loretta hesitated with, "I appreciate what you're saying, but there's a disconnect between the Scrum Team EHR configuration tasks and work involving other requirements and resources, like the WAT and HTAC."

"Exactly," declared Jonesy. "We just spent weeks defining Scrum assumptions, estimating our velocity, to prepare our configuration part of the overall project schedule. How can we rely on our schedule, based on Scrum assumptions, when we depend on dissimilar work, like workflow analysis, chart abstracting, and clinical documentation prepared by others, who don't have Scrum assumptions and estimating techniques?"

Uncertainty

"That's what this meeting is about," Nolan said. "None of us expect to eliminate uncertainty. The future is unknown and this means we all suffer from an imperfect understanding of scope, an incomplete grasp of the tasks within it, and an inability to forecast the unexpected. Tasks, other than those involving Agile, don't establish predictability based on actual value-driven work completed repeatedly and incrementally for the customer. The project schedule must rely on a combination of Scrum and other assumptions defined to increase the credibility of our estimates. Agency decision-making depends on it. If our assumptions are wrong, we waste money and time, cause disputes, lose credibility, and provoke project cancellation.

"I'm struggling. Am I making any sense?" asked Nolan.

Everyone confirmed they got it.

"I'm not sure why, but I'm having difficulties communicating today," Nolan revealed. "Let me know if you don't understand what I'm saying, please.

"Oh well, let's start with the project management critical path method to identify other assumptions. Time is the critical constraint. The critical path is the longest series of dependent tasks the team must complete on time, or else they'll delay the entire project.

"The best way to calculate a critical path relies on a project scheduling software tool. This requires finding all project tasks, loading them into the software, estimating task duration, linking all task dependencies, and relying on the tool to calculate the critical path.

"When you assign resources to the critical path tasks, this starts the critical chain method. This assumes the project has limited resources to complete each predecessor task on time before going to its next successor. The critical chain method shifts the constraint from time to resources.

"The critical chain method requires resource leveling. Resource leveling adjusts task start and end dates for constraints like demand for people or other assets exceeding supply. Once again, this requires scheduling software to calculate resource availability. For example, we assign a resource ideal days of work per task. The tool adjusts the demand from other activities requiring this same resource by, for example, making tasks sequential instead of concurrent.

"Critical chain and path methods are the same at this point, except for resource leveling.[22] We could stop here and use these combined scheduling techniques to estimate a project schedule for those other tasks that don't involve Agile assumptions."

Tina said, "That's what I do. I use critical path method with resource leveling together to manage a project schedule. I don't get what's so important about critical chain method."

Nolan clarified, "Critical chain method helps reduce critical path uncertainty with resource leveling. What's important is that we still haven't dealt with the other assumptions about duration estimates that include uncertainty. Everyone insists their time estimates are correct, even though we make over-optimistic predictions constantly. There are complex mathematical techniques, based on deficient assumptions, to overcome this problem.[23] However, there are proven and simpler approaches that reduce uncertainty in assumptions used to estimate task duration. For example, borrowing from Agile, we reduce each work product to a set of small tasks with short individual time estimates and use frequent reviews to accommodate unexpected changes. We focus on prioritized work, track the highest-priority tasks on a Scrum or Task Board, start each task as soon as possible, and minimize interruptions. All these require finding a trained resource to estimate, own, and complete their task with Agent and Sponsor review and support to bolster achieving customer value.

"These are management techniques applied to uncertainty. Our configuration schedule is important to the project, and so is the timetable for all other work. Bottom line, uncertainty is a variable in the project schedule. Defining assumptions that drive estimates and apply proven methods, although imperfect, manages it. They include a repeatable standard set of steps on how we minimized uncertainty in our schedule estimate. We also reveal our assumptions candidly to leadership that relies on them, including imperfections. If leadership questions our assumptions, we collaborate with these decision makers and prepare revised assumptions and associated schedule estimates."

Tomo replied, "While I understand what you're saying, I must adjust my desire for certainty."

Nolan prompted, "Don't we all."

As this meeting ended, Nolan announced the final planning meeting's date to complete the project schedule. I waited for Renee in the hall outside the conference room. As she walked into the hall, I hesitated and then said to her, "Oscar wants to see us urgently. I don't know what it's about."

Renee said, "That doesn't sound good," as we walked down the hall to meet Oscar.

"What's going on?" I said, as we entered his office.

Oscar informed us that Mike Jen had withdrawn as county *acting* CEO so the BOS could promptly appoint him CEO. He then announced consolidation of all county health care under a new entity. The BOS received an early draft of ITAS's report recommending county health consolidation. The board shared this confidentially with the DHS director, asking for his input. He told the BOS to create an agency over all county health care for him to run.

"Wow! The crazy never stops," I responded. "Is this happening with no input from any of the affected departments?"

Oscar explained, "Department of Public Health, Jail Health, and Mental Health didn't know about what happened until the announced change. ITAS did the analysis without interviewing representatives from these departments. They'll get a token opportunity to review the decision and meet with the board. It really doesn't matter since the BOS already decided. Mike and the Third District probably stealthily created their plan long ago, building board support and then hiring ITAS, as an *independent* party, to confirm publicly what everyone decided to do previously."

"Mike is quite the strategist," remarked Renee. "How does this affect the Recovery Project?"

Oscar said, "The board will follow ITAS's recommendation, endorsed by the DHS director. That means Cerpix will supply their system to all departments included in the new health agency."

"Quite the win for Cerpix," reflected Renee.

I confirmed, "Cerpix stands to make a huge amount of money. At the same time, there is wisdom in county health care consolidation. Think about it. While the politics may be a worry, in some ways, consolidation makes our job easier. As you know, standardizing means all health entities will use the EHR vendor the county already selected. Cerpix has one of the best EHR solutions, underscored by the fact they and their sole competitor own over 50% of the acute care EHR market."

We ended the meeting with Oscar. I felt disconcerted by the choice of the new county CEO and health care consolidation.

As Renee and I walked back to my hotel, I talked briefly about Mike. "I'm troubled by not having a direct working relationship with him as the new CEO. He focuses on politics instead of principles. From an indirect standpoint, Samantha Edwards, his deputy CEO, is a constant, no matter CEO turnover. She is accessible and will take appropriate care of the project and us, but Mike remains a major concern."

SCRUM PLANNING

Nolan conducted a final planning session including the Scrum Team, Renee, me, Superusers, and a Cerpix product specialist to describe how the Scrum Team's contribution to the project schedule worked. Nolan smiled and started talking about the Scrum Planning Pyramid on the wall-mounted video display. With assumptions completed, Scrum planning requires moving through six levels, starting with strategic planning and ending with a completed product.

Nolan announced, "To date, we've finished three levels. When we started at the strategic level, or foundation, DHS prepared a purpose-driven vision plan with clinical IT improvement as the top priority and leadership-estimated time and cost to achieve all goals. DHS expected more refinement during later planning levels, including schedule and budget estimates.

"Next, at the portfolio level, DHS identified clinical IT product investments to achieve strategic goals linked to the vision. Following from this, DHS performed product planning, selecting an EHR, the top-priority product within that portfolio, for Recovery Project implementation. This included DHS SMART objectives that execute strategic goals tied to the vision, project organization resourced with the change management

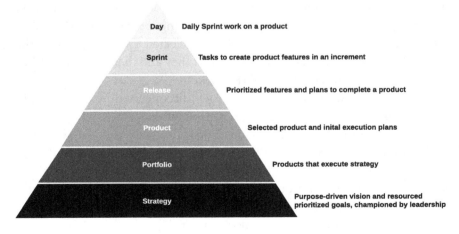

Scrum Planning Pyramid.

CAST, and a communication plan and reinforcement strategies to increase desired Target abilities and behaviors.

"Product planning also involved working on the EHR Product Backlogs supplied by NYHH and Jail Health. After analyzing this information, customers and their POs gained sufficient knowledge to prepare an inpatient Product Backlog tailored enough to contractually select Cerpix's EHR.

"This brings us to the remaining fourth, fifth, and sixth plans: release, iteration, and day planning, respectively. It is our team's responsibility to define and execute these plans, culminating in a high-value customer product. As we continue from strategic to the next Scrum planning pyramid levels, we increase our knowledge. This includes a better understanding of what the *product* looks like, how it works, and what features it includes. It also entails *project* knowledge, like how our Team works together to complete their value-driven work on schedule."[24]

Nolan explained we needed more to complete the remaining plans, like information from past similar projects. Unfortunately, the agency did not have a similar project using this team. We could rely on expert judgment, such as Cerpix, Jail Health, and NYHH project experiences. Once again, these were not particularly meaningful without the Team's actual experience.

Release Planning

Nolan explained Release Planning. This next progressively detailed plan focuses on prioritized requirements to configure the EHR product. This plan drives the Team's attention to start with minimum mandatory User Stories they must configure to complete the product, achieve customer value, and realize strategic goals and the DHS vision. Included are release goals, needed Sprints, and the associated schedule.

Jonesy wondered, "Can you explain a bit more using a real EHR product example?"

"Sure," said Nolan. "Suppose the PO sets a goal for a release on collecting documentation within the top-priority features in the clinical information module. The goal might be *enhance patient evaluation by collecting documentation that communicates how to improve health care delivery.* This goal relates to the agency's vision. It also helps identify what particular User Stories to include in a specific release."

Zara said, "How do we define multiple releases and assign User Stories to them?"

Nolan clarified, "Before answering, let's review some of our assumptions. To date, our Product Backlog has prioritized User Stories. Our customers previously prepared this backlog by updating the information supplied by NYHH. However, we never updated the Story Points defined by NYHH to express our Team's viewpoint, except for those Sprints completed previously to define our velocity.

"For Release Planning purposes, let's start with the number of Story Points we assigned to each User Story in the three Sprints executed to estimate Team velocity. We can then sum those Story Points and separately total NYHH's estimates for the same ones. Now, if we divide our number of Story Points by those from NYHH, we'll have a multiplier. We can then apply this multiplier to all NYHH Story Points in our Product Backlog to compute our own Story Point estimate for each User Story. We can then use this to prepare our release schedule."

Team members went to work. George calculated the Story Point multiplier and applied it to the Product Backlog listed on a spreadsheet.

Signaling Nolan, George confirmed, "Just to be sure, I updated the procurement Story Point estimate for each User Story based our Scrum Team's actual experience. This also means the priorities for these updated User Stories remain the same as established by the Kano model. These priorities are our minimum mandatory, highly desirable, and value-added releases organized by EHR module."

"You got it correct," said Nolan.

George leaned over the table and switched the video display source from Nolan's to his computer so everyone could see the Release Plan organizing the EHR product by the three priorities. The Team spent time discussing the plan, and George updated it on the screen based on their input about release priorities and their implications for interfaces, conversions, compliance requirements, security issues, and other product dependencies. When they completed this work, they had a Release Plan. They also had a schedule, including the sum of total Story Points in the three priority releases, divided by team velocity.

Nolan concluded the meeting with a final note, "To minimize uncertainty, we will communicate the Scrum Team part of the project schedule as a range. The low end is our total schedule estimate to complete all minimum mandatory features. The high end is the time to complete every remaining feature."

Sprint Planning

At the beginning of the following Monday session, Nolan announced, "This is our Sprint planning meeting. Sprint Planning refines the top-priority User Stories to set up what we will deliver in the next Sprint. George, as our current PO, starts with grooming. In our case, we'll re-estimate Story Points instead of relying on those we just updated by applying our Team's velocity to NYHH Story Points."

After grooming top-priority User Stories, George presented a subset of them to the team. The team asked questions to refine these User Stories into tasks and added them to a Sprint Backlog. This backlog included the work George and all other Scrum Team members agreed to deliver in the next Sprint to achieve a specific goal.

I then reminded them that George had worked with Targets to define an objective for each workflow. I said, "Now is the time where the PO, collaborating with the rest of our Scrum Team, integrates workflows and associated objectives with top-priority User Stories in the Sprint Backlog. These objectives inform definition of the goal the Scrum Team assigns to the Sprint. The goal sets up what the Team expects to achieve at the start of the Sprint and offers a potent way to measure and report that accomplishment."

Day Planning

Before completing the Sprint Planning meeting, Nolan said, "From now on, the team will conduct a meeting at the beginning of each day. You all know about the daily standup meeting. I still want to talk about it from an AIM reinforcement standpoint because it emphasizes teamwork.

"Our daily standup demonstrates how each Team member works, learns, and shares new knowledge. If we stand up and just stick to a playbook or plan, we're not going to deliver customer value. With our individual diverse backgrounds and experiences, we have a fierce unifying creative force to solve problems. Called upon during our daily standup, we use this force to strengthen our understanding of how to work together best and refine the release and Sprint plans for prompt and value-driven product delivery and project schedule update."[25]

Nolan paused, and then said, "I like to think of us as *The Avengers*, more than just a group of agency folks configuring an EHR."

Laughter erupted as Yolanda suggested each Team member select a nickname from the Avengers, like Iron Man, Hulk, and Black Widow.

NOTES

1. Stellman and Greene, *Learning Agile: Understanding Scrum, XP, Lean, and Kanban*, Chap. 2 and 9, Kindle. Republished with permission of O'Reilly Media, Inc., from Learning Agile: Understanding Scrum, XP, Lean, and Kanban, Andrew Stellman and Jennifer Greene, 2013; permission conveyed through Copyright Clearance Center, Inc.
2. Ibid., Chap. 5, Kindle.
3. Mike Cohn, *Agile Estimating and Planning* (New York, NY: Pearson Education, Inc., 2005), 156.
4. Ibid., 38.
5. Ibid., 37.
6. "Fibonacci Number."
7. S.A. Kushinka, "Workflow Analysis: EHR Deployment Techniques—Digital Collections—National Library of Medicine," *California Healthcare Foundation*, 2011, 2. Reprinted with permission from the California Healthcare Foundation 2021.
8. Ibid., 4.
9. Ibid., 4–5.
10. Ibid., 6.
11. Ibid., 10.
12. S.A. Kushinka, "Chart Abstraction: EHR Deployment Techniques—Digital Collections—National Library of Medicine," *California Healthcare Foundation*, 2010, 2. Reprinted with permission from the California Healthcare Foundation 2021.
13. Ibid.
14. Ibid.
15. Ibid., 3.
16. Ibid., 4–6.
17. Ibid., 5–6.
18. SA Kushinka, "Clinical Documentation: EHR Deployment Techniques—Digital Collections—National Library of Medicine," *California Healthcare Foundation*, 2010, 1–2. Reprinted with permission from the California Healthcare Foundation 2021.
19. Ibid., 3.
20. Ibid.

21. Ibid., 6–7.
22. "A Critical Look at Critical Chain Project Management," accessed July 22, 2021, www.pmi.org/learning/library/critical-chain-management-research-literature-5508, 25.
23. Ibid., 26–31.
24. Cohn, *Agile Estimating and Planning,* 36.
25. Ibid., 29–30.

11

Execution

Now Tina, the PM, could prepare the KDMC project plan, including the schedule and budget. After review and update, the Steering Committee approved both and execution began. Execution is about achieving the project plan to build the product while monitoring and controlling performance.

I told Oscar *execution* is a world within a laboratory. Everyone works under test conditions, experimenting, preparing, testing, and training. *Cutover*, in contrast, is continuation of execution in the wild or real world. Cutover is a period, not an event, before, during, and right after turning the new system on within all the operational components surrounding it. It's imperative that execution before cutover find and prevent the 20% of all EHR-related errors that cause 80% of the problems. When applied to health care, emphasis is on preventing patient safety risk while netting the greatest beneficial project outcomes. Thankfully, the underlying work in this project relies on Agile quality principles applied to project management, including Scrum configuration and workflow improvements, delivering the best patient care outcomes with minimal harm and cost.

Somehow months of execution went by. During this time, it was abundantly clear that there's theory, reality, and LA County. The Recovery Project was no exception. Nothing surprised me, yet the nature and context of LA County's problems were often uniquely severe. This made understanding the problem fully, finding suitable solutions, and implementing them successfully incredibly challenging.

Projects are complex systems; tweaking one part often has cascading effects, altering performance in unforeseen ways. This reminded me of Teri Amato's reference to *change anything changes everything* when she described how the GMIS's product relied on spaghetti code. When I am not sure how to solve project problems, I systematically apply different

DOI: 10.4324/9781003003809-11

change, Agile IT, and project management approaches until I find improvements that work.

SPONSORSHIP

To start with, I always focus on Sponsors. I prepared for my regular meeting with KDMC's top Reinforcing Sponsor and CEO, Jason Powell. It came as no surprise that I received a call canceling it one more time. As I found out later, once again, the dreadful reason was that KDMC killed another patient. Health care is a life-and-death business. Human beings deliver health care, and they make mistakes with grim outcomes. While extraordinarily difficult to accept, it's reality.

KDMC is a notable exception, with a decades-long pattern of deaths and injuries delivered by its providers. I often walk all over the hospital and see what is or is not happening. I interact with everyone, taking in their feedback about the project. Frequently, I receive unprompted comments from law enforcement at the ED. Officers guarded offenders and supported victims injured in violent crimes and auto accidents. Officers want to know who I am and what I am doing there. I explain, and then they offer, "If anything ever happens to you, don't let anyone take you here for medical care."

Today a patient died because of a prohibited practice. An ambulance rushed a patient to KDMC, based on the expectation a neurologist was available for the injured victim with a bullet in his spine from a drive-by shooting. The neurologist was not at KDMC. This provider checked in and then promptly left the premises to work in his private practice. Such banned double-dipping was a frequent KDMC way of doing things. The patient died in transit to another hospital after no one found the KDMC neurologist.

Such horror stories may not appear relevant to the Recovery Project. Scandals are hardly new to KDMC. Unfortunately, patterns like these engulfed the medical center in ongoing upheaval, distracting everyone from their duties to address investigations and improvements, raising constant suspicions, and heightening defensiveness, especially about change. This underscored why my meeting with Jason was critical to project success.

As an interim measure, I sought Layla, who, as KDMC's Chief Change Agent, worked with Jason directly. I called Layla on my cell phone. Luckily, she answered and agreed to meet for coffee at a nearby Denny's.

I saw Layla waiting for me at a table with two cups of black coffee. She leaned back in her chair against the wall and nodded as she said hello, with a face always ready to smile. Layla, a superb Change Agent, possessed solid listening skills, understanding of the agency's strategic plan and project imperatives, trust among Targets and Sponsors, knowledge of KDMC' culture and history, and successful leadership skills while promoting collaboration.[1]

"Hey, you," I said as I sat down. "Thank you for dropping everything to meet with me on short notice. Oh, and I'll buy next time"

"So, what's so important?" asked Layla.

"Jason often cancels our weekly meeting. I get that he's busy. I know there are higher priorities right now with an accidental death of a patient. I'm concerned since his cancellations are a bad pattern. He is the KDMC project lynchpin. So, with today's last-minute cancellation, I called. Given your project role, I thought you might share insights about what's happening here."

Layla looked away through a window as people milled about outside the restaurant. She returned her gaze and replied, "For starters, I don't think most Targets look up the chain of command at Jason as a leader who will help this project succeed. He's got his problems, like any leader, but he's also got every outside authority investigating KDMC and shouting at him publicly to fix whatever they find. KDMC is doing the best they can, barely surviving caring for their patients. Jason is new in his job, but no one will give him the time needed to fix the long historical problems that plague KDMC. Targets don't know if Jason can withstand the screw-ups he inherited and has yet to resolve finally."

"It's really awful," I agreed. "The thing is, Layla, it's always bad here; it's a way of life in L.A., created by a racist society that Jason cannot fix alone. Please don't misunderstand me. I'm not trivializing what you're saying. I've always found LA County extraordinary. It succeeds despite how bad it is. It's up to us to help the county get there. You've got one of the toughest jobs in this project, and Jason cannot succeed without you."

Layla didn't hesitate, "Oh, I get it. I'm here to see this through. I know I'm really good, but I don't have a magic potion for Jason."

"Tell me about your experiences to date with him, sparing no details, despite how trivial they may seem to you," I said.

Layla laughed and offered, "You sound like a sheriff's deputy interviewing a crime witness."

"You're the best witness I've got," I conceded with a smile.

Layla started with, "Jason says he's fully on board with this project, but his inaction and lack of reinforcement contradict this. He has too much on his plate. He knows time is the ultimate constraint. Everyone has 24 hours in their day, so the best way to complete anything requires setting priorities. To begin with, Jason says the Recovery Project is his top priority. Concurrently with a typical hospital CEO's job, Jason runs a facility known for staff injuring and killing patients out of disregard and incompetence. County leadership does not respond quickly with a permanent fix unless the LA Times prints another investigative exposé.

"There are too many *distractions*. I also meet with Jason less often than our standing weekly appointment. This isn't good, given he needs to rely on me more as a Reinforcing Sponsor with so many other competing demands. We meet 75% of the time we're supposed to because he's overwhelmed. I showed Jason a workflow Burndown Chart with initial delays that could soon affect configuration and training. The WAT examines processes involving a particular User Story and finds Targets unavailable, despite previously prepared schedule allowances. Given ongoing disruptions and investigations into wrongdoing, other priorities use these Targets' workflow time allotments. With these delays, workflow analysis is incomplete when the Scrum Team expects to start the next Sprint. Jason and I talk, and he resolves the problem. He follows through only after problems occur instead of preventing them."

"Okay . . . " I paused and took it in. "What are you doing to correct this?"

Layla calmly explained, "When I cannot get what I need, I have Jason's secretary schedule a face-to-face with him as soon as possible. I bring Cecilia Wells, his secretary, large slabs of Callebaut Belgian Chocolate about once a week. She's quite the baker, who shares her mouthwatering double chocolate caramel brownies, and bribery gets the job done.

"When we eventually meet. I communicate with him from his point of view, reflecting on the immense changes and demands weighing on him and KDMC while juggling so many serious hospital failings. He's appreciative and apologetic, but the pattern continues.

"My contract with Jason gives him only the smallest set of actions to show organizational alignment and commitment. I try to minimize his time and carry the load in my role, working with Targets on his behalf.

"While I keep him apprised, I leverage the next level Reinforcing Sponsors. I meet with them and their Agents to build internal follow-through without Jason. This includes assigning activities to subordinate Reinforcing Sponsors with built-in Target feedback and immediate positive reinforcement where it's due. This is no substitute when there's a poor senior Reinforcing Sponsor, but the situation is far from ideal."[2]

I ventured forward with, "It sounds like you're acting as a Reinforcing Sponsor on Jason's behalf. I'll meet with Oscar and tell him Dr. Zorn, as Authorizing Sponsor, must help Jason by meeting with him regularly and reinforcing his project roles and responsibilities. In the meantime, when you meet with Jason next, refresh him on his role and his priorities. I'll also get you a list from a couple of our clients, including Sponsor peers, who've done this before. Share this with Jason so he can get help from his contemporaries."

Layla and I parted with the understanding that she was to keep me apprised regularly.

SCOPE

To prepare for the monthly Project Steering Committee meeting, Oscar and I met to bring each other up to date. Oscar started with the county's poor financial condition, particularly the agency.

Oscar solemnly laid out the situation. "With the bad economy and the usual lack of full health services funding, we are taking drastic steps. Layoffs start next week. While not public until tomorrow, we plan to privatize RLAMC and change HDH to ambulatory services only. This will reduce agency expenditures."

My stomach tightened into a knot. RLANC is one of our nation's most renowned spinal and brain injury rehabilitation centers. It's a jewel the agency cannot lose and a potential showcase for Recovery Project implementation success.

I said softly, "This jeopardizes the entire recovery effort. KDMC is in turmoil, as usual, with providers maiming and killing patients. RLANRC privatization, HDH inpatient-to-outpatient transformation, and agency-wide layoffs will take their toll. Employees rightfully fearing for their jobs will make things worse at KDMC instead of focusing on change inherent in Recovery Project success."

There was a long silence before I finally said, "Removing RLANRC and HDH from the Recovery Project has an upside. We'll focus everyone and everything we have on fixing the project at KDMC."

SCHEDULE

Given impending RLANRC privatization and HDH inpatient-to-outpatient transformation, there was no point re-examining their portions of the Recovery Project. However, it was back to the drawing board to reflect layoffs in the KDMC project schedule. We expected uncertainty and accommodated this in the schedule already, but it was not enough. It was also time to frankly communicate the county's current financial problems and their impact on the project. We needed Authorizing and Reinforcing Sponsors communicating that while financial problems existed, including layoffs, KDMC would complete the project with necessary adjustments. I confirmed this with Oscar, and he agreed.

I met with Layla a week later and confirmed she met with Jason about improving his KDMC sponsorship at once. Following this, Layla told me that in her most recent meeting with Jason, he asked his subordinate Reinforcing Sponsors to rework schedules. Layla also saw Jason even found time to manage by walking around the Medical Center. Jason praised Targets for their work, reinforcing their support for the project. I assumed Dr. Zorn spoke with Jason, based on my communication with Oscar previously. Whatever the reason, hopefully, this was the start of his improved sponsorship role.

COST

"Oh, but there's more," continued Layla, after telling me about Jason's reinforcement actions. "An independent audit of the financial procedures at KDMC reveal mishandling of Recovery Project funds. KDMC's Fiscal Operations did not follow Recovery Project contract administrative procedures. Apparently, Cerpix implemented KDMC's cloud services at a lower cost than expected under the agreement. Cerpix invoiced for the original higher amount specified in the agreement, and KDMC paid it in full. KDMC and Cerpix then set up a hardware surplus fund and used it to pay for over $160,000 in purchases. The current county agreement with Cerpix prohibited creation of this surplus and the associated purchases without an amendment. Thankfully, no one stole funds, but they did mishandle them."

Oscar had not informed me about this new fiasco yet. When we met next, Oscar not only told me but explained the resolution. He was now in charge of all Recovery Project financial management. Previously, each facility assumed financial administration for the Recovery Project. This made sense, assuming no misconduct, because each hospital part of the project was sequential and self-contained, not requiring multi-hospital financial administration. Now that there was wrongdoing, Oscar explained the county planned to negotiate a settlement on this matter without upsetting the board. Oscar persuaded Cerpix to refund the total original surplus under the agreement, including any funds used by KDMC already. Oscar would go to the board with an amendment, requesting use of the surplus for more training services. I now saw firsthand how Oscar resolved agency problems successfully without causing political uproar.

RESOURCES

During my next regular update with Layla, Oscar took part, too. The project seemed on the brink of chaos. KDMC nurses threatened a strike. Nurses said they always have a staffing shortage, and layoffs had imperiled patient care to a point where it was intolerable now. The county usually hires temporary nurses in a strike. The county was in a bind with the nursing shortage. KDMC's management maintained it followed the Joint Commission's staffing requirements. While the Joint Commission accredits health care organizations, KDMC's deplorable history diminished the persuasiveness of their response.

Personnel from the agency Communications and Employee Relations departments kept collective bargaining informed of all decisions involving the EHR implementation. Agency and KDMC management felt blindsided. Staffing problems existed long before layoffs started. For example, prior budget cuts diminished nursing sick leave. It was as if the nurses already wanted to strike, and the layoff announcement gave them an excuse. This was unwelcome news for the Recovery Project. The EHR implementation staffing was already a challenge since it needed increased nurse staffing levels.

I explained, "The impending strike, coupled with staff shortages, will cause more delays in preparing nursing workflows. There's not enough staff available to work on them. The county could hire more nursing students as a stopgap measure, but they won't fully understand workflow complexity. Unfortunately, EHR benefits are elusive during and right after implementation. Benefits like increased nurse productivity, greater communication among caregivers, faster ordering, and fewer duplicate tests require staff adjustment time. KDMC needs a full nursing complement involved in workflow improvements and the EHR to build commitment to the change.[3] We have little choice but to extend the schedule to accommodate this resource constraint."

Oscar concurred and added, "We will extend the current schedule, assuming we cannot avert a strike quickly."

I worried privately about all the disruption. County layoffs, the strike threat, RLANRC privatization, and HDH inpatient to outpatient transformation created a long-term unstable project climate. The agency would have trouble filling open positions, including those essential to the project, even after the disruption ended.

COMMUNICATION

I attended the KDMC weekly PMT meeting. As usual, the PM handed me the Project Notebook, a meticulously kept hard copy of project documentation. It was backed up to electronic files. It was also a handy resource for distributing current and historical project information to third parties like myself. I wanted electronic access to everything involving the project. As is so often the case with my clients, agency IT security policy prohibited my remote access. Security required third-party access to a desktop computer within the agency. This wasn't workable since I was only on site part time.

I opened the notebook to the most recent project schedule report. To my surprise, it was nothing like those I had seen before now. The current project schedule report included significant delay. I didn't say anything. I studied the schedule, withholding my astonishment. I flipped pages and saw earlier schedule reports displaying similar critical path delays. At all my earlier meetings, schedule reports in the Project Notebook displayed various minimal non-critical path delays.

I smiled and shared it with the KDMC CIO and PM, Tina Green. "Thank you for this updated schedule report. Oh, what's causing this critical path delay?"

Tina paused briefly and avoided my eyes. She stared at KDMC's deputy PM, Tyler Avery. KDMC had two sets of books. I received the fake version, while KDMC had the real one. Not today, though. Tina and Tyler realized I had the *wrong* version.

I took in what Tina explained, "The lab interface was the source of all delay. They just reported it. This delay was new to everybody."

I didn't want to pursue her deceit now. I needed time to think, particularly since the delay started long before this most recent report.

The meeting continued as if nothing had happened. As it ended, I looked directly at Tina and saw cunning triumph in her eyes.

I said, "I'm so glad we all have the correct schedule now. I'll take this notebook with me so I can examine the extent of this delay. It must be difficult for you to share information about such a significant project setback. As you know, I will do everything necessary to overcome all project obstacles. It's so good to know that by sharing this unwelcome news with me, you agree. I will start on it now. It's important we find successful solutions, not attribution for causing or solving problems. I do not expect to vary from this principle. Of course, though, you'll be the first to know if I'm forced to do so."

I stared into Tina's eyes and saw fury.

I called Oscar at once after the PMT meeting. He agreed to clear his calendar so we could meet at his office when I was available. I suggested I'd need three hours, knowing LA traffic and requiring more information before we met.

RISK

While there were countless project risks to manage, KDMC's PM was the highest. Had she caused more damage? I had to know before I could do anything about it. Oscar needed all the information to define and execute a solution.

While heading back downtown from KDMC to Oscar, I called Renee. I told her what happened and requested she assemble the KDMC PMT in a meeting without Tina or Tyler. She agreed to assemble this small group, and we arranged to meet at the Starbucks outdoors on the plaza at the County Hall of Administration.

Even though I raced through traffic, I was the last to arrive. As I sat down, I said, "We're going to review the entire project quickly. We'll then decide what more we need to investigate to fashion a solution. I'll share our results with Oscar when I meet with him in two hours."

PROCUREMENT

When I met with Oscar, he said, "After your call, Max, I spoke with Jason. I told him what happened. He expressed genuine alarm. I tried to schedule time to meet him as soon as possible. Unfortunately, he's leaving tonight for the Healthcare Information System Society annual conference. He plans to return to the office Thursday. He'll meet with Tina to get her perspective before meeting me next Friday. In the interim, he told Tina to step down temporarily and appointed Tyler as acting KDMC CIO and PM."

I kept my mouth shut but knew that enraged Tina. I then told Oscar that the PMT and I just met moments ago, without Tina or Tyler. I explained that while we discussed the project status, we needed more time to investigate the extent of what Tina had done. Oscar and I agreed that the time available due to Jason's absence offered an opportunity to understand the full extent of project damage.

I then shared copies of the fake and genuine schedule reports from meetings with Tina and the KDMC PMT.

Oscar said gravely, "I'll make copies of this information and join you in the KDMC project review. Assume the conference room in my office suite is available. I will attend all meetings as my schedule permits. Please conduct these meetings whether I am present or not. Let's also meet at the end of each day so we can establish where we are and what we need to do next."

On a brighter note, Oscar offered, "I spent this morning in negotiations with Cerpix. The scope of the contract between the county and Cerpix covers an agency-wide EHR solution. This includes all Recovery Project hospitals despite RLANRC privatization and HDH inpatient to outpatient transformation. It's easier to put all hospitals in the contract now than it is to add them later if agency financial conditions improve. The current Recovery Project is still under a stopgap amendment to the Jail Health contract. At the end of my Cerpix meeting today, we agreed in principle on everything. The county is putting the agency-wide final draft contract together for review by both parties. There are a few small administrative changes, but we're almost done."

County Counsel appointed their *best* attorney to lead negotiations, but this did not meet board requirements to assign an attorney with IT contract experience to all agreements over $3 million. To accommodate this requirement, Oscar sent me each draft. I reviewed them with our attorney, Mitch Sugarman. Mitch worked on IT contracts for our clients. Mitch's firm was not willing to get on the county's master agreement, given byzantine public sector requirements, so he did not contract with county counsel directly. Instead, Mitch was a subcontractor on our county agreement. This approach also saved time by avoiding the lengthy process needed to procure an IT contract attorney through county counsel.

Mitch's work was significant, including frequent reviews greater than 35 pages. For example, while the contract said Cerpix had to fulfill the county's EHR requirements, it did not include or reference the Product Backlog. It also did not include a statement of work with Cerpix and county tasks, milestones, and deliverables defining county and vendor management and administrative roles and responsibilities. It even omitted warranties from Cerpix for its EHR products and services compliant with specified health care industry standards.

The county updated the draft, including Mitch's changes. With outside counsel input, Cerpix and Oscar finally negotiated a deal.

REQUIREMENTS

During the remaining time before Jason returned, I met with various PMT members in the conference room provided by Oscar. I met with Nolan first. It was late in the day.

Nolan was not happy. "I have enough trouble coordinating external vendor dependencies. You'd think KDMC could manage their own damn resources. Tina lies about their progress instead of fixing problems. I'm finally getting the Scrum Team velocity to a stable cadence. What am I supposed to do now, stop and wait for the lab interface?"

I countered, "Jason re-committed to his Reinforcing Sponsor role. He's taken ownership, so let him deliver on his commitment. We'll add more time to the schedule to accommodate the staff shortage, strike threat, and financial constraints. We have time to solve this problem.

"Nolan, no project exists in a vacuum. Internal and external dependencies are the bane of every project, not just your Scrum Team. These dependencies are exceedingly difficult to control."

Nolan just shook his head.

I continued, "While we have less control over third-party vendors, we've tried to estimate accurately the amount of effort needed to complete their dependent tasks by bringing them into our assumptions. It's frustrating, I know. Bottom line, everyone underestimated the complexity of this project, despite retrospective reviews and project management monitoring. We all need to take this as a challenge where we learn and test the power of our skills."

"I know," Nolan said, smirking. "The lab interface delay is not my only problem."

I suggested we order takeout dinner delivery. I hoped to change course, giving Nolan another one of his needed moments to cool down, before proceeding.

We took time to order from Yang Chow. It was a short delivery trip from Chinatown, which is near agency headquarters. I was hungry and needed fuel without delay. I was looking forward to my slippery shrimp order. When the food arrived, we took time from work and enjoyed exceptional Sichuan.

Nolan, more settled, began with, "Requirements revealed another problem. For example, although we estimated the schedule based on 1115

Waiver Sprints from New York's experience, Cerpix was not working on the code, so we couldn't test it in a timely manner. There was a misunderstanding. Cerpix thought we would define and then supply required modifications to them. The county thought Cerpix planned to demonstrate the existing 1115 waiver functions already within the EHR before we supplied our modifications. Each party was waiting for the other. No one was doing anything. I just found out about this yesterday afternoon."

Nolan looked up from his finished paper plate, explaining, "Oscar shared the latest draft county contract with me. That's where I found this problem. The stopgap Jail Health contract amendment did not offer details about the 1115 Waiver. It was in the final agency-wide draft agreement. We were on the hook to define User Stories first and meet with Cerpix to figure out the amount of needed configuring and new programming."

"The agency just started working on its part based on my findings. This affects Scrum Team, WAT, and training schedules, at a minimum. I was going to ask Tina to revise the schedule. Obviously, someone else will do that."

I pulled out my Mac, looked at the Project Issue Log, and asked. "Why isn't this on the log?"

Nolan put his PC on the table, punched in keystrokes, and looked at me, puzzled. He spun his laptop around and pointed to the item on the log. Putting our computers together side by side, I shook my head. "KDMC has multiple issue logs."

It's part of a project lifecycle to experience all kinds of disrupting issues. Unlike risks, which may occur, issues are happening. It's another matter when there are multiple logs, causing conflicts, inconsistencies, and omissions threatening product and project success. I was just beginning to understand why Nolan was so frustrated.

Nolan leaned back in his chair, shaking his head, and said, "There's nothing more irritating than unresolved issues creating more problems because no one bothered to tell us for whatever reason. We've got enough going on that we can hardly resolve already."

I shared this problem with Oscar during our meeting late that day. "Tina is responsible for this. Can you call Tyler and have him consolidate the logs?"

Oscar agreed as we both shook our heads in dismay.

INFRASTRUCTURE

In a meeting with Nolan, SM; Billy Davis, CPO; Shirley Walker, WAM; Walter Ming, CSU; and Kabir Patel, PMT senior systems engineer, we found a problem with POC devices. At first, KDMC found it difficult defining the best solution or solutions: mounted PCs, computers on wheels, or handheld mobile devices. It was complicated. KDMC's chief nursing officer, with help from Walter, had recently endorsed a more traditional approach including wall-mounted personal computers hardwired directly to the network. Nursing had previously organized a vendor fair involving each device choice. Nurses took part in the fair with invited vendor representatives and their products. Nurses evaluated these products, with the wall-mounted solution as the winner, followed by computers on wheels and handheld devices.

This solution simplified implementation, mitigating inherent risks associated with wireless technology, for example, controlling mobile device checkout and return, charging batteries, losing devices, and so on.

The project planned to go ahead with wired computers mounted in patient rooms when Shirley raised a regulatory issue.

"California's Office of Statewide Health Planning and Development must review any physical modifications to permanent structures in a patient room. Mounting a computer in a patient room requires this review. The time needed to get their approval will delay the project even more."

Billy said, "Each KDMC patient room has a freestanding wardrobe. They're heavy wooden closets against a wall but not connected to any permanent structure. We could mount a monitor and even a keyboard tray on the side of each armoire and put the computer inside of it if space is not available for a desk. We could even mount each monitor on a small desk, and the computer hardware could sit under it without any permanent structural modifications. We have LAN wiring in each patient room already. Computers on wheels could supplement and support wherever this did not work, avoiding regulatory delays and mobile device concerns. They do require a wireless network upgrade, but that's in the works already for future mobile device connectivity after the Recovery Project."

"Brilliant!" I replied. "Let's plan on KDMC testing this device setup."

Kabir said he would make sure that happened.

I made a note to add this to the single KDMC issue log.

The meeting participants and I then spoke about the significant volume of hardware, cost, and impact on the project. Thankfully, KDMC planned to test all equipment components, for example: fixed workstations, laptops, monitors, printers, keyboards, suspension arms, and computers on wheels; wireless network hardware and software, hardwired network connections; power connections; and all other assorted peripheral devices. I confirmed these tests included nurses and physicians working with the equipment and confirming acceptability before submitting a costly purchase order for the entire facility. This was good news. It lessened the risk of making a large-scale equipment purchase without fully understanding and confirming its usefulness in patient-care settings by clinicians.

NETWORK

Everyone thought KDMC's internal network was undergoing a massive upgrade. Before his abrupt departure, county CIO Clarence Willoughby mandated standardizing on Cisco, but KDMC preferred their incumbent, Aruba. The county CIO never approved the budget for KDMC's necessary project network upgrade because of this conflict. Now that he was gone, at least temporarily, Tina decided to go ahead with Aruba.

Renaldo Campo, a 30-year IT veteran, was now the county CIO. The county CIO was no longer independently reporting to the BOS. Even though Willoughby was still on administrative leave, county CEO Mike Jen demoted the county CIO. The position now reported to Mike directly, with Campo as the acting CIO. I had no idea what had happened to deputy CIO Homer Jons.

The KDMC and county CIO were in a tug of war. Without approval, KDMC's CIO committed to an Aruba solution included in the project schedule. Project participants approved it without KDMC disclosing the conflict with county CIO policy or the outcome, a stalled network implementation.

Before Willoughby's departure, the county bought and was implementing a massive wide-area network and telephony upgrade with Light Force, Inc., called LACnet. Cisco supplied the components in the contract. I knew about this county upgrade. Light Force and the State of California announced a project dispute the day before the LA County Board planned to approve a similar agreement. Jane brought me in to review the contract.

Of course, Sugarman did his review. Together we negotiated a revised contract, safeguarding the county from succumbing to a dispute like the state had with Light Force.

Oscar, who joined our meeting in the afternoon, said, "I'll resolve KDMC's network standardization issue with the county CIO."

I knew county CIO standardization outplayed Tina's Aruba commitment. KDMC's extensive network upgrade was a prerequisite for the EHR, due to increased network traffic and necessary facility-wide wired and wireless access. I was glad Oscar was managing it. I didn't want to mess in any way with Mike if he got involved.

Regrettably, it wasn't that simple. While we would get KDMC's Cisco compliance, this added project delay, and LACnet was at issue. The LACnet link between KDMC and Cerpix's cloud already had outages.

I asked, "Did anyone investigate why this was happening?"

Nolan responded, "I know about this because it affects our configuration work. Apparently, KDMC found the problem and a solution within one week."

Concerns about LACnet reliability involved two downtime incidents. The first involved a power outage, and the second included an incorrect router configuration. Neither was a result of failures with LACnet, contrary to earlier reports.

Nolan continued, "There's even good news. KDMC will add a backup to avoid future outages. There's an alternative pathway undergoing planning now and installation at once afterward. I'm referring to an alternate connection between KDMC and RLANRC, where that facility keeps an existing connection to LACnet. KDMC currently has a router at the Downey Courthouse that previously failed. The alternative entry point will deliver necessary redundancy during an outage. It is also a model for use at all other facilities."

"Well done!" I said.

CONVERSION

KDMC adopted Cerpix's solution that assigned a unique identifier to each individual patient. Once patients received their unique identifier, the county-wide conversion ensured the entire health agency could drastically improve access to individual medical records. Implementing Cerpix's solution ended the county's 16-year EMPI project. This was a huge county-wide win.

In other good news, it appeared that HIM and HTAC's work on chart abstracting and clinical documentation continued as planned. Docs objected, as usual, but the medical director prevailed as needed.

There was a problem from a technical standpoint. KDMC had a conversion plan for the legacy system that the EHR replaced, based on manual updates to patient records. Given staffing shortages and a strike threat, KDMC now needed an automated conversion. Since this occurred later in the project, the Scrum Team had time to complete this revised conversion, including custom software development. Still, this was another unexpected event for both Cerpix and the Scrum Team.

INTERFACES

Next, the meeting participants found that work had stopped on the KDMC lab system interface. According to Kabir, the lab vendor had yet to upgrade the agency's system, which Cerpix's interface specialist needed before starting work with KDMC. No one bothered to figure out why there was a delay. Complicating matters further, KDMC had a *new* hematology system. Now KDMC and Cerpix had to build a previously unexpected hematology/lab interface.

I suggested, after BOS approval of the Recovery Project, that each facility start examining all EHR interfaces and conversions. These two always cause problems, particularly because they involve third-party dependencies outside project control. So, it's best to begin work as early as possible to prevent delays.

Unfortunately, KDMC and SampleDX, the lab system vendor, wasted months trying to start work on the EHR interface. As of the previous week, LabPlatform, a competitor, had bought SampleDX. KDMC tried to find who was working on the Cerpix interface, the original SampleDX staff or the new owner. Meanwhile, Cerpix's interface specialist couldn't wait for resolution of this problem. Cerpix kept all their staff billable, so they assigned this specialist to another customer. KDMC didn't know when they needed him back, so Cerpix reassigned him.

I told Kabir, "I'd expect nothing less at this point."

In a later evening meeting with Oscar, he confirmed, "I received a courtesy call from SampleDX's general counsel, Joel Ferguson, letting me know to expect a written notice per our contract about their upcoming acquisition. It's a letter executing a standard clause that defines what the parties do when transferring obligations and rights under a contract to another party. In this case, the county receives a formal notice from the current lab vendor that their obligations transfer to the new owner. The acquiring vendor honors the county agreement. That's where I get involved. The parties discuss how to go ahead, hopefully at once, in this case.

"The good news was Joel and I negotiated the original agreement. He assured me there were no changes expected for at least a year, and the buyer expected KDMC work to continue uninterrupted. I thanked him and arranged a meeting to review the acquisition details and the mechanics of the transition to new ownership. We agreed to meet this morning.

"I joined the meeting as planned. The conference call included three of Joel's staff, who greeted me politely. We waited an hour, but Joel never showed up. Finally, his frazzled assistant joined the conference call briefly. Apologizing profusely for the delay, she announced that LabPlatform released Joel from employment just moments ago. They would contact me by the end of the week concerning next steps."

"So much for progress," I declared.

WORKFLOW

As acting CIO, Tyler took charge of the Recovery Project as the temporary PM. We met in Oscar's conference room. In addition to multiple issue logs, in countless instances, KDMC stopped tracking issues altogether. KDMC reported issues verbally to Cerpix directly instead of using their facility's Service Desk software.

According to Tyler, Cerpix tracked and kept these issues in their tracking system only, limiting shared understanding with KDMC to weekly PMT meetings. Coordination between KDMC and Cerpix faltered even more. For example, a Cerpix application specialist visited KDMC to help address an EHR and workload issue that the WAT resolved previously.

I recommended, "KDMC's current issue log, not part of anything provided by Cerpix, works only if it includes *all* project issues."

Oscar, who once again joined us during our meeting, added, "From now on, you, Tyler, are the only individual to contact Cerpix except me. I'll notify Cerpix of this change. Also, I'll ask Cerpix to direct any other KDMC caller to me. It will be the responsibility of the offending party's Reinforcing Sponsor to resolve this matter at once with their subordinate if anyone other than you or me contact Cerpix."

SECURITY

In our following evening meeting, Oscar did not share his source as he gave me copies of correspondence concerning KDMC IT security. Tina wrote the top letter to a consulting firm, hiring them to review KDMC's security requirements, define necessary improvements, and document the associated schedule and budget to implement them.

Tina sent the consultants a later letter after that firm completed and documented their findings. This second letter told the consulting firm they caused all KDMC's security issues identified as needing improvements. She also accused the firm of neglecting to meet required contract deliverable dates, causing Recovery Project delay and receiving payment for undocumented professional fees. Consequently, the vendor was in breach of their contract.

The follow-up letter from the security vendor's CEO, Roger Cummings, documented point by point that Tina's letter was false. A copy of the vendor's letter went to their attorney, who would handle all future communication. The problem was that KDMC's current security installation included several consumer instead of commercial-grade network devices. I saw this previously and thought it was very strange. The security consultants did not install these consumer devices and then claim KDMC had to replace them.

Oscar reasoned, "All the security consultant's deliverables included dates on their documents and copies of their email with matching dates. All of them met the dates in the contract."

He also noted invoices included professional fees tied to supporting time entries with the date and a memo field documenting what each security consultant did to perform specified contract tasks. Billing was unarguably correct.

Oscar concluded, "Tina's letter accused the consulting firm of breaching the contract without any evidence. The consulting firm's response demonstrated Tina had no basis for her accusations, but she still executed the contract termination clause."

I said, "While I was not aware until now, I know this security vendor. Roger Cummings was Portland, Oregon's former chief security officer. We worked together on Portland projects. Previously, Roger was a senior official with System Strike, a highly regarded global security firm. I trust Roger. We even discussed authoring a book together. It was about how to respond swiftly and effectively to security breaches. We're all victims of prevention failures, so there was no reason to write about that.

"Your experience with Cummings reinforces the vendor's documented position. However, we cannot act without meeting with Jason to explain what we've found and what must change for project success," said Oscar.

TESTING

In the next meeting with Nolan, he explained how the Scrum Team tests every configuration change before completing a Sprint. This includes verifying that completed configuration changes meet the requirements in a User Story. It also involves testing technical requirements like security, performance, and usability. A PO, Superuser, and Workflow Analyst make sure the team configures and tests each Sprint to meet customer value. They also use automated testing tools, where possible, given how little time they have in each Sprint. They apply the standard of pairing developers with testers to maximize communicating and analyzing defects. Finally, they work with the PO to define User Acceptance Test criteria and perform this test to complete each Sprint.

Oscar noted, "I've received positive feedback from POs about the Scrum Team's work. They do an excellent job testing, finding defects, documenting them, correcting them, and conducting retrospectives to avoid repeating them."

Renee, whom I had asked to attend this meeting, noted, "The biggest problem I've noticed to date is unfinished work the Scrum Team has at the end of a Sprint. This is a frequent Agile problem. The difficulty occurs in estimating the time required to complete this carry-over work in the next Sprint. A typical problem occurs where the Scrum Team, for example, completes 85% of the work. Scrum teams often assume they won't need more time to complete this carryover work. They refuse to increase the original time estimate needed for the remaining 15%. The solution is to start decreasing the amount work included in each Sprint to minimize carryover. Even if there is extra time remaining when the Scrum Team completes a Sprint, there's always more work for the team to do."

Nolan shook his head, "It's not about the Scrum Team. Cerpix is the problem. KDMC receives new software releases from Cerpix and finds defects. Cerpix applies *patches* on the fly to fix these defects instead of distributing a fully updated and tested software release. This practice lets Cerpix make changes rapidly. It may result in poorly documented and tested modifications that the vendor might overlook in later releases."

"If you're right, Cerpix knows better than that," Oscar said. "What's going on with them?"

Nolan continued, "I'm worried about their testing abilities. Earlier, as part of the procurement, Tina and I had a conference call with New York about their 1115 Waiver modifications. They offered helpful insights so KDMC could begin to understand software modifications we did or did not need. New York also told us about Cerpix's software testing problems.

"As I've already said, KDMC discovered software deficiencies when testing Cerpix software patches before implementing them. This fact alone is not alarming. What is significant is New York discovered software deficiencies in what Cerpix refer to as their *product* version of the software. Cerpix defines *product* in this context as their COTS software without customer modifications. During pre-implementation testing, New York discovered a substantial number of product defects. Generally, based on my experience testing other vendors' software, most defects discovered involve customer-specific software code.

"In Cerpix's case, during the latest version test, Cerpix acknowledged they found more software deficiencies than expected. In addition, there are situations where the quality of third-party software, like a form application used with the EHR, causes product software defects.

"The cause relates to factors throughout the software design, development, testing, and distribution process. As you know, vendors rely on QA testing during their software development process to find and resolve defects before distribution to their customers. Cerpix has a mature product installed in hospitals throughout the country. We should not expect to find significant software defects during KDMC testing. Unfortunately, this was not the case in New York. It looks like we may have the same problem here."

Oscar promised, "I will discuss this problem with Cerpix directly before meeting with Jason. Cerpix must prove they resolved it before KDMC begins integrated test and cutover tasks. In addition, the agency could now include liquidated damages terms in our new Cerpix contract. This means defining and agreeing now on how to address certain harm, like software defects, and a schedule of fees the agency collects from the date of finding a bug to its correction by Cerpix."

Nolan affirmed, "Tina and I already discussed this defect issue with Cerpix more than once. Their response was a combination of acknowledgement followed by the assertion that defects would not occur if KDMC ran the most recent version of Cerpix's EHR software. That's a legitimate point. However, since Renee's involvement, KDMC's newly implemented stringent testing protocol is more rigorous than testing performed by other existing Cerpix customers. KDMC refuses to implement the latest release when they find so many defects. Although comforting to know KDMC's testing is thorough, the county should not assume this costly and time-consuming QA role on behalf of Cerpix.

"Another crucial factor that contributes heavily to the quality of Cerpix's EHR is the software maintenance process. Their process lets KDMC find software issues, report them to Cerpix's Service Desk, followed by quick analysis and application of patches to the software. Unfortunately, this short cycle for complex software can increase defects. For example, KDMC reported multiple times about the same defects. It took Cerpix multiple software updates to correct them and eliminate newly created problems.

"Although I recognize the county cannot avoid all software defects, I recommend the county examine Cerpix's software maintenance process. The needed improvement includes the requirements gathering process, which occurs very quickly at the time of defect reporting only. The process can result in incomplete or mistaken information for the Cerpix programmer analyst to develop quality updates. I also recommend reducing the frequency of software updates. Cerpix reported the county has a nonstandard software update schedule. Other Cerpix customers use a quarterly schedule, depending on the functional significance of these updates.

"Finally, an important background to these quality issues is that Cerpix supports the County Jail. Even without RLANRC and HDH, this is a daunting staffing challenge for any organization. The jail requires significant new software to accommodate criminal justice standards. In a broad sense, Cerpix's organization and distribution of human resources across its product lines and to their customers may be the primary factor influencing the quality of their product delivery."

Oscar agreed to meet with Cerpix and to resolve this issue promptly, particularly given his leverage with the unsigned agency-wide contract.

TRAINING

During the last of the investigative meetings Loretta reported, "The results of the training proficiency survey indicated 22% of 1,400 trainees need basic computer proficiency education before participating in EHR product training. The product training plan calculated the total number of trainees and the training duration, based on the assumption all trainees achieved the required computer proficiency minimum. Unfortunately, this plan included a mismatch between training time required and available calendar days. The available number of calendar training days was too low for the volume of training hours per student, trainers, and facilities. KDMC had to extend the schedule unless they prepared and offered online classes accessible by trainees from anywhere at any time.

"I've recalculated the training schedule to accommodate more training. I assume we will start supplying online training to overcome current training constraints. We know we will incur project delay given everything else we've been talking about already. Taking all of this into account, my goal is to fit training into the revised schedule without contributing to project delay.

"Now we must include the impact of training delay on the ability of students to retain and apply their newly acquired skills. Reinforcing Sponsors must make sure their Targets have time allocated to their schedules for EHR training and practice. Practice should include using the sandbox. This also means making sure Reinforcing Sponsors track their Targets' hours working in the sandbox and meet with them to increase accountability."

Loretta finished with, "There's good news, too. We have a growing group of trainees who have a minimum 80% competency score to receive system access. This group is leveraging Cerpix-provided scenarios, testing the usability and safety of our configured EHR and workflows."

As the meeting concluded, Oscar and I went to his office to discuss a solution that would put the project back on track.

PROJECT MANAGER

Oscar called me late Thursday afternoon, requesting we meet in his office to discuss last-minute details involved in the appointment Friday with Jason. I told Oscar I'd be there in about 30 minutes.

Oscar waited for me to sit down and then said, "Just before I phoned you, Jason called me about his meeting with Tina. She claims the two sets of books were your idea. You and Tina had a standing appointment before each weekly PMT meeting. She said you made up the details she needed to lie about at the next PMT meeting because you were afraid to disclose the Recovery Project failure.

"I don't believe a word of what she said. Unfortunately, my position doesn't matter, putting you in a horrible position. The LA County Office of the Inspector General will investigate. You cannot work on the project until they complete this investigation. It could take months, which is damaging to both you and the project."

Wearily, I said, "I thought this would happen eventually. I put together a bulletproof response to stop anymore of Tina's lies. I can prove Tina is responsible for all of this in a matter of minutes. There won't be an investigation."

"What?" gasped Oscar.

"A long time ago, I had a manipulative client try to blame me for his mistakes. He eventually suffered the consequences. During that time, I experienced extremely debilitating stress defending my integrity. I vowed to never let that happen again.

"From then on, I've kept a careful diary of all my client interactions and experiences. At the slightest instance of even an inkling of client misbehavior, I copy and mail my notes to myself. The postmark on the envelope shows the past date the Postal Service delivered the letter to me, which I keep unopened. Early in this project, I started applying this same technique to all my interactions with Tina. It is impossible for Tina to change what I documented in the past by making up stories now. I have everything documented for months sealed in envelopes with postmarks through last week when I discovered her two sets of project schedules."

"Why can't Tina deny what's in the envelopes and still suggest it was all your idea?" asked Oscar.

"Several reasons," I said as I handed Oscar Tina's PMT meeting minutes and a copy of my corresponding diary, also included in sealed and postmarked envelopes in my backpack. "Go to page 127 of my diary and notice the detail. You'll see my diary includes more detail when you compare it to Tina's meeting minutes. While both documents report no project delay, Tina's *minutes* summarize the PMT meeting.

"Now turn to page 139 in my diary. Notice you and I had a meeting together that started at 11:00 and ended at 1:15. I had a standing noon pre-meeting with Tina and the 1:00 PMT meeting the same day. Early that morning, you called me to schedule the 11:00 meeting. I agreed and scheduled Renee to attend the pre- and PMT meetings in my absence. Renee had a noon conflict, so she attended the PMT meeting only.

"After my massive infection, I designated Renee as my Recovery Project backup. Renee and I meet often and exchange email daily about the project so we're always up to date, and she can take over if I'm not available.

"Let's suppose Tina claims I give her details during our pre-meeting to lie about during the PMT meeting. When Renee attends both of those meetings, she includes details about those sessions in her daily email to me."

I opened my portfolio and retrieved Renee's project update email for the date coinciding with my absence from the KDMC pre- and PMT meetings, due to my appointment with Oscar. I also included the copy of that meeting's minutes where Tina lied about project on-time performance.

I handed these documents to Oscar and explained, "This specific meeting reviewed work scheduled and expected to begin on the interface between McKesson's Admission, Discharge, Transfer (ADT) and the Cerpix EHR systems. Tina's minutes say work is underway on the interface, including on-time project performance. Renee's email confirms Tina referred to current work on ADT and message sharing involving Health Level Seven, data transfer standards.

"Renee knows McKesson well. Yesterday, Renee called her friend Jerry Rossini, one of McKesson's ADT Health Level Seven Certified Professionals.

Jerry confirmed KDMC and McKesson have yet to start work on the Health Level Seven interface. Jerry said he had a copy of Dr. Zorn's letter, sent months ago, that said the agency plans to implement an EHR and requires support from McKesson on the ADT interface. Jerry noted he was wondering about the agency because he never heard anything more about the interface."

"Good form!" exclaimed Oscar. "I'll call Jason and suggest waiting on launching an inspector general investigation until after we meet with him tomorrow."

"I have another idea," I offered. "Let me explain what has to happen to keep this entire fiasco from going any further."

I sat in Tina's office on Friday morning as she arrived to start her day.

As Tina walked into her office, she sneered, "What are you doing here? I have a meeting with Oscar, not you."

"Oscar asked me to join him. We just spoke, and he's delayed. He asked that I start without him."

"What do you want?" she said contemptuously.

"Is it your intention to deceive everyone about the Recovery Project delay?" I asked quietly.

"Absolutely not," she shot back.

"Well, that's not my experience," I said calmly. "You made up a story that the ADT interface was underway without delay. I've seen you prepare multiple issue logs, causing confusion and delay. You also accused the security vendor of causing the problems they uncovered at KDMC to hide your responsibility instead of fixing them. You kept two sets of books, sharing a false on-time schedule with me rather than the real one with project delay."

"You can't intimidate me," said Tina.

"Oh, I'm not," I said with a smile. "'I'm just beginning to explain there are consequences for your actions. For example, you caused project delay and significant budget overrun. You defamed a security vendor, who could embroil the agency in a legal battle it will lose."

"I don't know what you're talking about," she hissed.

I leaned over to my portfolio and pulled out a stack of sealed envelopes. I stood up and placed them on her desk in chronological order as I explained their contents and the lies about the ADT and EHR interface. I returned to my seat and concluded with total indifference.

I had to give her credit. She was a pro. As if insisting she did nothing wrong, she said, "So what do you expect me to do about this mail you supposedly sent to yourself and your hopeless story containing a pack of lies?

"Tell Jason the truth and resign by 4:00 p.m. today, or I'll disclose the contents of these letters to Jason and Dr. Zorn."

"Don't you dare threaten me," raged Tina.

I got up, gathered the envelopes from her desk and just looked at her quietly. Finally, I repeated, "I never threatened you. I just finished explaining the consequences of your actions."

I walked out of her office.

Oscar called me before 3:00 p.m. Tina announced she'd taken a new job with one of Cerpix's competitors. Tyler was the acting project manager until KDMC recruited Tina's replacement. Jason promised Oscar he would do whatever was necessary to ensure Recovery Project success. Jason also promised to meet with me the following Monday.

Renee and I met at Starbucks on the County plaza. We walked to Oscar's office for our 5:00 p.m.

Oscar smiled and said, "You did it!"

Renee explained, "While the source is gone, Tyler is a milquetoast and woefully unqualified as KDMC's project manager. He's a good tech lacking the courage needed in a manager."

"We can't malign the poor guy for his personality," remarked Oscar. "Can we train him or prop him up somehow?"

When Renee finished sipping her coffee and using a napkin to wipe her lips, she said, "I could be *consulting CIO* and help Tyler as KDMC's acting CIO and Recovery Project PM."

"The county has a tough time recruiting, especially when competing with private industry for IT staff and the current layoff environment," noted Oscar. "We could sure use your help recruiting Tina's replacement while offering Tyler temporary support in the interim. I expect Jason would welcome your contribution."

"That works for me so long as it's okay with you, Max," offered Oscar.

I explained, "Renee and I talked about this previously. It was her idea. I confirmed it made sense to me."

Oscar said he would speak with Jason. Assuming he agreed, Oscar clarified that he wanted Jason to explain Renee's new role to Tyler. Oscar also said he would prepare an amendment to our agreement once Jason gave him the okay.

Renee then spoke about how to improve Tyler's performance.

Renee said, "Don't hold your breath. I understand Tyler doesn't even know how to use Microsoft Project. I'll give him training. Hopefully, we've found all known project delays, so he can update the schedule and report revised dates promptly."

On Monday, during my meeting with Jason, I said, "What are your plans beyond the CIO personnel change?"

Jason began, "I have an all-hands meeting with Reinforcing Sponsors and Agents. I will honestly state KDMC has a culture of deceit. We have a big job to do. Patient care is number one, and the Recovery Project enables it. Our accountability system for this project restarts at once. Most work so hard to do the right thing, while a few rig the system. We will measure Target behavior and how it affects project success at once. This includes immediate feedback on positive and negative behaviors. Our goal is to reinforce positive contributions while making it difficult to engage in negative ones.

"Each Reinforcing Sponsor will conduct a weekly one-on-one session with their Targets, where they will give and receive feedback on the prior week's project activities. Every month, Reinforcing Sponsors will summarize feedback patterns across their Targets. They will also share these patterns with their Targets, update them as necessary, and summarize and distribute them up the Sponsorship chain, making them widely available throughout our organization.

"I've broken the project chain of Sponsorship. I am responsible for it. I will fix it with widespread evidence on truth-telling about all behaviors. Collaboration and feedback with all Targets will reveal what is happening and how we are responding to it. This adverse situation does not have to be the case. We will take aim at deceit, measure our progress, and adjust the ways we address it until we eradicate it. This in turn will help drive EHR implementation success."

I confirmed, "I appreciate what you said, Jason. I see this for what it is, resistance. Right now, KDMC struggles and resists this project. To make this project work, you must do more. What you've offered is a start only. You are now suggesting project reinforcement, which can only begin to succeed if you understand and communicate from the viewpoint of your Targets. This also applies to every Reinforcing Sponsor and their Targets.

I applaud your enthusiasm to add rewards for desired behaviors and to take them away for the undesirable ones. This must occur at once and explicitly when Targets act. You must communicate this to all Reinforcing Sponsors and Targets, not only in words, but *you* must model and reward it consistently and continually. It won't stick otherwise. Finally, put all Agents together as a team and ask them to review and update the current reinforcement index to encourage wanted and discourage unwanted behaviors. This includes reinforcements that make undesirable behaviors more difficult to perform when compared to desirable ones."[4]

We talked more about the details. Jason and I agreed he would rely on Layla for help where he could delegate. Even so, the burden was his. Jason had to actively drive his plan continuously and consistently. I made sure Layla would let me know at once if there was any deviation whatsoever from Jason's commitment.

NOTES

1. Harrison, *Introducing the Accelerating Implementation Methodology (AIM) A Practical Guide to Change Project Management*, 21.
2. Ibid., 51.
3. Ibid., 91.
4. Ibid., 115–119.

12

Cutover

It took months for KDMC to plan and execute a successful turnaround. While KDMC struggled with ongoing safety issues, Jason revitalized the chain of sponsorship with reinforcement and training that refreshed project leadership effectiveness. Tyler, Renee, Nolan, and Layla prepared an extended schedule, including solutions to change and Agile IT project management problems Tina caused. Nurses did not strike, and the county fiscal crisis lessened without privatizing RLANRC and HDH. This good news restored the original Recovery Project scope, along with improved Target engagement.

Given this progress, my staff conducted an implementation risk forecast. The respondents included all Champions, Agents, Sponsors, and Targets randomly selected throughout the agency and KDMC specifically. The results suggested probability of implementation success was moderate to high across ten key categories.

CUTOVER PLAN

Excitement actually filled the air in the meeting when I said, "We're ready to prepare for cutover. Remember, cutover is not an event. It is an integrated process of pre-, go-, and post-live tasks. Cutover starts only after minor-severity and medium-priority defects remain in the EHR software. Frontline Reinforcing Sponsors will repeatedly remind their Targets that project support mechanisms and Cerpix staff will do everything possible to help cutover succeed. Even if Targets got testing and training right, it's impossible to achieve perfection using the EHR in a live and unpredictable

DOI: 10.4324/9781003003809-12

environment. So instead of Targets burdening themselves with perfection during go-live, Reinforcing Sponsors will remind them about available help from Superusers, trainers, and staff dedicated to the project at the Service Desk. Also, Reinforcing Sponsors will remind their Targets that EHR and workflow stabilization occur during optimization, after cutover."

Renee, Marissa, and I were working together with Tyler and Layla at the cutover planning meeting, where I explained, "Renee, Marissa, and I are here to ask you two to prepare KDMC's cutover plan. This plan is the map transitioning the EHR and workflow from the *test* to the live environment, where skilled and willing Targets expect to use and improve these two work products.

"Because so much of what happens during go-live is technically and operationally centric, KDMC must integrate everything into a single cutover plan. Tyler, you are KDMC's acting CIO and PM, so you, Renee, and I will work on the Agile IT project management. Layla, as KDMC's chief change agent, you, and Marissa, as the project change manager, will work on the people and their operational perspective of cutover. All of us will work together to combine everything as it becomes a whole cutover plan."

Objective

Tyler said, "I get the difference between what Layla and I will do, but it's difficult to know where to start."

I said. "I'd start with the cutover plan objective. It defines how KDMC will transition from the current state to the future live EHR environment. This includes the IT and operational environments and how Targets will transition to them.

Readiness

"Readiness means KDMC project participants are fully prepared. When this happens, it means they can transition to the EHR now. While the work began months ago to instill technical and operational readiness to use the EHR live, the PM administers a checklist to ensure everything is in place to go ahead. This checklist includes change and Agile IT project management items."

Tyler looked at me quizzically and said, "I understand there are absolutes needed to go live. Some of these preparations occur shortly before go-live only, like pre-loading the Operating Room (OR) schedule. How do we confirm readiness for these items?"

I related, "In this and similar cases, the KDMC portion of the Recovery Project includes a fully tested pre-load process that occurs right before go-live."

Tyler asked, "Are you saying in some situations, the assessment must forecast readiness?"

"Yes," I said. "It's not really that much different when compared to other items on the readiness checklist. Preparedness relies on testing everything whether it occurs a long or short time before go-live."

I continued to explain that readiness also applies at the conclusion of post-live. Post-live ends when KDMC achieves a previously defined status. Like the status for readiness needed to go live, there's preparedness at the end of post-live that begins the transition to optimization. This involves another checklist. Assuming the results state post-live can end, KDMC begins to wind down the cutover part of the Recovery Project as optimization ramps up to continuously improve patient service delivery.

Approach

I moved on to the cutover approach and described how it involves preparing a plan reviewed and approved by a multi-disciplinary group including PMT, CMT, Cerpix, and the Steering Committee in consultation with HTAC. The plan includes tasks scheduled in shorter intervals as the cutover date nears and reverts to longer intervening periods afterward. For example, the end of pre-live week has multiple tasks for each day. The weekend before go-live includes myriad tasks by hour. This continues with briefer time intervals into the next day right before go-live. Once go-live occurs, the remaining two weeks gradually shift from hourly to daily tasks as post-live approaches. Adherence to this time sequence varies depending on go-live success.

Schedule

I noted the schedule includes detailed tasks, resource assignments, durations, and dates. It starts with pre-live, about a month before go-live, to verify readiness. During the final days of pre-live, Targets finish their checklists, like confirming they passed all training tests, resulting in credentials allowing live EHR access.

Go-live lasts up to two weeks depending on its success. Following this, post-live user training and Service Desk support continue, but issue reporting declines and then stays at a steady level. This, coupled with administration of the post-live checklist and acceptable results, marks the end of cutover and the transition to optimization.

Support

Tina and Tyler continued to listen without questions as I described the role of support. Support includes a variety of elements. From a logistical standpoint, there's setting up a Command Center in a conference room within KDMC. The Command Center functions during pre-, go-, and post-live, run by the PM and supported by the chief change agent. Other staff, such as trainers, Superusers, Agents, and individuals dispatched by the Service Desk work on the hospital floor delivering user help. The schedule includes tasks showing these and other resources who, when, and where they take part and what they do. This helps Reinforcing Sponsors know whom to relieve from their normal duties to work during cutover. Additionally, cutover trainers working throughout KDMC wear a brightly colored T-shirt, making their role readily observable to anyone needing help.

Tyler inquired, "Is there peer-based assistance, like physicians receiving help from other docs?"

Marissa noted, "Actually, there is. For example, it's important to continue using physician trainers, who are also doctors. It's also beneficial to consider using a dedicated Service Desk line for physicians and staffed by physicians if such resources are available. Finally, plan to use dedicated Service Desk staff who receive all calls during cutover. These resources receive training focused on the EHR configuration and workflow instead of IT only. They're trained to resolve a user's issue at first contact, or the first tier, avoiding a second-level response from IT staff where possible. It's also important to use software that tracks user feedback to improve Service Desk staff performance during cutover.

"Working the Service Desk can be grueling under normal circumstances. This role is stressful for Service Desk staff because they must respond with issue resolution promptly, especially during go-live. To minimize this, Service Desk staff receive supplemental training on FOR. Apart from this Service Desk staff education, users receive training in their role requesting help. While Service Desk representatives have excellent troubleshooting skills, users must assist too by knowing how to clarify what they need to accomplish, what went wrong, and when the problem started."

Communication

Marissa continued with, "There are other critical go-live areas that apply to preparing the cutover plan. For example, communication. To begin, Authorizing Sponsors, especially the agency CEO, will announce the go-live date. Reinforcing Sponsors will also meet weekly with their Targets. These meetings include reviewing Target roles and responsibilities and creating and completing checklists they need to finish during pre-live.

"Once go-live begins, the Command Center communicates critical events and milestones so everyone understands what's happening and how to respond. Clarity is necessary for project service delivery and accountability, especially under limited time constraints during go-live. Tyler, you post critical events on the Commend Center's electronic bulletin board, like the EMPI final conversion start, finish, and results. Reinforcing success deserves immediate praise. Likewise, failure requires a prompt remedy. For example, the Command Center executes a previously prepared backup plan, while IT finds the cause of the failure to solve the problem. This plan includes notifying users electronically and contacting their frontline Reinforcing Sponsors directly, so everyone knows they must execute pre-defined steps.

"It's also critical to respond to issues identified in data reporting that help dictate how to allocate go-live resources and distribute information. For example, clinicians often complain the EHR is far more difficult to use when compared to paper records. Let's assume clinicians report this to the Service Desk repeatedly during go-live. In response, IT posts an immediate follow-up to accumulated data on this issue. For example, they post a FAQ and notify clinicians an associated link directs them to the training library with instructions on how to use templates and available speech-to-text software. In addition, JIT trainers go directly to physicians and guide them at the elbow on how to complete templates.

"It's so important to set and communicate go-live expectations. Reinforcing Sponsors must remind their Targets regularly that IT and operational support cannot fix everything at once. Go-live requires responding to individual defects and issues but also stepping back and assessing severity and priority for optimized resource allocation. All issues will get a response. However, after evaluation, IT and operational support resources are available only to respond to issues based on the highest priority and severest criticality.

"As part of this expectation setting, users need clear instructions on where to report an issue and who will provide support. The Service Desk dispatches resources based only on issues reported to them. Each issue receives a unique identifier. The Service Desk centralizes and prioritizes issues so they can dispatch resources to resolve what's most critical first. Dispatched resources cannot respond to issues found by users who happen to see IT and operational support personnel on the floor. This may appear harsh to users. To minimize this, IT and operational support staff receive training to help explain this patiently, Reinforcing Sponsors communicate this to their Targets during meetings right before go-live, and a FAQ defines how users request Service Desk help.

"Finally, go-live is short, but it includes a checkpoint report at the end of each 12-hour shift. These times include the PM reporting to the PMT, CMT, agency chain of Sponsors, and Targets. Presentation occurs at the Command Center and virtually, including posting the report on the KDMC intranet. Each checkpoint report includes general status of the go-live, high-priority issue resolution since the prior report, newly identified issues, and those issues still undergoing resolution."

Monitoring and Controlling

I concluded with, "The EHR has a massive effect on the hospital, so it's essential to monitor safety, compliance, vital operational data, and project metrics. The cutover plan accounts for these, relying on RBM information. For example, during go-live, it's imperative that KDMC conduct chart audits and monitor daily revenue reports. These and other RBM information sources direct the PM to communicate action on training, configuration, workflow, and other updates to control initial and long-term EHR use and impact."

"What more can you say about the details to include in the cutover plan?" asked Layla.

In response, I handed Tyler and Layla a list of Cutover Plan Requirements. "I want to clarify this is not a cutover plan. For example, this list references interfaces collectively. A cutover plan names each interface individually, including multiple action items. I'm sharing this list to help you prepare and supplement your own plan with details from other plans prepared by NYHH, Jail Health, and Cerpix customers. After building a plan, you must confirm your draft, including tasks, resources, dates, and times, with project participants before starting the approval process."

Cutover Plan Requirements

Cutover Plan Requirements Pre-Live (30 Days Before Go-Live)	Done
Schedule	
Authorizing Sponsors announce cutover go-live start date to all Targets	
Reinforcing Sponsors meet with Targets weekly to complete cutover checklists and to receive feedback	
All third parties notified of forthcoming go-live, including requests for their help	
All patients notified of go-live before admission, during admission, and while receiving KDMC care	
Frontline Targets schedule and workload reductions ready for cutover	
Twice daily check-ins ready to supply feedback on go-live	
Shift changes ready to include go-live updates	
Test	
Infrastructure platform performance and capacity test success	
User device and connectivity test success	
Interface acceptance test success	
Conversion and pre-load test success	
Security test success	
Software configuration and programming acceptance test success	
Workflow acceptance test success	
RBM	
SMART objectives or progress milestones achieved	
Pre- and post-live data collection metrics ready for reporting	
Chart audits and revenue reporting ready for EHR operational assessment	
Training	
Operational and technical support assignments distributed	
Impact sheets on workflow and EHR distributed	
User device training certification	
User workflow and EHR training certification	
Minimum hours of user practice on workflow and EHR certification	
Minimum hours of user POC role play on workflow and EHR certification	

(CONTINUED)

Cutover Plan Requirements

Cutover Plan Requirements Pre-Live (30 Days Before Go-Live)	Done
Trainers receive day-glo green T-shirts to wear during go-live	
Departmental user groups created to share their experiences among peers, including reporting to Agents and Reinforcing Sponsors	
Support	
KDMC and Cerpix named key contacts and backup individuals	
Procedures ready for KDMC and Cerpix cutover issue escalation process	
Procedures ready for internal staff and external vendors' technical and operational support	
Reinforcing Sponsors confirm with Targets patient safety is go-live top priority	
Reinforcing Sponsors confirm with Targets that EHR functions and workflows may not work as planned, but technical and operational support are available to help	
Backup	
Processes ready for system downtime, including completed Target and IT training	
Catastrophes defined and senior officials named and trained to stop go-live, if needed	
Rollback procedures ready, with completed Target and IT training, if needed	
Pre-Live (One to Three Days Before Go-Live)	
Schedule	
Reinforcing Sponsors confirm Targets complete cutover checklists	
All third parties reminded of go-live date and needed help	
All patients reminded of go-live before admission, during admission, and while receiving KDMC care	
Go-live schedule verified	
Reinforcing Sponsors meet with frontline Targets and confirm roles, responsibilities, checklists, and schedules	
Frontline Targets reminded to arrive one hour early before their shift begins on go-live day	
Readiness	
Users have correct EHR access privileges	
Users know how to log into the EHR with their user ID and password	
Successful go-live rehearsal	
Successful integration test	

Cutover Plan Requirements Pre-Live (30 Days Before Go-Live)	Done
Support	
KDMC and Cerpix confirm key contacts and backup individuals	
KDMC and Cerpix confirm issue escalation procedures	
KDMC and Cerpix confirm technical and operational support procedures	
Trainers ready to supply instructions at specified locations and for named individuals and user groups	
Users confirm they understand procedures for contacting the Service Desk and reporting issues	
Go-Live (One to Two Weeks)	
Schedule	
Each conversion and pre-load performs on schedule completely and correctly	
Each interface performs on schedule correctly	
Targets arrive one hour early before their shift begins	
Targets conduct walkthrough of their workflow and EHR functions and receive help, as needed	
Targets prepare for their incoming patients	
EHR goes live successfully	
Training	
Trainers deliver JIT user instructions and coaching	
Clinicians receive at-the-elbow training	
Support	
Break rooms provisioned with extra drinks and snacks	
Internal and vendor operational and technical support are on the floor delivering JIT aid	
Agents and all Sponsors walk the frontline multiple times a day to reinforce, observe, communicate, and receive Target feedback	
Command Center conducts daily support call with department heads and user groups for feedback and status reporting	
DELTA Team tackles operational and technical issues proactively with users	
Post-Live (Four to Eight Weeks)	
RBM	
Chart audits and revenue reports delivered on EHR implementation impact on KDMC for corrective action	
Pre-live versus go-live data compared for technical and operational support and corrective action	
EHR RBM metrics posted on Web and distributed to user groups for progress reporting and corrective action	

(CONTINUED)

Cutover Plan Requirements

Cutover Plan Requirements Pre-Live (30 Days Before Go-Live)	Done
Training	
Trainers remain ready to assist users for the long term	
Trainers, IT, and Workflow Analysts review EHR technical and operational updates to identify and deliver more training	
Trainers supply JIT EHR and workflow support where and when needed	
Support	
Reinforcing Sponsors meet with Targets to confirm expectations on optimizing the EHR once cutover ends	
Agents and all Sponsors walk the frontline daily to reinforce, observe, communicate, and receive Target feedback	
User groups meet weekly with Agents and Sponsors on EHR technical and operational support, training, workflow, and configuration issues	
Service Desk reviews all outstanding issues, removes duplicates, and sets priorities for corrective action	
Service Desk analyzes all prioritized issues for EHR technical and operational support, training, workflow, and configuration requirements	
Service Desk keeps staff with EHR and workflow experience to help users during optimization	
KDMC and Cerpix staff prepare to execute EHR and workflow optimization training and help	
Trainers, IT, and Workflow Analysts review EHR technical and operational requirements for transition to optimization	
Reinforcing Sponsors meet with Targets to review and resource optimizing the EHR after cutover	

Tyler asked, "Where does the PM fit in cutover?"

I stressed, "Project management is about process. We are currently in the project management *execution* process. Cutover includes Agile IT and change management tasks that project management ensures occur promptly and completely."

"Cool," responded Tyler.

PRE-LIVE

Layla and Tyler did an excellent collaborative job putting the cutover plan together. They completed a final draft and weathered the approval process.

Now, Tyler handed Renee, Marissa, and me the Go-Live Readiness Checklist.

Go-Live Readiness Checklist

Requirements to Go Live	Completed Successfully
Purpose-driven vision	X
Project business case	X
Cascading sponsorship	X
CAST roles and responsibilities	X
Communication plan	X
Reinforcement management index	X
Infrastructure capacity and performance testing	X
Project SMART objectives or progress milestones	X
Product Backlog	X
Workflow testing	X
Configuration testing	X
Frontline Target roles and responsibilities	X
All Targets certified on EHR	X
All Targets certified on workflow	X
All Target certified on minimum practice time	X
Infrastructure capacity and performance testing	X
Network capacity and performance testing	X
All interface testing	X
All conversion and pre-load testing	X
All security testing	X
Service Desk roles and responsibilities assignments	X
Trainer roles and responsibilities assignments	X
Cutover plan	X
Post-live transition optimization checklist	X
Pre-, go-, and post-live metrics	X
Go-live rehearsal	X
Integration test	

KDMC appeared ready for integration testing. This test combined the completed Project Backlog, converted data, and interfaces to confirm everything worked together as users expected. Once finished successfully, KDMC could go live.

Nolan asked Layla, "It is relatively easy to prove the completeness of the IT portion of the checklist by reviewing test results. It's not the same for the organizational change. What other steps, if any, did you perform to confirm KDMC readiness for the more intangible parts involving people?"

Layla explained, "I worked with the Change Agent Team and their Targets. I requested Agents meet with their Targets and ask for the top three to five reasons they think they're ready for go-live and a similar list of reasons why they are not. The Agents and I then met and discussed the results from the two sets of questions. Targets reported high willingness and readiness. These results, completion status of all relevant items on the go-live checklist, and the findings reported earlier on the implementation risk forecast confirmed readiness from a change management perspective."

"Your concrete work, including what you just confirmed, will help patients on a daily basis!" claimed Nolan.

Layla beamed. "Thank you. Using my strengths to help others feels great."

On Tuesday, Tyler reported the integration test results to the Steering Committee. "The final EMPI conversion took longer than expected. We found lab interface errors sending orders and receiving results. We also discovered deviations between new workflows and EHR configuration changes. We can still resolve everything for Sunday go-live."

Renee bit her lip. Earlier she told me Tyler had agreed to a KDMC delay. Postponing go-live gave the vendors and Scrum Team time to fix defects and perform regression tests. Regression testing must happen because it helps ensure the software still performs as expected after making changes, like removing defects. Delay also let users complete another full integration test. This added two weeks to the schedule. It also required refresher training and additional practice time because the delay reduced user readiness.

Tyler could not tell the truth. He was a classic pleaser, unable to speak up because he didn't have the courage. He was a kind person with no evil intent, but this inaction could have grave consequences. He spoke very softly, almost ashamed, as if he were personally responsible for the defects.

So much came before him, and he overcame all of it except for the identified defects in the integration test. The test served its purpose. It found defects before go-live. When the KDMC part of the Recovery Project ended successfully, no one would remember there was an added two-week delay to correct these defects. In contrast, everyone would remember a failed go-live that went ahead without completely retesting corrected severe and high priority defects.

I said, "The test results tell us that we are not ready. Don't you think we should avert risk of failure and complete another round of integration testing after correcting these defects?"

Tyler shifted in his seat and nodded. His non-verbal communication slowly released enough tension in the room that he regained confidence to speak.

Tyler continued, "I agree with you, Max. If the rest of the Steering Committee concurs, we will delay go-live for two weeks, fix the defects, and conduct another integration test. To be sure, let's assume I'll notify the Steering Committee a week from today if we need more time."

Dr. Zorn said, "Thank you, Tyler. Does anyone have any comments about Tyler's recommendation?"

No one did, and the Committee approved the delay unanimously. The conference room emptied except for Oscar, Layla, Renee, Dr. Zorn, and me.

I never cared about donuts. The folks staying enjoyed the still-fresh Krispy Kreme breakfast treat supplied by Oscar. I joined in drinking Starbucks coffee. I wasn't a fan, even though I live near Seattle. However, it had a burnt aftertaste worth tolerating today. I worried during the night needlessly about the go-live delay.

"What's the best way to announce this go-live delay?" asked Dr. Zorn.

Layla proposed, "We have a revised go-live date already confirmed by the PMT and vendor. This date also assumes KDMC expects low hospital bed occupancy and admission rates and limited ED activity. As an Authorizing Sponsor, Dr. Zorn, you must communicate the delay with an honest and clear reason for it. Consider each Target group, tailoring the message to their individual perspectives. For example, underscore the benefit of how this delay minimizes defects to help offset undermining Target confidence in this long-awaited change. It's a big deal, so the more in-person communication, the better. Finally, allow for questions and give consistent and complete answers, including prompt follow-up on all feedback."

"That makes sense," answered Dr. Zorn.

On Friday, Tyler reported the KDMC did not need to extend the go-live delay beyond two weeks. The pre-live corrections and Scrum Team unit tests results showed KDMC was ready to conduct integration testing again.

The two-week delay had below a 20% attendance rate at refresher training. Go-live couldn't arrive soon enough.

GO-LIVE

Go-live is never without difficulties because there are too many moving parts for it to happen flawlessly. For me, it's an enormous high. Two years of work, and then everyone crosses the finish line simultaneously. Or, at least, that's what's supposed to happen.

I went to the Command Center, and there was no one there. Quickly, I searched for Tyler and found him under the counter at a nurse's station.

"What are you doing, Tyler?" I asked. I received no response. Fortunately, Tyler didn't hear me.

A nurse I did not know announced, "I was just entering my shift assessment for a patient and my computer crashed. I couldn't restart it. Luckily, Tyler walked by, and he could help me."

Tyler popped up from behind the counter and said to this nurse, "Your computer's power supply is dead. You need a new PC."

I waited for them to finish their conversation. It would be counterproductive if I let Tyler know how much this situation irritated me. I deadpanned, "Tyler, you're needed in the Command Center now."

He looked at me briefly and then pointed to the other computer in use at the station and said to the nurse, "I'll have a replacement PC installed here in about 15 minutes. In the interim, log on to this other computer when it becomes available."

Tyler and I walked back to the Command Center while I insisted, "You are exceptionally good at technical support. Now, you're responsible for centralized control of this go-live. In this leadership role, you monitor what's happening and order resolution to identified problems rather than fixing them yourself."

Annoyed, Tyler recounted, "I was just walking by when Millie asked for help. What was I supposed to do, tell her to call the Service Desk?"

"As a matter of fact, yes," I imparted as patiently as I could. "Go-live needs the data on what's happening and how to assist users best. Centralized Service Desk calls provide that data for the prioritized dispatch of technical and operational support responses. What you just did was outside that necessary centralized reporting process."

"I've known Millie Jessup for over 15 years, and I couldn't do that to her," pressed Tyler.

"Tyler, this is not the time or place for either of us to argue," I insisted. "Let's go back to the Command Center where KDMC needs you most. Okay?"

Tyler acquiesced with a nod, and we walked back to the Command Center in silence.

We arrived to pandemonium. The lab system wasn't working. Everyone was talking at once. Tyler froze.

I saw a tech with a telephone amid the chaos. "Are you calling the vendor lead assigned to this go-live?" He looked confused. "Give me the phone!" I demanded. Startled, he complied.

Moments later, I retrieved the number on my list of key contacts that I had in my portfolio and placed the call. I took Tyler by the arm as the call went through. Loud enough for him to hear, I said, "This is the KDMC go-live Command Center. Our lab system is not working correctly, and we just began our EHR go-live. I have the PM in charge of the go-live here, Tyler Avery, who will take this call now." I handed Tyler the phone and watched as he took over. Within ten minutes, the vendor had the lab system running and the interface communicating with the EHR.

Tyler announced this success in the Command Center, and everyone appeared relieved. We completed physical IT launch of go-live. The lab interface problem made this a disruptive process. It was particularly crucial that we help users through this upset and make progress.

I walked to the reception counter at the ED, behind the inch-thick bulletproof glass. It was eight deep out the door in the ED, and this was a light load. Everywhere I went, KDMC go-live remained stable late into the night. Training and technical and operational support were helping users as planned.

Because Renee never slept, we agreed she would relieve me while I prepared to go back to my hotel. I planned to return to KDMC in about four hours.

It was 2:00 a.m. in one of the worst parts of LA. The hospital doors locked behind me as I stepped outside in a gush of fresh air to relax before getting sleep at the hotel. Trying to remain calm and pay attention simultaneously, I tried reaching Renee on my cell phone, but my call went directly to voicemail. I took the sidewalk around the campus until I found a door. I grabbed the handle and found it locked. Nobody else was outside nearby. KDMC campus lights illuminated the sidewalk. Panicking, I managed to keep looking for an unlocked door and finally found my way to the emergency entrance. I needed sleep.

When I returned later that morning to KDMC, I toured the hospital on my way to the Command Center and found the fracture clinic overwhelmed in the waiting area. I helped the clinic manager, organizing the crowd into separate lines dedicated to those who needed x-rays, cast removal or change, orthopedic team review, and other. Schedulers working a specific line could concentrate on repeating mostly the same computer functions. As volume diminished, the clinic manager shifted schedulers so that they could serve different lines and use different system functions with minimal patient delay.

When I finally made it to the Command Center, Renee was already there, and the shift briefing was about to begin.

Tyler announced, "The EHR is operating as expected. Since the prior period, the report generated to compare pre- and post-order volumes by department is now available. As expected, we are working slower than pre-live but keeping up with the volume. Likewise, although there was a delay with the lab system at go-live, it is functioning correctly now.

"Currently, our severest and highest priority issue is the lab interface, not the lab system itself. We're getting errors caused by the integration engine. We plan to work with the interface engine vendor to update tables and eliminate these errors. I will notify everyone when we expect to resolve this problem.

"Also worth noting are sporadic printer issues occurring now throughout the facility. The Service Desk dispatched hardware and software staff, who are stabilizing the printing environment now. I hope to announce resolution of this issue by our next meeting."

Layla reported, "I have one priority to report. Even with lower patient loads, Targets get upset and flustered as they learn real time and cause patient delays. Training and coaching staff, with interim support from Reinforcing Sponsors, continue to work with these Targets. Reinforcing Sponsors are on the floor explaining we are amid an EHR go-live, apologizing for the delay, and letting patients know we have not forgotten them. We also continue to add training aides for online computer access and trainers keep delivering assistance at the elbow."

Late morning of go-live day two, Oscar, Layla, Renee, and I met in Tyler's office. Tyler announced, "The vendor responsible for the interface engine had a contract dispute that Tina never resolved. The vendor wants to leverage settling this dispute now by refusing to help us during go-live. We can't delay. This interface is generating 800 to 900 errors per day. These errors prevent ordering departments from viewing results in the EHR. They also disrupt data flow through the system used for workload and cost reporting and other financial purposes, including hospital reimbursement."

"Why can't your IT staff fix this problem?" asked Oscar.

"I'm afraid we will cause additional difficulties if I take any of our existing IT staff away from their current go-live assignments," Tyler said.

Renee nodded in agreement as Oscar pondered other options. Oscar then revealed, "Our Cerpix contract has *pool dollars* for situations just like this. Pool dollars are a capped financial amount within the contract available only for previously unidentified but in-scope vendor supplemental services. To avoid an unnecessary and arduous contract amendment process, the agreement allows using change order procedures here instead. Can Cerpix load the integration tables correctly without this other vendor?"

Tyler ventured, "I think so. I'll confirm right now."

He picked up the telephone and called the Cerpix project director. After Tyler ended the call, he recounted, "Cerpix will proceed with their supplemental services at once and update the integration engine tables to eliminate the errors given their severity and high priority. I will prepare a change request and order now for signatures."

Renee volunteered, "I'll prepare those documents, Tyler. Since you know staff here better than I do, you should work with Cerpix and KDMC IT and lab resources to correct interface errors."

Tyler agreed.

Oscar said he'd negotiate with the integration engine vendor separately to resolve their support contract finally.

A bit of luck, good timing, and loads of planning came together. At least that was how it felt five days after go-live. While difficulties persisted, there were no more severe high-priority issues.

POST-LIVE

Cerpix completed the integration engine table updates as KDMC staff worked to remove the backlog of errors quickly. As promised, technical support staff also fixed the sporadic printer problems. Users continued to rely on the EHR and new workflows without significant issues reported. It was the unreported issues that mattered.

During the first post-live Command Center status meeting, Tyler distributed a report of project issues and began with, "We've had difficulty producing a consolidated list of issues during go-live because of Service Desk software problems and limited staff resources. We thought we reported all Recovery Project go-live issues previously. One of our Service Desk staff said her call tickets did not appear on the most recent report. After examining the report setup, we found the parameters, including the type of data retrieval, were incomplete. We updated the parameters and re-ran the report from go-live through today. We found a serious backlog of previously unreported uncharged orders from first use of the EHR. This backlog may affect patient accounting, billing, and month-end processing. Operations and IT management personnel indicated they will resolve this backlog within 30 days and plan to introduce changes to eliminate future backlogs."

Layla then told us, "Information on one KDMC objective is inconclusive because we are unable to accurately identify why we're not achieving the metric. The agency set an objective to switch 80% of all clinician ordering from paper to online. Our review suggests higher system ordering is not occurring as expected. The current report does not isolate specific locations for ordering and corresponding results reporting. We are developing a query that captures this information. The report should show which units generate high paper order volume and those that don't. We plan to identify what's wrong and how to resolve it promptly."

Except for Layla's findings, later Command Center meetings reported no significant severity and priority issues. At the end of week four of post-live, Layla announced, "We updated the EHR ordering query by department, unit, and shift and identified the location and source of the problem. Departments that kept paper order requisitions openly available for downtime occurrence only had the lowest level of electronic ordering. We received approval to remove paper requisitions from day-to-day work areas but to keep them available in each nearby department manager's office or desk. This negative reinforcement worked well for other Cerpix customers because it encourages reluctant department staff to use the EHR for order processing instead of paper requisitions.

"We then had a breakthrough that reversed EHR ordering under-utilization. Focusing on both ability and willingness achieved dramatic results. We removed paper order requisitions and audited selected locations to gather low system usage data. We then had Reinforcing Sponsors meet repeatedly with their underperforming Targets to keep them accountable and supplied refresher training as well. The revised query for all KDMC locations showed electronic ordering increased remarkably. For example, the ED increased electronic ordering by 300%."

Oscar chimed in with, "I applaud everyone's persistent effort to resolve this issue."

Layla smiled and concluded, "There was also a portion of the EHR that failed to match with workflow. The Scrum Team corrected and tested a setting so now nurses can access information supplied by physicians on a specific screen, which was not previously available."

Post-live intensity diminished. For example, the Service Desk reported, at another status meeting, that demand tapered to a workload level higher than pre-live but much lower than go-live, without any noticeable uptick. It was time for KDMC to move from the Recovery Project to optimization.

Tyler asked Renee, "Do we return Service Desk support to the original staffing level before we started cutover?"

Renee reckoned, "It's important we not reduce Service Desk support staff for now as patient loads increase to pre-live levels and the Command Center gradually shuts down. We already cut the Command Center from 24/7 to 12/7 operation. When it ceases operation entirely, all remaining Command Center workload transfers to the Service Desk. Once this workload transfer stabilizes, you may reduce Service Desk staff dedicated to the EHR. However, expect to keep resources to support the EHR, since it is a new addition to Service Desk ongoing operation."

Later at a Command Center status meeting, Tyler distributed the Optimization Readiness Checklist he and Layla had prepared previously. Tyler met with IT staff to confirm checklist results, and Layla completed meetings with the Change Agent Team to do the same.

Tyler summarized, "From an IT standpoint, this readiness checklist indicates KDMC can transition from the project to optimization. Layla has more to say, so I'll leave it to her to continue."

Optimization Readiness Checklist

Optimization Requirements	Completed Successfully
1. Leadership	
Authorizing Sponsor approve ongoing optimization budget and staffing	X
2. Alignment	
Sponsors reinforce adherence to strategic plan, including purpose-driven vision	X
Chain of sponsorship monitors RBM metrics to reinforce realization of near- and long-term SMART objectives and their benefits	X
Chain of sponsorship supports and reinforces direct report continuous achievement of metrics to improve patient care	X
3. Training and Reinforcement	
HR trains and onboards Targets filling changed and new positions	X
DELTA Team delivers ongoing JIT technical and operational assistance and training	X
Trainers update education materials continuously	
Authorizing and Reinforcing Sponsors, or agency leadership, maintain and support user groups	X
User group leadership receives authorization to attend vendor user conferences	X
4. Measurement and Feedback	
RBM metrics focus on aligning agency activities and processes to achieve strategic initiatives and objectives, including optimization	X
Service Desk continues to find trends to improve technical and operational support and training for EHR configuration and workflow optimization	X

Layla chimed in with, "I agree with Tyler from a change management perspective. The project is ready to start optimization."

Oscar clapped his hands, and the rest of the meeting participants followed.

OPTIMIZATION

Oscar, Renee, Marissa, Layla, and I stayed with Tyler at the Command Center to review optimization details, as it's a critical part of maximizing EHR benefits. Optimization includes sequential stages after cutover.

During each stage, KDMC performs at a greater level of EHR and operational effectiveness.

Stabilization

I said, "Following cutover, optimization begins stabilization. Think about it. Everyone has a first day performing new EHR tasks with go-live. This is an unstable state. KDMC must achieve EHR stability before taking more steps. This involves a learning curve. Users don't master every new job responsibility and supporting EHR task on the first day of go-live. It takes time to apply training in a live environment. The more users rely on their job roles, responsibilities, and the EHR, the better they get. At some point, they reach a stable state, confident with the basics. To measure this, RBM metrics will indicate EHR user productivity trends toward pre-live levels. At this time, KDMC should also see resolution of significant priority and severity issues reported to Cerpix and the Scrum Team. Also, revenue reporting metrics will trend toward pre-live levels."

As part of stabilization, I also explained Tyler and Layla should review their plans for closing the KDMC portion of the Recovery Project. This involved changes in project staff assignments. Some remained as part of the Recovery Project governance structure, allocated to implement the EHR at RLANRC and then HDH. Others returned to their pre-Recovery Project positions. The rest went to modified or new positions created because of the EHR implementation and associated changes to KDMC's work environment. Authorizing and Reinforcing Sponsors ensured HR had previously trained these individuals in new skills and onboarded them with accountability measures to reinforce skill adoption.

Marissa leaned forward, pointed to the optimization readiness checklist, and said, "Optimization readiness is *not* EHR final acceptance. Final acceptance is the previously defined contract date indicating Cerpix will deliver the EHR product successfully and begin vendor technical support services. Thankfully, we did this, and the Steering Committee approved that momentous achievement. While acceptance of the vendor's EHR implementation is important, optimization signifies transitioning to a new and sustainable future, built on continuously improved patient care using the EHR. This is the agency's responsibility.

"KDMC did not implement the EHR and then return to pre-live conditions. AIM and Agile IT project management took the agency to organizational maturity Level 5; optimize, and it is here to stay. Agency leadership, or Project Sponsors, have a tool including separate categories in the optimization readiness checklist. These leaders can use this tool to confirm what they need to do to keep an ongoing improvement environment. It's a brief list reminding leaders whether KDMC maintains an organization that helps Targets not only do their job but improve continually. Ultimately, KDMC's key EHR success measure is improving patient care, driven by organizational change that connects operational RBM metrics to the agency's vision directly. As KDMC achieves current metrics, it can explore and implement new ones."

"Yes, of course; we understand," responded Layla.

I noted, "Anyone observing KDMC now sees that this project succeeded because Sponsors and their Targets adopted and now sustain the motivation to continuously deliver improved patient care."

Competency

I then said, "As optimization continues after establishing a foundation with the basics in place, users move up the learning curve and explore more advanced EHR features. At this point, their interests focus on competency. Also, Cerpix, the Scrum Team, and Workflow Analysts complete all items deferred before go-live.

"As competency increases, KDMC administers an assessment of all users concerning EHR and workflow use. The outcome typically names three general user categories. The first group includes early adopters, who not only know how to use the system but also find diverse ways of taking advantage of the EHR never considered by the Scrum Team and WAT. The second group, majority adopters, use at least 20% of the EHR, originally set up as the minimum needed for go-live. The remaining group, which I call constrained adopters, continue to resist change and struggle with skill and motivational factors.[1] Agency leaders or former Reinforcing Sponsors use this information responsibly for re-training and reinforcement. This helps KDMC strive to bring everyone to a minimum competency skill and motivational level, necessary for the next optimization stage, continuous process improvement."

Continuous Improvement

I added, "As this project ends, it affects core clinical functions, requiring ongoing changes long afterward. Continuous improvement is about constantly and incrementally making those changes beneficial while simultaneously minimizing their costs. For example, POs working with departmental user groups prepare User Stories for configuration updates that improve EHR use. Similarly, Workflow Analysts collaborate with these user groups, too, creating process improvements. The Scrum Team adds these User Stories to the prioritized Product Backlog for EHR configuration updates. Concurrently, the DELTA Team serves KDMC departments, minimizing Service Desk support calls, supplying JIT training, and surfacing improvements for user group consideration and contribution to the Scrum Team and Product Backlog.

"AIM and Agile IT project management remain as underlying and basic principles flourishing as integral parts of the agency. For example, there are updates to SMART objectives linked to the agency's strategic plan and purpose-driven vision, expectations set to continue the chain of sponsorship or leadership, changes made to RBM metrics on achievement of new imperatives, modifications to training, and reinforcements for frontline Targets."

Tyler said, "You're saying KDMC completed their part of the Recovery Project, but they'll never finish optimizing."

"That's about it," I said.

NOTE

1. Rogers, *Diffusion of Innovations*, 281.

13

Closing

Closing is the point where ending a project occurs, whether successful or not. A project, by definition, is always finite, including a start and end. An unsuccessful project stays disconnected from the organization. A successful one fully integrates with it. In an IT project, this includes stabilized system and workflow aspects and achievement of widespread user competency needed for continuous process improvement. The Steering Committee applauded this success of the KDMC part of the Recovery Project and closed it with unanimous approval.

LESSONS LEARNED

After the Steering Committee meeting, a group of us remained in the conference room. Tyler planned to prepare a Lessons Learned Report. He and Layla wanted input from those of us in the room plus other invited project participants. The meeting included Renee and me; Oscar; Tyler, acting PM; Nolan, SM; Layla, chief change agent; and Billy, CPO.

Tyler said, "I know our Lessons Learned Report is essential because RLANC and HDH will use it to guide their EHR implementations."

Renee responded with, "Agreed, and I know you've done this before. Do you have a standard for a Lessons Learned Report?"

"Yes, KMDC does," Tyler answered, nodding. "Layla and I plan to begin with group meetings of project governance and department user groups. I always start these meetings by asking what the three to five best and worst aspects of the project are. Discussion starts at once, and common themes surface. We collect these themes gathered during all our meetings,

DOI: 10.4324/9781003003809-13

supplementing them with information from project documentation. We will also use these themes to prepare guides for individual interviews with Authorizing and Reinforcing Sponsors. Themes become the basis for how to maximize successes and minimize failures documented in the report.

"The report also includes sections noting final acceptance and achievement status of objectives, scope, schedule, and budget. For example, there's a section on objectives, including those the agency achieved and others with the status of milestones attained to date. Other sections describe the scope as defined by deliverable achievement status and project schedule and budget adherence, including the original and those adjusted with approved change orders and amendments."

I got up from my chair and went to the whiteboard. I then asked everyone to go around the table naming what they found most beneficial to project success. I said I would record these findings on the electronic whiteboard, which included a printer, and distribute the results to all meeting attendees.

Uncharacteristically, Tyler started first. He said, "The DELTA Framework was key to our success. As a certified PM, I struggled with the PMBOK Guide. Although I've studied it, you only need flip through it to see how it relies heavily on the input-process-output model, used in systems theory, to define virtually every project management knowledge area. For example, to plan communications management, the PMBOK Guide depends on inputs like a project charter and project management plan. It then applies tools and techniques, or processes like expert judgment and meetings, to produce the output or plan. While this is a great tool for illustrating theory, it neglects the reality of human behavior and how that affects everything included in the PMBOK Guide. For example, during the process of planning communications management, people interact with each other, including not doing specific tasks because they don't know how to do the work, they don't believe in it, they're scared of failing, and so on.

"DELTA principles logically embrace the human effect required for project success by unifying complementary ingredients from change and Agile IT project management. For example, the DELTA communication principle combines PMBOK Guide communications management with AIM human behaviors of expressing, modeling, and reinforcing to increase change success."

Nolan jumped in with, "I like your idea. Let's focus on DELTA principles to communicate what we learned during the project. If we include a finite set of them in the Lessons Learned Report, they will help the remaining Recovery Hospitals immensely."

Nolan then suggested, "DELTA was especially helpful to me because it applied Agile and other assumptions to PMBOK Guide time management. DELTA scheduling assumptions minimize human tendencies to underestimate time needed to complete a project. This was particularly beneficial when preparing a reliable project schedule."

Billy explained, as CPO, "I thought I would struggle with Targets all the time trying to prioritize User Stories to achieve the highest customer value. It was not as if all Targets were the same and shared identical thoughts about these priorities. I had to find a way to resolve their differences. I didn't struggle at all. The DELTA prioritizing principle used the Kano model, included in Agile, to rank all IT requirements for vendor selection during procurement and organized the Product Backlog for every Sprint.

"Even after we completed that, we embraced constant change. DELTA approached this by requiring a feedback loop in all communication, which came from AIM and complemented the PMBOK Guide. As CPO, I met with project participants, who communicated information and expected meaningful feedback from me. This DELTA feedback principle meant I had to pay attention to each Target's FOR, to understand what the change meant to them, to increase adoption of new skills and behaviors needed for successful change

"Likewise, the DELTA involvement principle, founded in AIM, reduced resistance by combining it with the Agile value of customer collaboration. For example, we conducted four different meetings during each Sprint: planning, daily standup, review, and retrospective. Each meeting invoked involvement, which fostered feedback, collaboration, change, and ongoing improvement to deliver the best customer value."

Nolan added, "DELTA fostered collaboration throughout change and Agile IT project management. Think about it. We employed self-managing team collaboration for project work, like software development, governance, and Target involvement."

Layla noted, "We all knew sponsorship was the most important success factor in our project. The PMBOK Guide emphasized the executive sponsor only. AIM added a chain of Authorizing and Reinforcing Sponsors. The DELTA sponsorship principle joined project management executive sponsorship and change management Authorizing and Reinforcing Sponsors, cascading from the top of the organization to frontline Targets, to deliver successful change.

"Spending the time to understand stakeholders as a CAST revealed the project scope in a way I never saw before. It pinpointed the formal and informal cultural dimensions of the agency and how they interact. DELTA scope principle integrated PMBOK Guide scope and stakeholder management with AIM CAST identification. This principle identified all Champions, Agents, Sponsors, and Targets who participated in the project and unveiled how to estimate scope and dependent time and cost.

"Many Targets told me they'd never experienced IT project training that spent so much time on their job change, instead of the new system only. It was such a refreshing concept! Looking back, I realized the PMBOK Guide focused on staffing and other resources needed to execute the project. AIM concentrated on future state change requirements, including what Sponsors reinforced so Targets could achieve project objectives. The DELTA resource principle identified required behaviors and skills that created a capacity-building process based on managing resistance and reinforcing Target change readiness."

Oscar reminded all of us about how inferior quality contributed to earlier project failures. He then said, "When the Recovery Project began, I knew nothing about change management and Agile, but I knew poor project and product quality was a significant part of our past. Then Renee explained how DELTA put it all together. I realized quality was key to everything involved in the EHR product creation, during and after the project, including users embracing ongoing optimization."

Oscar then recounted how the strategic planning process was his first introduction to DELTA. He explained, "Max started telling me how the agency was stuck, failing because it repeatedly used an inadequate approach to IT projects. We never owned up to what we did or explored how we could change for the better based on understanding our history or climate. I told Max all about our history. Afterward, he administered a climate assessment. The results weren't startling or new, but this time we began learning from our failures instead of repeating them.

"I began to see how DELTA integrated change and Agile IT project management. I knew project management started after strategic planning and visioning and the ensuing business case. I also knew IT projects relied on a business case for justification. I learned AIM required a compelling business case, translated into Sponsors', Agents', and Targets' FOR, as the foundation for defining a project.[1] DELTA helped us own and understand our past; identify insights about our future; and integrate how to define, prioritize, and plan for sorely need change."

I waited a moment and made sure no one had more to offer. I then printed the results and told everyone I would send them a copy. I also suggested including this list in Lessons Learned interviews to get updates before including it in the final version of the report.

Three weeks later, Tyler shared the final version of the DELTA Principles with me.

DELTA Principles

DELTA Principle	Description
Definition	Own the past to understand the risk of future failures and to supply insights to define a vision and business case as the foundation for future change
Sponsorship	Combine project management executive sponsorship and change management Authorizing and Reinforcing Sponsors, cascading from the top of the organization to frontline Targets, to deliver change successfully
Scope	Identify all Champions, Agents, Sponsors, and Targets to unveil how to estimate project scope and dependent time and cost based on the people responsible for the change
Prioritizing	Use the Kano model to prioritize all IT requirements, included in the vendor procurement and Product Backlog, to select the product and deliver the project that achieves highest customer value
Assumptions	Prepare a reliable schedule using Agile and other assumptions to minimize human tendencies to underestimate time needed to complete a project
Quality	Put project and Agile IT quality management together in creating the product, during and after the project, including users embracing ongoing optimization
Risk and Uncertainty	Rely on team trust to define what the project can do to overcome uncertainty or situations where it is exceedingly difficult to prepare a plan that mitigates an adverse impact
Resources	Unify project management resources with AIM future state requirements to identify behaviors, skills, and the capacity-building process needed to manage resistance and reinforce Target change readiness

(CONTINUED)

(CONTINUED)

DELTA Principles

DELTA Principle	Description
Communication	Join project and change management communications, using expressing, modeling, and reinforcing to increase adoption of new skills and behaviors required for successful change
Feedback	Utilize feedback loops in all project and change management communications to understand Target groups' FOR, appreciate what change means to them, increase their trust, reduce their resistance, and cultivate adoption
Involvement	Reduce resistance by combining change management involvement with the Agile value of customer collaboration to foster feedback, collaboration, change, and ongoing improvement to deliver the best customer value
Collaboration	Employ self-managing team collaboration for all project work, such as strategic planning, software development, governance, and Target involvement

NEXT

It was five years since starting the Recovery Project, and Oscar and I were eating lunch together at a classic oceanside restaurant in Manhattan Beach. Each of the three Recovery Project hospitals enjoyed a successful EHR implementation. The project died peacefully instead of lingering painfully like others from DHS's history. I said, "The agency did it!" Oscar artfully coaxed me into saying *we* had completed Recovery Project success together. He always showed such grace.

Renee left KDMC, filling the CIO position, after 16 months. Renee, using a recruiting firm, helped KDMC hire a candidate responsible for overall leadership, planning, development, and management of IT resources across the facility and its ambulatory health centers. Relieved, Tyler returned to his deputy CIO position.

The county also prevailed in the Medi-Cal suit against the state. The result was full reimbursement of $39 million in claims.

It wasn't the end, really. We had an LA office, serving county clients. One of our projects even included the county CEO, implementing a real estate portfolio management system. Mike saw us as an asset.

While *Recovery* was officially over, we worked with one of the non-recovery hospitals. This included preparing for EHR implementation at LAC+USC Medical Center.

Surprisingly, we had a project with the county CIO. The county did not prevail in their investigation of Clarence. In fact, Clarence was back at his old job, but now reporting to the CEO as a subordinate, instead of directly to the board. Clarence replaced Renaldo Campo, whom Mike ousted callously.

I can't explain it, but Clarence wanted my opinion on a troubled project with the Department of Public Works. He and I always respected each other at an intellectual level. Now we were working together and enjoying a productive relationship.

Three months after my lunch with Oscar, I was in San Francisco with a client in my last on-site meeting before returning home to Seattle. My phone was on stun to avoid disturbing anyone. My phone vibrated. I looked, and it was Mike. I apologized to the meeting participants and stepped into the hall. "Hello, Mike. What can I do for you?"

"Good afternoon, Max," said Mike. "LAC+USC Medical Center's telephone system keeps having unexplained outages. The latest one occurred during a call between the hospital's CEO and the board's third district supervisor."

I held my breath and then released it slowly. "That's awful," I said.

Mike responded, "Yes, and now with the whole BOS agitated, we need to investigate and fix this problem quickly. What's your availability?"

"I'm completing a client visit now in San Francisco. I can fly to LA later today and meet with you tomorrow morning."

"Excellent. I'll see you at 9:00 tomorrow.

NOTE

1. Harrison, *Introducing the Accelerating Implementation Methodology (AIM) A Practical Guide to Change Project Management*, 10.

Appendix 1

Delta Framework

CHANGE MANAGEMENT

Accelerating Implementation Management Methodology[1]

Road Map

Define the Change
Build Agent Capacity
Assess the Climate
Generate Sponsorship
Determine Change Approach
Develop Target Readiness
Build Communication Plan
Develop Reinforcement Strategy
Create Cultural Fit
Prioritize Action

PROJECT MANAGEMENT

Project Management Body of Knowledge Guide Methodology[2]

Process Groups

Initiating
Planning

Executing
Monitoring and Controlling
Closing

Knowledge Areas

Integration Management
Scope Management
Schedule Management
Cost Management
Quality Management
Resource Management
Communication Management
Risk Management
Procurement Management
Stakeholder Management

IT MANAGEMENT

IEEE Software Body of Knowledge Methodology (Derived)

Knowledge Areas

User Requirements Management
Infrastructure Management
Network Management
Conversion Management
Interface Management
Security Management
Workflow Management
Software Configuration/Development Management
Test Management
Cutover Management
Support Management

AGILE PHILOSOPHY

Values

"The Agile Manifesto"

We are uncovering better ways of developing software by doing it and helping others do it. Through this work we have come to value:

Individuals and interactions over processes and tools
Working software over comprehensive documentation
Customer collaboration over contract negotiation
Responding to change over following a plan.

That is, while there is value in the items on the right, we value the items on the left more."[3]

Principles

"The following 12 Principles are based on the Agile Manifesto:

1. Our highest priority is to satisfy the customer through early and continuous delivery of valuable software.
2. Welcome changing requirements, even late in development. Agile processes harness change for the customer's competitive advantage.
3. Deliver working software frequently, from a couple of weeks to a couple of months, with a preference to the shorter timescale.
4. Business people and developers must work together daily throughout the project.
5. Build projects around motivated individuals. Give them the environment and support they need and trust them to get the job done.
6. The most efficient and effective method of conveying information to and within a development team is face-to-face conversation.
7. Working software is the primary measure of progress.
8. Agile processes promote sustainable development. The sponsors, developers, and users should be able to maintain a constant pace indefinitely.

9. Continuous attention to technical excellence and good design enhances agility.
10. Simplicity—the art of maximizing the amount of work not done—is essential.
11. The best architectures, requirements, and designs emerge from self-organizing teams.
12. At regular intervals, the team reflects on how to become more effective, then tunes and adjusts its behavior accordingly."[4]

NOTES

1. Harrison, *Introducing the Accelerating Implementation Methodology (AIM) A Practical Guide to Change Project Management.*
2. Project Management Institute, *A Guide to the Project Management Body of Knowledge (PMBOK Guide)*, 556.
3. Beck et al., "Manifesto for Agile Software Development."
4. Beck et al., "12 Principles Behind the Agile Manifesto."

Appendix 2

Assessments and Checklists

ACCELERATING IMPLEMENTATION MANAGEMENT[1]

Project Overview
Change Agent Assessment
Organizational Change Stress Test
Implementation History (Climate) Assessment
Sponsor Assessment
Readiness Assessment
Communication Audit
Target Reinforcement Index
Implementation Risk Forecast

OTHER

Social Network Survey
Kano Questionnaire
Training Assessment
Computer Proficiency Assessment
Go-Live Readiness Checklist
Optimization Checklist
Competency Assessment

NOTE

1. Harrison, *Introducing the Accelerating Implementation Methodology (AIM) A Practical Guide to Change Project Management.*

Bibliography

Beck, Kent, Mike Beedle, Arie van Bennekum, Alistair Cockburn, Ward Cunningham, Martin Fowler, Robert C. Martin, et al. "12 Principles Behind the Agile Manifesto." *Agile Alliance*, 2019. www.agilealliance.org/agile101/12-principles-behind-the-agile-manifesto/.

———. "Manifesto for Agile Software Development." *Agile Alliance*, 2019. https://agilemanifesto. org/.

Bohns, Vanessa K. "A Face-to-Face Request Is 34 Times More Successful Than an Email." *Harvard Business Review*, no. April (2017): 1–4. https://hbr.org/2017/04/a-face-to-face-request-is-34-times-more-successful-than-an-email.

———. "What Makes Storytelling So Effective for Learning?" *Harvard Business Publishing*, 2017. www.harvardbusiness.org/what-makes-storytelling-so-effective-for-learning/.

Brooks, Fred P. *The Mythical Man-Month, Essays on Software Engineering*. Vol. 10. Reading, MA: Addison-Wesley, 1975. https://doi.org/https://doi.org/10.1145/800027.808439.

Chang, Florence. *Transforming Strategy into Operational Excellence*. Seattle, WA: Multicare Health System, 2011.

Cohn, Mike. *Agile Estimating and Planning*. New York, NY: Pearson Education, Inc., 2005.

Cross, Rob Prusak, Laurence. "The People Who Make Organizations Work." *Harvard Business Review* June (2002). https://doi.org/10.1093/oso/9780195159509.003.0017.

Franklin, Benjamin. "Poor Richard's Almanac." In *The Astronomical Calculations*. Annual Illustrated ed. New York, NY: John Doggett, Jr., 1849.

Goldratt, Eliyahu M. *The Goal: A Process of Ongoing Improvement*. 30th ed. Great Barrington, MA: North River Press, 2014. https://doi.org/https://doi.org/10.4324/9781315270456.

Harrison, Don. *Introducing the Accelerating Implementation Methodology (AIM) A Practical Guide to Change Project Management*. Lakewood, CO: Implementation Management Associates, 2017.

Johnson, Jim. "ROI, It's Your Job." In *Third International Conference on Extreme Programming*. Alghero, Italy: Standish Group, 2002.

Kushinka, S.A. "Chart Abstraction: EHR Deployment Techniques—Digital Collections—National Library of Medicine." *California Healthcare Foundation*, 2010.

———. "Clinical Documentation: EHR Deployment Techniques—Digital Collections—National Library of Medicine." *California Healthcare Foundation*, 2010.

———. "Workflow Analysis: EHR Deployment Techniques—Digital Collections—National Library of Medicine." *California Healthcare Foundation*, 2011.

Malnight, Thomas W., Ivy Buche, and Charles Dhanaraj. "Put Purpose at the Core of Your Strategy." *Harvard Business Review*, no. September–October (September 1, 2019). https://hbr.org/2019/09/put-purpose-at-the-core-of-your-strategy.

McCarthy, Claire, Douglas Eastman, and David E. Garets. *Effective Strategies for CHΔNGE™*. *Effective Strategies for CHΔNGE™*. New York, NY: HIMSS Publishing, 2018. https://doi.org/10.4324/9780429055010.

Menting, Ann Marie. "The Chill of Fear." *Harvard Medicine Magazine*. Boston, MA, 2011. https://hms.harvard.edu/magazine/science-emotion/chill-fear.

"Pirates of the Caribbean: The Curse of the Black Pearl—Wikiquote." Accessed May 30, 2021. https://en.wikiquote.org/wiki/Pirates_of_the_Caribbean:_The_Curse_of_the_Black_Pearl.

"Planning Poker—Wikipedia." Accessed July 9, 2021. https://en.wikipedia.org/wiki/Planning_poker.

Project Management Institute. *A Guide to the Project Management Body of Knowledge (PMBOK Guide)*. PMBOK Guide. 6th ed. Newton Square, PA: Project Management Institute, 2017.

Quinn, Robert E., and Anjan V. Thakor. "How to Help Your Team Find Their Higher Purpose." *Harvard Business Review* July–Augus (2018): 78–85. https://hbr.org/2018/07/creating-a-purpose-driven-organization.

Raz, Tzvi, Robert Barnes, and Dov Dvir. "A Critical Look at Critical Chain Project Management." *IEEE Engineering Management Review* 34, no. 4 (2003): 24–32. https://doi.org/10.1109/EMR.2004.25048.

Rogers, Everett M. *Diffusion of Innovations*. 5th ed. New York, NY: Free Press, 2003.

Sisodia, Rajendra, Jagdish N. Sheth, and David Wolfe. *Firms of Endearment: How World-Class Companies Profit From Passion and Purpose*. 2nd ed. Upper Saddle River, NJ: Pearson FT Press, 2014.

Skinner, B.F. *Science and Human Behavior*. 1st ed. New York, NY: Free Press, 2012.

Stellman, Andrew, and Jennifer Greene. *Learning Agile: Understanding Scrum, XP, Lean, and Kanban*. 1st ed. Sebastopol, CA: O'Reilly Media, 2013.

Tversky, Amos, and Daniel Kahneman. "Judgment Under Uncertainty: Heuristics and Biases." *Science* 185, no. 4157 (1974): 1124–31. https://doi.org/10.1126/science.185.4157.1124.

Wikipedia. "Agile Software Development." 2018. https://en.wikipedia.org/wiki/Agile_software_development.

———. "Burn Down Chart." 2021. https://en.wikipedia.org/wiki/Burn_down_chart.

———. "Capability Maturity Model Integration." 2021. https://en.wikipedia.org/wiki/Capability_Maturity_Model_Integration.

———. "Fibonacci Number." 2021. https://en.wikipedia.org/wiki/Fibonacci_number.

———. "Kano Model." 2021. https://en.wikipedia.org/wiki/Kano_model.

———. "Martin Luther King Jr. Outpatient Center." 2020. https://en.wikipedia.org/wiki/Martin_Luther_King_Jr._Outpatient_Center.

———. "Scrum (Software Development)." 2021. https://en.wikipedia.org/wiki/Scrum_(software_development).

———. "Servant Leadership." 2021. https://en.wikipedia.org/wiki/Servant_leadership.

———. "Waterfall Model." 2021. https://en.wikipedia.org/wiki/Waterfall_model.

Index

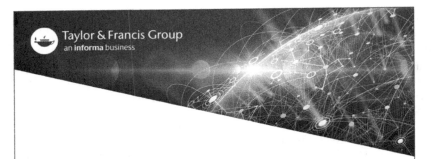

Printed in the United States
by Baker & Taylor Publisher Services